SUCCESS LIFE SKILLS FOR TEENS

4 Books in 1

Learn Essential Life Skills, Master Social Skills, Become Financially Savvy, Find Your Future Dream Career and Turn Your Life into a Huge Success

EMILY CARTER

TABLE OF CONTENTS

Your Free Gift vii

THE BIG BOOK OF ADULTING LIFE SKILLS FOR TEENS

Introduction 3

Part 1: Living Away From Home 6

Chapter 1: **Renting and Moving** 7

Chapter 2: **Cooking and Meal Planning** 17

Chapter 3: **Cleaning and Organization** 25

Chapter 4: **Home Maintenance and Repairs** 29

Part 2: Financial Literacy 40

Chapter 5: **Healthy Finances Are the Foundation of a Happy Life** 41

Chapter 6: **Credit Scores, Credit Cards, and Debt** 51

Chapter 7: **Investing and Planning for the Future** 59

Part 3: Relationships and Communication 68

Chapter 8: **Different Relationships, Same Foundations** . 69

Chapter 9: **Developing Healthy Communication Skills** . 79

Part 4: **Health and Wellness** 90

Chapter 10: **Physical and Mental Health Go Hand-in-Hand**
. 91

Chapter 11: **Self-Care and Healthy Habits** 99

Chapter 12: **Medical Matters** 111

Part 5: **Personal Development** 118

Chapter 13: **Time Management and Goal Setting** 119

Chapter 14: **Growth Mindset, Self-Confidence, and Resilience**
. 133

Conclusion 141

MONEY SKILLS FOR TEENS

Introduction 145

Chapter 1: **Understanding Money** 147

Chapter 2: **Making Money** 157

Chapter 3: **Banking and Financial Services** 175

Chapter 4: **Budgeting** 195

Chapter 5: **Spending and Paying Bills** 211

Chapter 6: **Credit, Credit Cards, and Debt Management** . . 231

Chapter 7: **Investing** 241

Chapter 8: **Insurance** 255

Chapter 9: **Big Purchases and Paying for College** 259

Chapter 10: **Retirement** 265

Conclusion 269

SOCIAL SKILLS FOR TEENS

Introduction 275

Chapter 1: **Self-Awareness** 281

Chapter 2: **Self-Confidence** 303

Chapter 3: **Social Skills.** 321

Chapter 4: **Social Anxiety** 341

Chapter 5: **Connection** 359

Chapter 6: **Handling Difficult Social Situations** 375

Chapter 7: **Social Sustainability** 393

Conclusion 409

CAREER PLANNING FOR TEENS

Introduction 415

Chapter 1: **Understanding Yourself.** 421

Chapter 2: **Exploring Career Options** 433

Chapter 3: **Developing Essential Skills** 447

Chapter 4: **Seeking Guidance** 467

Chapter 5: **Planning for Education and Training** 477

Chapter 6: **Gaining Practical Experience** 491

Chapter 7: **Making Informed Decisions** 503

Chapter 8: **Taking Action** 517

Chapter 9: **Transitioning to the World of Work** 531

Conclusion 543

About The Author. 549

References 551

YOUR FREE GIFT

Having the right mindset is the key when it comes to achieving success in any area of your life. As a way of saying thank you for your purchase, I want to offer you my book *Unleashing Your Potential: A Teenager's Guide to Developing a Growth Mindset and Opening Your Path to Success* for completely FREE of charge.

To get instant access, just scan the QR-code below or go to: https://lifeskillbooks.com/success-skills-free-bonus

Inside the book, you will discover...

⬧ The difference between a fixed and growth mindset, how your mindset impacts your personal growth and success, and why a growth mindset is the one you should adopt.

⬧ Practical strategies to cultivate a growth mindset, from daily habits to overcoming obstacles.

⬧ How to utilize a growth mindset to supercharge your academic and career success.

⬧ And much more!

But wait, there's more to come...

In addition to the *Unleashing Your Potential* eBook, I want to give you two additional special bonuses:

BONUS 1

The Essential Summer Job Handbook: The Teen's Guide to a Fun and Profitable Summer

Inside this exciting guide, you will discover...

✧ The many benefits of having a summertime job, from earning extra cash to gaining valuable experience and skills that will set you up for success in the future.

✧ The different types of jobs available for teens at different ages, and how to market yourself effectively to potential employers.

✧ Practical tips for avoiding being taken advantage of, and advice on tax considerations that every working teen needs to know.

BONUS 2

Raising Teens With Confidence: 10 Exclusive Blog Posts on Parenting Teens

I know this sounds boring if you're a teen, and that's completely fine. But for you parents out there, these unreleased blog posts offer a great opportunity to learn some new effective ways of parenting your teen.

Inside this compilation, you will discover...

✧ Invaluable insights and practical tips on how to navigate the challenges of parenting teenagers, from setting boundaries and dealing with mood swings to managing serious issues like drink and drug use.

✧ How to pick your battles wisely and let go of the small stuff, while still maintaining a strong connection with your teen and encouraging them to open up to you.

✧ Effective strategies for getting your teen to help out more at home, and how to strike the right balance between being a supportive parent and allowing your teen to develop their independence.

If you want to really make a change in your life for the better and get ahead of 95% of other teens, make sure to scan the QR-code below or head to the web address below to gain instant access to your bonuses.

https://lifeskillbooks.com/success-skills-free-bonus

THE BIG BOOK OF ADULTING LIFE SKILLS FOR TEENS

A Complete Guide to All the Crucial Life Skills They Don't Teach You in School for Teenagers

EMILY CARTER

INTRODUCTION

> *For in every adult there dwells the child that was, and in every child there lies the adult that will be.*

> –John Connolly

The moment my parents drove away after dropping me off at my college dorm was a shock to my system. It was at that moment that I realized I was alone. I was responsible for myself, from what and when I'd eat to what time I'd go to bed at night. It was at that moment that I realized I'd made it. I was an adult with adult responsibilities.

In my sophomore year, when I opted to rent an apartment with a friend near campus, I realized that I'd been wrong. Living in a dorm is like adulthood on training wheels. You have a meal plan and dining halls. There are Resident Assistants (RAs) there to help with conflicts with roommates or other problems. In your own apartment or house? You're responsible for it all, from cleaning and cooking to making sure all the bills you've never had to think about before are paid.

Moving away from home for the first time is a big deal. Whether you're leaving the nest for a dorm for the school year or choosing an apartment, it's a big responsibility. From renting and moving to keeping yourself fed and your home organized, there's enough to consider to make your head spin, and don't worry—that's normal. This is your first major step into independence and adulthood. Once you move, you'll be responsible for feeding yourself, keeping your home clean, and doing maintenance on your home and car. You won't have your parents to fall back on the second something goes wrong, and while you may be able to call them to ask for help, they probably won't be cooking and cleaning or doing your laundry for you.

The first time my apartment sink backed up, I had no clue what to do. It wouldn't drain, no matter how much I ran the garbage disposal. It wouldn't budge. I was equally clueless the time my car's tire blew out mid-winter one year until I was informed that the tire pressure was well under what it should have been.

There were so many things I didn't know about adulthood that, looking back, should have been taught in school. After all, if school is meant to prepare us for the world, why are we spending time memorizing the Pythagorean theorem instead of how to handle debt? Why aren't we taught how to take care of ourselves and our homes?

Ultimately, now as an adult, I understand the importance of teaching children how to *be* adults. That begins with an understanding of all the things you'll need to do living away from home.

That's why I put together this book. It's all about the skills I wish I'd learned sooner. I'm sure they would have saved me a lot of time learning via trial by fire. I don't regret the past or the struggles I faced growing up—they certainly taught me valuable life lessons that I've used to thrive later on. However, if I can save even one teen from making all those same mistakes or going into adulthood blindly, I've done my job.

As you read this book, you'll get a preview of what it takes to be an adult. This means being able to manage your own household and finances to managing your relationships and conflicts. You'll learn about keeping yourself healthy and also what it takes to have a mindset that will set you up for success.

Before you dive in, there's one thing I want to emphasize. You never stop learning, growing, or changing. Even if these things seem tough to remember or do at first, that doesn't mean you won't be able to do them later. You may be an adult or approaching adulthood, but that doesn't mean that you'll suddenly have all the right answers. You don't magically get any brand new insight the moment you hit adulthood. But, you do get handed a whole lot of new responsibilities as you prepare to set off on your own.

Approach these skills with an open mind and a willingness to learn, even if it takes you several tries to get something done. As long as you keep on trying, you'll get to where you want to go. After all, you haven't failed unless you've decided to give up or not participate at all!

PART 1

LIVING AWAY FROM HOME

Never underestimate the power you have to take your life in a new direction.

–Germany Kent

CHAPTER 1

RENTING AND MOVING

When it's time to move on to your own place, it's normal to feel nervous, excited, and maybe even a little bit scared. As you say goodbye to your parents and shut your door on them for the first time, it's strange. It's like shutting that door breaks a tether that's held you to them for your entire life. You entered this world knowing only them. You held their hand as you grew, watched them as they taught you, and lived with them your whole life, and now? You've left the nest.

It's a bittersweet moment for you and probably your parents too. They're probably brimming with pride as they drop their precious baby off for the last time, but they're probably also a little bit afraid, sad, and not quite ready to let go.

Whether you're moving into a dorm, a rental, or buying a house, there's always a huge transition shift when you finally walk out the door of your parents' home for the last time. There's a finality to it, but that doesn't have to be a bad thing. It just means you've grown up, and you're ready to start your own life. That's normal. It's only natural.

Of course, this comes with a little caveat—you suddenly find yourself responsible for all the things you probably took for granted growing up. Bills being paid, chores getting done, milk magically appearing in the fridge... These things take time and mental labor. And now? That's all yours. Congratulations!

But, before it's time to say goodbye and start your new life, you have to get somewhere to live first. Moving into a dorm is relatively simple for most people. You put in the application, you get assigned a room on campus, and you pay for it for the year. However, moving into an apartment on your own requires a lot more thought. From knowing lease terms to how to avoid a scam, there are some things to keep in mind.

Don't forget that your parents or guardians can be a major support during this process. They might cry when you get your first set of keys, but they can be just the people to turn to if you have specific questions. After all, they want what's best for you and they've got the experience to boot.

Everything You Need to Know

Before renting and moving, you'll want to familiarize yourself with several steps in the process. What are the terms of your lease? What utilities does the rent cover, if any? What about furniture and appliances? Why do you have to pay two or three months' rent upfront? Does renter's insurance really matter? Why? What is it? For a brand-new apartment hunter, there's a lot that you need to know that you may never have considered before, and that's okay! We all start somewhere and this is the perfect starting point.

Lease Terms

Leases are the contracts you sign when renting an apartment that grants you exclusive use of an apartment, room, house, or any other rental unit in exchange for an agreed-upon price. They're more than just that, though. They also list out the rules and guidelines that you need to abide by while renting, and if you violate the terms of the lease, you may break the contract and lose your right to remain in the unit.

Each lease will be different, so you'll want to read it all prior to signing it and ask any questions about terms you're unsure about or don't understand. The leasing agent will be able to walk you through it all.

Keep in mind that leases will also vary around the world. While in the US, it's standard for leases to include appliances; other countries may give you an entirely empty unit without a fridge, cabinets, or counters. While in the US, you can expect to have a background check run, be required to verify your income, and provide valid identification; other countries may also have additional requirements. You may be required to provide structural repairs in other countries as well.

Another thing to remember is that your lease will likely dictate whether you're allowed to have long-term guests to prevent unintended residencies. In many places, someone residing in a unit for longer than a month is enough to establish tenancy, even if they're a guest, and that can create a lot of legal headaches for the landlord if they refuse to leave. Even without a valid lease for that long-term guest, they may be forced to legally evict them if they can prove they've been there long enough.

Are Utilities Included?

Sometimes, utilities are included in your rental costs. This is especially common if you rent a room in a house. However, most rentals in the US will require you to have utilities in your own name, including electricity, gas, water, sewer, and garbage. You'll also likely have to pay for your own internet costs. Verify what's included in your lease beforehand to avoid any surprises, such as having to have the utilities transferred prior to moving in.

Deposits and Move-In Costs

Before you move in, you'll usually be responsible for the first month of rent. This seems pretty straightforward, right? Well, there are other expenses that will likely come into play too. Most rentals will charge a security deposit for any damages beyond normal wear and tear, which is any expected damage accrued by regular use, such as a wobbly doorknob or scuffs and wear on flooring.

The exact amount of your deposit will depend on what the state or country allows. For example, in Seattle, where I live now, a landlord can't charge more than one month's rent for a security deposit or nonrefundable fees, and renters have up to six months to pay off the security deposit, nonrefundable fees, and the last month's rent in a payment plan. This is a city-specific regulation, while the state of Washington has no such cap. Colorado has no caps on security deposits. Connecticut allows two months' rent for most tenants, but for those 62 or older, that number is halved to the equivalent of one month.

Make sure you know what's considered a legal deposit in your location prior to signing a lease and remember, if the deposit doesn't seem to align with what the law allows, there's a chance you're walking into a scam.

Beyond the deposit and last month's rent, you may also be required to pay a pet deposit or pet rent, deposits to begin utility services in your name, or other fees that may be dictated in your lease. You may also have to pay for movers, rent a moving truck, or pay someone to help you to get your belongings where they need to go.

Renters Insurance

Your lease may or may not require that you keep a renters insurance policy, but even if it's not obligatory, it's still a good idea to have. Renters' insurance typically covers unexpected events, which in the insurance world are known as covered perils. Each policy will vary in both coverage and cost, so make sure you speak with an agent who can help you understand which plans will work best for you. It typically comes with three types of coverage:

- ✧ **Personal Property:** This covers the cost to replace or repair any of your belongings that have been damaged, including furniture, electronics, and other items, up to the limit of your policy.

- ✧ **Liability:** This covers the cost of repairs if you accidentally damage the property or the cost of medical bills for a guest if they are injured on the property and you're found responsible, up to the limit of your policy.

- ✧ **Additional Living Expenses:** This covers any costs you may incur if your rental is damaged and you have to stay in a hotel.

Of course, there will be additional terms that will vary from company to company and state to state, such as what your deductible (the amount you pay before insurance pays out) will be, your premiums (the amount you pay monthly), and any covered perils.

Pet Policies

Pet policies can vary wildly, from allowing any and all dogs or cats to restricting you to specific sizes or prohibiting certain breeds. If you have a pet, this is probably one of the first considerations to make. Be sure to check your lease for pet policies, including a pet deposit, monthly pet rent, and any restrictions the property may have.

If you think you can get around the pet fees by hiding your pet, think again. This is a violation of your lease and you can be evicted and charged fees for pet damage. Likewise, if you have an apartment that doesn't allow pets at all, don't try to hide them.

Do You Need a Cosigner?

As a young adult, you'll likely start out without much credit unless your parents have been actively building it for you (more on this later). This means that you won't always look like the most attractive prospective tenant to landlords and they may be hesitant to rent to you since you won't have any sort of rental history. That's where cosigners come into play.

A cosigner is someone who co-signs your lease and agrees to be responsible for any fees, unpaid rent, or damages if you don't pay them. Typically, your cosigner will be someone with a much more established credit history and financial position, like your parents. Just remember that the cosigner is also on the lease and will have the same access to the property as you will. An alternative to a cosigner is a guarantor, who promises to pay the rent if you don't but does not have access to the apartment.

Choosing a Rental

If it's time to begin your rental search, hold your horses. Before you get too excited and start circling all the chic rentals with a million amenities and upgraded features, you've got some planning to do. I know how tempting it is to scroll through available units and dream of your new life in the best of the best, but the reality is most of us start small and work our way up. Choosing a rental takes a whole lot of planning, research, and time, and even then, you may not get the first one you apply for.

What's Your Budget?

The biggest factor in the entire apartment search is your budget. After all, you have to be able to afford your new place. Getting in over your head, even if you may qualify for an apartment that is, on paper, unaffordable, is a good way to start on the wrong foot.

Generally speaking, your budget should be less than 30% of your monthly income. This is where things get tricky, especially with the housing and rental markets skyrocketing. If you're making the U.S. minimum wage of $7.25 per hour while working a full-time job, that puts your annual pay at $15,080, or an average of about $1,257 per month. Using the 30% rule, you can only afford to pay about $377 per month in rent.

If that's looking bleak to you, you understand exactly what problem so many young adults of today face, and that's being unable to afford to live alone. If your pay alone is not enough to cover the average cost of rent in your area, you have some options. The most popular one is to rent with friends or roommates and everyone contributes to the monthly cost. This can make rent more affordable. Alternatively, you may need to consider living with parents or family members while gaining work experience, going to college, or pursuing a trade to boost your earning power.

To calculate your budget, take your hourly pay and multiply it by the number of hours you work per week. Then, multiply that number by 52 (for 52 weeks in the year to get annual pay). Divide that number by 12 to get your monthly average income. Then, multiply your monthly average income by 0.3 to see what the most you should be paying for rent is.

What Do You Want or Need?

Once you know how much you can pay, you can start considering amenities that matter to you. Start with a list of all the things you need out of your home, such as the distance to where you work or go to school and non-negotiable amenities.

- ✧ **Parking:** If you drive, you probably want somewhere that has available parking. Some apartment complexes may have assigned parking spots. Others may not offer any parking at all and require you to park on the streets.

- ✧ **Neighborhood:** Do you have a particular neighborhood you're partial to or neighborhoods you'd like to avoid? Check out crime statistics in the area you're considering, and spend some time looking around the area in person if you can to get a good feel for it.

- ✧ **Amenities:** Are there any amenities that you absolutely must have? For many, appliances like dishwashers and washers and dryers are required. Others may consider having an on-site gym or pool essential.

- ✧ **Closeness to work or school:** What is the farthest you're willing to move from your work or school? Remember, even if prices are cheaper for you to live further away, you may be spending so much more on transportation that it's actually more expensive than living closer.

Make a Short List

With your list of wants and needs and with your budget, you can then go searching for vacancies. Make a list of three to five rentals that you'd like to check out, that you can afford, and that meet your list of needs. You can search for rentals through word of mouth, asking around if anyone knows of vacancies, or online. Check out local property management companies to see if they have anything that will work for you.

View Apartments

Contact the apartments on your shortlist and ask if you can schedule a tour. It's strongly recommended that you never rent a place sight unseen because there may be problems that aren't obvious in photographs online. Take the time to tour the units and neighborhoods, and if you can, bring a trusted, experienced adult to take a look at everything, too.

Apply

Once you've decided on an apartment in your budget that meets your needs, it's time to apply. Be aware that most places will have non refundable application fees to cover background checks, and applying isn't a guarantee you'll get the place, especially in areas with a lot of competition. If your application is accepted, make sure you review the lease carefully before signing it.

Chapter Summary

Getting your first place is probably going to feel a little overwhelming at first. After all, you have to figure out what you need and can afford and then find somewhere with the availability that works for you. It might be with roommates, or you may truly be on your own for the first time. Either way, these tips are meant to try to smooth out the process. Don't forget that you can always ask for help from people around you!

And, once you've got your very own place to call home, you get to experience something new—managing your diet. From cooking to meal prepping, the next chapter will dive into everything you need to know.

CHAPTER 2

COOKING AND MEAL PLANNING

W e all need to eat at some point. Once you've settled into your new place, that responsibility falls firmly on your plate. Or, you might have roommates and decide to split up the responsibilities. Either way, there's no more Mom or Dad taking care of this for you, so it's time to get comfortable in the kitchen if you're not already.

I had roommates at one point and we rotated between cooking and cleaning on various nights. I've also had roommate situations where we were each responsible for feeding ourselves and cleaning up our messes after using the kitchens. You'll want to hash out expectations with your roommates before moving in together so you're on the same page. Will some items be free for everyone to use? Will you have different shelves in the fridge and cabinets for your food? These are all considerations to make.

Then comes meal planning, shopping, and keeping yourself satisfied, hopefully with healthy foods.

Dive Into Meal Planning

Meal planning is one of those things that sounds intimidating but is far easier than most people think. It's all about setting up a calendar with what you'll eat and when and making sure you have all of the ingredients on hand. This can really help you if you're the kind of person who gets overwhelmed with choices and doesn't know what to make, so you end up choosing to order out or buy something easy, which can be a big drain on your budget.

Meal Planning Steps

Meal planning really is as easy as following four simple steps that will keep you on track and help you to stretch your budget while still eating healthy foods that will keep your body running. If you reach for empty carbs and snacks like potato chips when you're busy and hungry, you aren't doing yourself any favors. You'll be hungry again a short while later. With meal planning, especially if you prep your meals in advance, you'll always know what's available and have something easy to eat.

Step 1: Take the Time to Plan

Each week, dedicate an hour or two to planning your meals for the next week. Try to plan breakfasts, lunches, and dinners. If you know there are days in your schedule when you're busy, make sure you have quick meals for them. Write down the meals and ingredients you'll need to make them.

While you're at it, choose meals that use similar ingredients so you can buy in bulk and lower costs. For example, maybe you make a chicken stir fry one night and then chicken fajitas the next. This lets you use up everything without waste.

Step 2: Check What's Already in the Kitchen

Once you have a list of ingredients, check your kitchen to see what you already have. Make sure that you check the use-by dates to ensure everything is still good, and if you have any ingredients that are about to expire, consider altering your meal plan to include those foods to avoid waste.

Step 3: Make Sure You Like the Meals

The key to sticking to a meal plan is making sure you're excited to eat the food. If you decide on recipes to use up items that you don't really like much, you'll be more tempted to ignore them and order in.

Step 4: Cook in Bulk and Use Your Leftovers

Choosing meals that make multiple servings can help make your meal-planning process easier. Even better, you can use the leftovers for lunch the next day. Just make sure that any meals that you choose to cook in bulk will reheat easily.

If you like big casseroles or dishes that usually result in a lot of food, you may be able to freeze them too. Foods like pot pies, casseroles, lasagna, spaghetti sauce, and stews all tend to freeze well, and you'll be able to pull out servings for lunches or dinners on busy days.

A Well-Stocked Kitchen is Key

Part of meal planning successfully is relying on some essentials in the pantry and fridge. When you first move to your first place, there are some things you should just keep stocked if they're part of your usual rotation of foods. These include:

Pantry Goods	Refrigerator Goods	Freezer Goods
Rice and grains	Milk	Frozen meats
Pasta	Butter	Frozen vegetables
Canned meats	Cheese	Frozen potatoes
Potato flakes	Eggs	Frozen fruits
Snacks	Yogurt	
Veggie and chicken broth	Fresh fruits and veggies	
Jarred peppers and olives	Meats	
Cream soups	Condiments	
Oils		
Flour		
Sugar		
Salt		
Baking soda		
Baking powder		
Seasonings		
Dried herbs		

A good way to help build up this stockpile is to buy in bulk when there are good sales and put items in your freezer. For example, maybe there's a good sale on chicken, so you buy more than you'd normally need and vacuum seal the extras to put in your freezer. This is a great way to cut down your costs.

Sprucing Up Cheap Meals

While ramen is hardly a balanced meal on its own, it's also one of those go-to foods that young adults eat regularly. After all, it's cheap, filling, and can be pretty tasty, too. I get it! I've had more than my fair share of instant noodles over the years.

When you go for cheap meals, there's no reason you can't spruce them up a bit. Toss in some frozen mixed veggies, a hard-boiled egg, and some chicken, and you've got a full meal. You can do this with other meals, too, like tossing vegetables into pasta or making fried rice with leftovers.

Meal Planning Tips for Young Adults

If you're planning out your weekly meals and trying to keep to a strict budget, you've got some options. These are some of my tried-and-true tips that I use to keep my food costs down without sacrificing much in the quality department.

Shop With Weekly Ads and Coupons in Mind

When you sit down to meal plan, review all the weekly ads and coupons at the store or stores you plan to shop at. You might notice that certain meats go on sale at certain points in the month or catch some killer deals on produce that you can use to implement into your meal plan. You might even be able to add some meat to your stockpile if you plan accordingly.

Stretch the Proteins

Especially in the US, there's this idea that protein has to be the main part of a meal. While planning around a protein can be helpful, it doesn't have to be the main dish. For example, instead of making burritos with lots of ground beef, you can cut the beef with a can of whole black beans to make it go further.

Throwing proteins into casseroles or pasta dishes can also help them feel like they go farther. Meat, in particular, is expensive, but by mixing it with other foods, you may be able to get more out of it.

Reach for Filling Foods

Foods that fill you up should be the bulk of your diet. When you shop, that means looking for whole foods that are on the perimeters of most grocery stores. The center aisles tend to be full of other foods that won't be as satisfying. Stick to the produce, meat, dairy, and whole grain areas as much as possible.

When you're hungry, grab satisfying foods like nuts, whole veggies, and fruits. Pair a carb with a healthy fat to boost feelings of fullness. After all, when you're satisfied with healthy foods, you're not going to be reaching for so many snacks, which can get expensive.

Cook at Home Whenever Possible

Just because you decide to meal plan doesn't mean that you can't eat out from time to time. But you'll want to focus on your meals at home, giving you healthy meals without breaking the bank.

Have Easy-to-Grab Foods Available for Those Busy Mornings

I get it—mornings are busy. I skipped my morning meals way too much when I was younger. Why bother eating if I need to rush out the door when having breakfast means waking up earlier? Why not just pick up a coffee and pastry at my favorite cafe on my way? Why not just pick up something from one of the dining halls? Well, the problem with this is that it gets expensive quickly.

Breakfast is the most important meal of your day. It stabilizes your blood sugar, which can help you feel more alert and energetic throughout the day, which also reduces the chances you'll be tempted by that afternoon's unhealthy snack.

I recommend keeping some easy grab-and-go foods on hand so you can have a complete breakfast any time you're in a rush. I love keeping DIY breakfast burritos and sandwiches in my freezer, so all I have to do is pop it onto a plate and warm it up for a minute while I get my coffee going. It saves my wallet and keeps me satisfied and full throughout my morning.

Chapter Summary

As one of the most basic needs that you require, food and thinking about food will probably be a pretty major part of your life for the foreseeable future. That's why implementing meal planning can be so useful—it takes thinking about food out of the equation. With minimal time spent handling and planning your food, you'll be able to free up time for other important things, like chores and staying organized.

CHAPTER 3

CLEANING AND ORGANIZATION

One of the biggest shocks to my system when I moved into my own place was just how much work goes into maintaining it. A good, solid cleaning schedule is key to keeping a clean environment, and that requires discipline. When I first got my own apartment, I realized that my parents did a lot more than I initially thought. They kept the floors vacuumed and mopped. They kept the bathrooms clean and the living room organized. While I had chores that I was responsible for, they paled in comparison to the regular upkeep of a home.

The best way for you to maintain your home is to have a schedule for daily, weekly, and monthly chores so you know what you're doing and when. This helps to keep you accountable and builds a routine where the cleanup is completed.

A Place for Everything

Any time you bring something home, it needs to have a dedicated place. This is one of the easiest ways to keep clutter down. If you don't have room for something, then it probably shouldn't be brought home. When you finish using something, return it back to its designated spot.

If it Takes Five Minutes, Do it Right Away

How often do you make a small mess and then tell yourself that you'll get to it later? This is an easy trap to fall into, but all those quick, little jobs can build up over time until what should have been easy tidying up becomes needing a deep clean or a more extensive scrub-down of an area. For example, if you spill something on the counter, you might tell yourself that you'll clean it when you do the dishes. Sure, it's not a big deal, but if you do that with all the little messes you make throughout the day, they all add up to a longer cleaning session.

The rule I use and that I teach my children is that if a cleanup task only takes five minutes or less to do after making a mess, then do it right away. If you spill your coffee, wipe it up right away. By doing the little tasks as soon as they pop up, you help maintain the cleanliness of your home so your cleanup routine stays consistent.

Develop a Regular Cleaning Schedule

Setting up a regular cleaning schedule can feel a little too reminiscent of chore charts for some new adults, but that's kind of the point. The chore chart helps keep everything done on time and makes sure nothing slips through the cracks. In my home, we divide chores into three categories.

Daily	Weekly	Monthly
Make your bed Do the dishes Wipe counters Tidy up clutter Take out trash/recycling	Scrub bathrooms Mop Vacuum Wash bedding Clean out fridge Dust surfaces	Wipe baseboards Wipe light switches Deep clean appliances Replace filters Vacuum underneath furniture Clean windows and tracks Scrub out trash cans

Of course, you might have other chores that you need to take care of, too, like cleaning out cat boxes, water changes for aquariums, watering plants, or yard work. Fit those in as needed as well.

From there, you have a few options. You can designate one day per week as your deep cleaning day or you can choose to do one or two weekly chores each day. For example:

✧ Sunday: Clean bedding and empty fridge
✧ Monday: Monthly chore
✧ Tuesday: Monthly chore
✧ Wednesday: Monthly chore

✧ Thursday: Dust surfaces

✧ Friday: Mop and vacuum

✧ Saturday: Scrub bathrooms

By adding in a few monthly chores on days you don't have weekly chores to complete, you can spread them out throughout the month so you don't find yourself overwhelmed on one or two days trying to get to everything on the list.

Chapter Summary

Keeping a tidy home can do wonders for your mental health, and it doesn't take much. Following these tips and setting a schedule can help you keep your home in tip-top shape—until something goes wrong and you have to fix it, that is. That's why the next chapter's here to prepare you with everything you need to know about maintaining your home—and which repairs to leave to the pros.

CHAPTER 4

HOME MAINTENANCE AND REPAIRS

The first time I had an apartment, I thought everything would be taken care of. After all, that's what maintenance is for, right? Well, there are a lot of maintenance things that the apartment isn't responsible for. Yes, they'll repair major issues with plumbing, dead appliances, and make sure that the environment is livable. You'll need to know what your responsibilities are and what your landlord is responsible for. Most of this is going to be dictated in your lease, outlining what you need to do.

Beyond when not to do your repairs, there are several common issues that you'll likely run into at one point or another that you'll need to be able to repair on your own.

When Not to Do Your Own Repairs

Some repairs are major and aren't your responsibility. In particular, these are habitable issues, problems with safety, or emergency requests.

✧ **Habitable issues:** If you have an issue that makes the environment uninhabitable, like issues with the electrical system, heating, air conditioning, or plumbing, these are usually concerns that maintenance will handle. Other issues include faulty appliances and pest infestations.

✧ **Safety problems:** Safety problems may include issues with smoke alarms, locks, or carbon monoxide detectors. While you may need to do battery replacements in alarms, your landlord has to make sure these devices function properly. Likewise, the entire property needs to be maintained. If there are trees outside that appear unstable, for example, the property owner has a duty to keep them safe.

✧ **Emergency requests:** Some emergency issues also warrant a call to maintenance for help. These include gas leaks, flooding, water leaks, or mold. If you notice these issues, you should contact maintenance and have them handle the situation.

How to Unclog a Drain

A clogged drain can really bring your daily routine grinding to a halt, especially if it's in your kitchen. However, other clogs can also occur, like in your toilet or bathtub. Thankfully, there are a lot of easy ways you can fix a clog without having to wait for maintenance.

Use a Plunger

A plunger is most commonly used for a toilet but can also be useful in other drains as well. Just be sure that any plunger used in your kitchen isn't shared with the toilet or make sure that it's thoroughly sanitized before using it. These work by forcing water down into the drain pipe to push the clog through and work well in many cases.

Use a Drain Snake

A drain snake or an auger is a long, flexible cable that you can use to push down a drain to pull out major clogs that you can't force through the plumbing with a plunger. With most of these, you simply put the coiled end into the drain and then turn the handle until it catches on something. Then, rotate it around to either catch the clog or break it apart. Recoil the snake and see if you pulled anything out, then flush the drain with hot water. If it's still draining slowly, you can repeat the process with the snake or move on to a liquid drain cleaner to chemically break down the clog.

Use a Liquid Drain Cleaner

Liquid drain cleaners are products you buy from the store that are poured down the drain to chemically break it down. They're great for breaking down clogs in drain systems, like hair or grease, especially in areas you can't easily reach the plumbing, like in a bathtub, but that also means that they can be dangerous if they get on your skin too. Make sure you follow the directions on the product's packaging to remove the drain and take care to avoid getting it on you.

Cleaning a Sink Trap

You may also be able to remove a clog by removing a sink's p-trap and then manually removing whatever is blocking it up. However, this can be messy, too, and you'll need to be careful to have a bucket or some other large container ready to catch any water stuck inside.

The p-trap is the u-shaped pipe underneath a sink and is designed to keep smelly sewer smells from coming through the pipes. This is usually done with a water seal, which means as soon as you remove it, water will spill.

To clean your p-trap, you'll need a flexible wire brush as well as pliers or an adjustable wrench, depending on the setup of your pipe. If you have a hard time visualizing the steps listed below, there are dozens of videos online that can also walk you through the repair step by step.

1. Turn off the water faucet and remember, even if the faucet is off, water will still leak once you remove the trap.

2. Many p-traps can be removed by hand. Twist the big nuts holding the p-trap onto the rest of the plumbing until it loosens. If it's tight, use a wrench or pliers. Be ready to catch the water because it'll start spilling as soon as the nut is loosened.

3. Once you've removed the p-trap, you can clean it out by pulling out any clogs. If needed, use a wire brush to force any clogs through the other end.

4. Put the pipe back into place and tighten the nuts again. Use the wrench or pliers if necessary to get a solid seal. Then run the water for 15–20 seconds to make sure there's no leakage from the nuts. If water

leaks, turn off the faucet and tighten the nuts before testing it again.

Cleaning the Garbage Disposal

Is your garbage disposal getting smelly? This is one of those appliances that you'll want to clean out at least monthly, but every week or every other week is often preferred. While garbage disposals see a lot of water pumping through them, there are areas that aren't easily rinsed clean when used, and that's what you'll need to clean.

It might seem daunting to stick your hand inside an appliance that exists just to break down foods, but you can remove the risk simply by turning off the power to the device at the breaker box. Before you begin, make sure you flip the switch to see if the disposal has been disabled. If it doesn't turn on, flip it off again, and then you can begin the cleaning process.

You'll need:

- ✧ a kitchen sponge
- ✧ a sink stopper
- ✧ dish soap
- ✧ ½ cup baking soda
- ✧ 1 cup vinegar
- ✧ ice cubes
- ✧ 1 cup rock salt
- ✧ water

✧ rubber gloves (if you want them)

Once you've got your tools handy and the power is off (this is important enough to repeat!), it's time to scrub.

1. Put on the gloves if you want to keep your hands clean, and then take the sponge and add dish soap to it. First, you'll want to scrub the baffle, which is the rubber part that leads down into the drain and keeps food from flying back up and out of the drain when using the disposal. Scrub it thoroughly, rinsing the sponge regularly to get rid of all the built-up gunk.

2. Use the sponge to clean out the grinding chamber, scrubbing the walls around the top and sides, and once again rinsing frequently until you stop seeing gunk come up on your sponge. This is enough for a weekly scrub of your disposal, but if it's extra stinky or it's been a while since you cleaned it thoroughly, you'll want to keep cleaning.

3. Dump the baking soda down the drain, then slowly follow up with the vinegar. Place the drain stopper over the drain to keep all the foam inside the garbage disposal, where it'll do its work. Leave it for at least 10 minutes. While waiting, go switch the power back on to the garbage disposal, and after the time is up, rinse the drain with hot water while running the disposal.

4. Turn off the disposal and fill up the drain with ice cubes. Dump in the cup of rock salt, then run the disposal to grind up the ice and salt. This will get any last bits of gunk left behind. Once the ice is ground

up, run some hot water to wash everything through, and your garbage disposal should smell fresh.

How to Clean Washers and Dryers

Washers, in particular, can start smelling dank if you don't take good care of them. The care for these will change based on whether you have a top-loading or front-loading washer. Front-loading washers tend to build up mold inside the door. The easiest way to prevent them from stinking is to remove wet clothes from them promptly and make sure you leave the door open when not in use to dry them out.

If your front-loading washer is starting to stink, you can wipe it down with a mix of 1:9 bleach to water solution and a small scrubber like a toothbrush. From there, the process of cleaning out any residue buildup is the same in both top- and front-loading appliances.

To clean it, you'll want to run a hot cycle with a cup of bleach on the long cleaning cycle. Then, run a second cycle with hot water and two cups of vinegar. Let it sit, then run another long cleaning cycle. Finally, run a long cycle with just hot water.

To be safe, you'll want to make sure the first load of laundry you do after bleaching your washer is just whites. I've learned this the hard way after turning my favorite pink shirt into a shell of what it once was, covered in bleached spots.

Dryers don't need as thorough of a cleaning since there are only clean clothes going into them, but lint can build up. Make sure you remove the lint trap and clean it out before every load of laundry to make sure that lint doesn't build up in the duct. This can be a fire hazard!

Try fitting a vacuum hose into the lint trap to suck out the remaining lint, then wipe out the drum with a mild detergent. You'll also want to clean the exhaust on the back of the dryer if you can. Loosen up the clamp on the back and use your hands to take out as much lint as you can. You'll want to shove your vacuum hose into this as well to suck out any remaining lint.

How to Clean Dishwashers

You might not know this but your dishwasher *also* needs to be cleaned frequently. Yes, the device that sanitizes your dishes can get dirty! If you've noticed that your machine isn't washing as well as it used to or you're getting funky smells coming from it, there's a good chance that the filter needs to be cleaned out. The good news is this is usually an easy cleaning process and with maybe ten minutes of active work, you can have it working as good as new.

You'll either want to have dishwasher cleaning products or baking soda and vinegar so you can break down any grease or soap scum stuck in the appliance.

1. Remove the racks, utensil holders, and the filter from the dishwasher. If you're unsure how, look up the model online or consult the instruction manual. The filter, in particular, will probably look pretty gross if you haven't cleaned it in a while. Scrub out the filter to remove any food, scum, or mold that

may have built up, then soak it in vinegar and warm water while you finish the rest of the scrubbing.

2. Wipe down everything you can see, including spray arms, side walls, and corners where gunk may have gotten stuck. Use a toothbrush or toothpick to get stubborn bits out.

3. Place the filter, racks, and utensil holders back into the machine and either use a dishwasher cleaning product on its own according to the instructions or set a bowl with a cup of vinegar into the bottom of the dishwasher. Run the cycle (sanitation cycle if you have it!).

4. After the vinegar cycle, remove the bowl and toss in a cup of baking soda across the bottom. This will deodorize the dishwasher and also remove any stains that may have gotten stuck. Run an express cycle with the baking soda and you're done!

How to Replace an Air Filter

Air filter replacements should happen frequently, every other month or so, or more often if you have pets or live somewhere that's dry and dusty. This is often a part of maintenance that you're expected to do on your own. You may have a reusable filter that needs to be vacuumed out from time to time, or you may need to replace it on your own. To change it, follow these steps:

1. Find the location(s) of your air filter. There may be more than one that needs to be changed.

2. Make sure you know the right size and get a new one. You'll need the right length, width, and thickness.

3. When you have the new filter, open up the housing and remove the old one. Wipe out any dust or grime from the housing and then place the new filter into the duct, paying attention to the arrows. Then, close the grille and secure it in place.

How to Replace Lightbulbs

If you have a lightbulb that doesn't turn on or is flickering a lot, it's probably time to replace it. Before you crack a joke about how many young adults it takes to change a bulb, know it's really simple. All you have to do is make sure you have the right light bulbs on hand, make sure the light is switched off and that the lightbulb is cooled off, then unscrew the old one and place the new one in.

If you have light fixtures, you may have to remove those first by unscrewing them to gain access to the bulbs. That's okay too! While you're changing your bulbs, consider picking up LED bulbs, which last much longer and are also energy-efficient and can lower your overall energy bill.

Chapter Summary

Doing basic maintenance on your home can be really intimidating if you were never taught to do it before, but it's not so bad after practicing it. Even better, knowing how to maintain appliances can actually help you to keep some money in your pocket instead of rushing out to replace them at the first sign of a problem or if you get a clog somewhere in your drain. Practice, check out tutorial videos online, and trust that you can learn and do these things just like other adults. After all, the handiest person around the house that you know once knew nothing about maintenance too.

With that money you save on repairs, you can throw it toward your savings. The next section of the book talks all about how to manage your finances and keep your spending under control while saving for the future.

PART 2

FINANCIAL LITERACY

Financial literacy makes it okay for you to make small or big mistakes. On the other hand, being financially illiterate only makes those mistakes dire and regrettable

–Anas Hamshari

CHAPTER 5

HEALTHY FINANCES
ARE THE FOUNDATION
OF A HAPPY LIFE

One thing I regret never being taught as a child and a teen is the value of saving money. It's easy to spend when it's sitting in your pocket or bank account, which makes saving all the more difficult when you know you have enough money to buy that new video game, phone, dress, or whatever else has caught your eye. As we'll talk about a few chapters from now, though, saving money, especially when you're able to grow it with interest, is one of the best things you can do for yourself, even if you have to give up a little bit for now to have it later.

While money can't buy happiness in the truest sense, in my experience, it's incredibly difficult to be happy *without* it. That doesn't mean that you need to strive for lavish vacations, designer brands, and partying it up without a care in the world to be happy, but feeling secure is difficult if you're scraping every last cent together to pay your bills or buy that cheap pack of ramen to have something to eat for the day. Having your finances in order means that you can alleviate some of that stress, and it all begins with budgeting. Through budgeting, you can save money and manage it better. The result? Less stress and more time to enjoy yourself, even if you're skipping out on that fun event everyone else is doing or not eating out as often as before.

The Basics of Budgeting

Budgeting is as simple as meeting three simple steps: Tracking your income, your expenses, and managing what's left over. The hard part is finding the willpower to stick to your budget. I personally manage my budget weekly and monthly using a spreadsheet with all of my family's expenses against the income we receive. Once per week, I tally up all of my expenditures and check them against my budget to make sure I haven't gone over.

Sure, my family gets by well enough that I don't have to count every last dollar or worry about whether I can buy something, but I've found that the only way to grow and *maintain* any wealth is through avoiding lifestyle creep and living well within our means. That means that sometimes, I tell my children no, we won't be going out to a restaurant for dinner when they request it. Could we? Sure. Should we? Not if we've already used our fun money for the week. Staying accountable and true to the budget is the best way that I've found to really help my family financially, and it's a skill I learned a decade later than I should have.

Your budget will help you understand exactly how much money you have for different things. If you decide to spend less in some categories, you may be able to free up additional cash to use elsewhere. For example, if you budget $100 for clothing every month but only spend $50, you've got $50 free that you can use on something fun or to put into savings.

Track Your Income

Income is any money that you have coming in that you can spend from all sources. Whether we're talking about money from a job, royalties, money you get refunded from student loans for living expenses, cash from your parents, or any other source, it's important to count it here so you'll know how much usable money you have. Start writing down all the sources of money you have, the amount you get, and how frequently you get it.

Make sure that, when counting money from jobs, you rely on the after-tax (net) income amounts since the taxes will likely be deducted immediately if you work a traditional job, or if you freelance, you'll have to pay those taxes at some point.

Once you have that number, hold onto it. It might not be as much as it looks like at first when you realize how much money you're spending. That's why it's so important to track your income.

Track Your Expenses

Next, it's time to track your expenses. Either write them down or put them into a spreadsheet for easy access. This will include recurring expenses, like any streaming subscriptions, credit card bills, rent, utilities, and car costs. It should also include a set amount that you spend on living necessities like food, clothing, haircuts, and similar budget lines.

Part of your budget should also include savings for emergencies, car repairs, or other unforeseen expenses. It should also include a line for money that you can use for fun.

With your spreadsheet ready to go, you can now track your expenses. Every week or two, you should sit down and check out all of the expenses from your bank account to see where you're spending money and then deduct that from the monthly allotments for those categories.

Once your budget of expenses is done, you can also begin a plan to save cash.

Pay Yourself First and Build Savings

No matter who you are or what your life plans are, having savings helps bring those goals to life. If you want to buy a house, you'll need healthy savings to do so. If you want to travel the world? You'll need money for that. Starting a business, paying off student debt, and generally just living life require money. Getting into good saving habits now means that it'll be easier to get to a comfortable position later.

One way to see this play out is in a 1960s psychology study by Stanford professor Walter Mischel. He studied the reactions of hundreds of children to determine their ability to delay gratification. The test involved setting a child in a private room with a marshmallow. The child was then told that the adult would leave the room and if the child didn't eat the marshmallow, they'd get two marshmallows later, but if they decided to eat the marshmallow while the adult was out, they wouldn't get the second marshmallow.

Some children ate the marshmallow immediately in the 15 minutes they were alone. Many others tried to wait but gave in a few minutes after. A few children were able to delay their urge to eat the marshmallow and got the second one. This is called delayed gratification—these children wait to enjoy more later.

Even more interesting, the children who were able to delay gratification also tested to have higher SAT scores, lower levels of substance abuse and obesity, and scored better in several other categories than their peers who didn't, including better stress responses and social skills. You can do the same thing with money.

Saving Money Now to Have It Later

If you learn to delay gratification, you get a wealth of benefits, and one of those is in your financial life. If you can turn down the invitation to that concert or choose to eat at home instead of going out, you can quickly build up cash savings that other people squander away on instant gratification.

The sooner you start saving, the less of your income you'll have to save just because your money will have more time to grow and accumulate interest, especially if you choose to invest it. It's recommended that you save 10–15% of your income for retirement if you start in your late teens or early 20s.

Emergency Savings

An emergency fund should be considered fully funded when you have enough in it to cover six months of expenses. Yes, this is probably a lot more than you'd expect, but it's important to have on hand. You never know if you'll get sick or hurt and need to take time off work, or you could lose or leave a job and need time to get a new one. This can also cover major expenses, like buying a new car if you suddenly need to replace it or covering the cost of medical expenses. Try to place at least 10% of your income into emergency savings.

Money Management Tips for Young Adults

Looking for some ways to manage your money and stick more into savings? These are some of my tried and true tricks to free up extra cash.

Skip the Debt. Pay with Cash

You pay a lot in credit card interest, which we'll discuss in the next chapter. Even if you only pay a minimum payment on a credit card, the final price of your purchases are inflated by interest. Pay with cash. If you can't afford it with cash now and it's not a necessity, don't buy it.

Stick to Your Budget

Your budget helps allocate every dollar you have so you know what's available to spend and what's already earmarked for something else. By making sure you stick to your budget, you can make sure that you hit your savings goals each month.

Manage Your Grocery Budget

Groceries are one of the biggest expenses we have. According to the U.S. Department of Agriculture, the average cost for groceries for one person is between $300 and $540 per month, but this can vary widely based on where you live and what kind of diet you eat. Make sure that you keep a close eye on the budget line and plan your meals to help manage your costs.

Consider Generic

Generic brands can help cut out a lot of extra costs. Those few cents between items can add up quickly, and often, generic food is just as good as the name brands. Figure out which foods you're happy to have the generic versions of and buy them to save money.

Coupons and Grocery Store Memberships

Coupons and memberships can help cut the cost of food as well. Make sure you're checking weekly ads and digital coupons to see what you can save, as well as signing up for grocery store loyalty discount memberships where you shop the most.

Cut Out the Subscriptions and Memberships You Don't Need

Do you really need three video or music streaming subscriptions? Are you actually using your gym membership or online gaming? These little subscriptions can be easy to sign up for since they're pretty cheap on their own, but they can quickly add up if you're not careful. Double-check any subscriptions you currently have and see if any of them can be cut out.

Transfer Money to Savings Automatically

Did you know that a lot of banks will allow you to transfer money to your savings account automatically? This is an easy way to put money out of sight immediately before it ever hits your checking account. Consider setting this up with your direct deposit if that's how you get paid.

Be Wise With Unexpected Income

Any time you get a sudden windfall, whether it's some cash for a holiday or birthday or you managed to win a sum of money. You could also wind up inheriting money, depending on your family setup, or getting a bonus at work. Be wise when you get unexpected income. Instead of running out to spend it, consider putting it into savings or investing it instead.

Pay Attention to Taxes

Part of being an adult is paying taxes. If, when you file your taxes, you receive a large tax refund, there's a chance your taxes aren't set up properly.

Spending Freeze

Have you ever heard of a spending freeze? It's a sort of challenge where you don't spend any extra money at all. Don't buy anything nonessential for a month and see how much cash you save.

DIY

While there are some things best left to the professionals, a lot of things can be done yourself, from sewing up minor tears in clothing to refurbishing furniture to give it a nice facelift.

Choose Secondhand Items

Buying things you need secondhand is a great way to pocket the extra cash that would otherwise go toward buying a boxed or brand-new item. While some things should be bought new for sanitary reasons, most things can be bought on secondhand marketplaces like Facebook Marketplace or Craigslist.

Chapter Summary

Making the most of your money is all about stretching your dollar as far as you can and building up savings so you're ready to cover any expenses that may arise. By managing your money, you can better get a handle on any potential debt you may accrue. In the next chapter, we'll be discussing how to safely use credit cards in ways that are beneficial to your financial health.

CHAPTER 6

CREDIT SCORES, CREDIT CARDS, AND DEBT

C redit—it's one of those things that you can't live without but building it can be dangerous. Part of building it requires you to take out loans and credit cards, but if you're not smart about how you use them, you'll do more harm than good.

As a young adult, you most likely won't have any credit, or if you do, it'll probably be pretty bad unless your parents helped you build it by adding you to credit accounts while you were younger to help you piggyback off their scores. Unfortunately, that makes it difficult for you to get housing, rent an apartment, or buy a car if you plan on using a loan. It can be hard to get credit cards, too, unless you know where to look.

This can make a loop where you can't take out lines of credit that won't put you at risk of serious interest payments, which means you can't build your credit easily. If you're like me, you'll fall into the trap of using credit cards as a sort of bridge between what you want and what you can afford. Don't do this! One of the worst things you can do is put yourself in debt over wants.

Credit Scores

If you live in the US, you have a credit score that's tracked by Experian, Equifax, or TransUnion. Many other countries have similar programs used to track creditworthiness that use similar factors in calculating a score.

In the US, this credit score is determined by considering several factors, including:

- ✧ **Debt owed:** The amount you owe versus how much available credit you have is a major component of your credit score. If you use most or all of your available credit, the assumption is that you are making ends meet with your credit because you don't have enough money to cover your monthly expenses, making you a higher risk for defaulting on future credit accounts.

- ✧ **New credit:** This considers how many accounts have been opened recently. People who have recently opened several credit accounts are usually considered a higher risk, so multiple new accounts can lower your score.

- ✧ **Length of credit history:** This is a tough one for young adults, but it's going to be helpful later. Credit scores are calculated in part by how long you've had credit, the age of your oldest account and newest account, and how long it's been since you've used accounts. The length of your credit history plays a part in calculating your score.

✧ **Credit mix:** This refers to the types of credit and loans you have, such as credit cards, installment loans (like cars or student loans), mortgages, and finance company accounts.

✧ **Payment history:** This is one of the biggest factors considered. All payments you make to your credit lines and loans are reported, and if you make them 30 days late or longer, they will be negative marks on your credit.

How to Judge Your Credit Score

Most credit scores range from 300–850, and those scores are divided into several categories that can give you a good idea of how your credit looks. These are:

✧ **Excellent:** 720–850

✧ **Good:** 690–719

✧ **Fair:** 630–689

✧ **Bad:** 300–629

We don't start out with a credit score—the first one is calculated based on your credit usage once you open your first line of credit. For many young adults, this is a student loan, but it may also be a credit card. Your first credit score will be calculated after having at least one credit account open and reporting to one of the three major bureaus for six months. Once you get your first account set up, make it count! Don't run out to celebrate that shiny new Visa card if you can't afford to pay it off.

What if You Miss a Payment?

If you miss a payment, a few things happen. One, you'll probably have some late fees associated with missing it. Two, if it's not paid within 30 days of the due date, it may be marked on your credit report as a missed payment, which will negatively impact your score. Some lenders don't report late payments until after 60 days past due, but you should still always pay your bills on time. Your late payments will remain on your credit report for seven years, which is why it's so important to avoid them whenever possible.

Credit Cards and Debt

Credit cards work by loaning you money to make purchases. In exchange, you owe the lender a debt that has to be repaid with interest. The interest amount will vary based on the terms of the card that you select. The vast majority of credit cards have a pre authorized limit based on your credit score. Many new cards start out with just a few hundred dollars but can go up into the thousands as your credit improves.

Carrying a balance on your credit card means that you owe money even after making the assigned payment, and that balance will be charged interest based on the annual percentage rate (APR) that you agreed to when taking out the card. Many cards use a variable APR that changes over time, and being 60 days late on your card can trigger a penalty APR, which will dramatically increase what you owe.

Some credit cards also come with fees, such as monthly and annual membership fees. While these cards often are easier to get with little or no credit, they're also incredibly expensive and you're essentially paying for the privilege of having it.

Other potential fees you may accrue include balance transfer fees, where you move the balance of one card to another, over-limit fees when you go over the card's credit limit, or late fees for missing the payment.

Credit cards aren't all bad, though. Many of them have perks that can make them worth using—wisely, of course. Credit cards tend to be safer than cash, coming with liability guarantees. It's often easier to dispute a credit charge than it is to fight a debit. Other benefits include:

- ✦ They're easy to use.
- ✦ Some offer rewards and cash back.
- ✦ They boost credit scores when used correctly.

On the other hand, before taking out a credit card and using it, be aware of the cons:

Interest and fees add up when you carry a balance.

They can harm your credit score if you carry a high balance or miss payments.

They make it easy to spiral into debt.

When Should You Use a Credit Card?

As dangerous as credit card usage can be, that doesn't mean that you should never use yours. Learning to use credit cards responsibly is the best thing that you can do for your credit score.

To Access a One-Time Bonus

Some credit cards will offer incentives for you to use them, such as offering a one-time bonus if you spend a set amount of money in the first few months the account is open. If you have an offer like this, using a credit card for your monthly expenses, like food and bills, allows you to then pay it off in full with the cash you'd normally use, avoiding the interest and earning access to the reward.

For Cash Back

Some cards also offer cash back for your purchases. If you have one of those cards, like with the one-time bonuses, you can build up cashback points. Some cards may offer up to 5 or 6 percent cash back on certain purchases, though they often have spending caps.

For Rewards Points or Frequent Flyer Miles

Other cards opt for rewards points or frequent flier miles when you use them. The more you spend, the more points you rack up, which can be used up later.

To Prevent Fraud

As we already discussed, credit cards are much easier to work with to fight fraudulent charges than when you pay with a debit card or cash. Because of this, your credit card offers a safe option for paying for your purchases.

This can also be used for making large payments toward vendors or handymen. If someone does a shoddy job, if you've paid with a credit card, you can get the charge reversed and have access to the money sooner rather than later. If subpar work is done after you've paid for it and you paid in cash, you run the risk of having to spend months fighting to claw back your money through legal avenues.

For Hotels or Car Rentals

If you plan to rent a car or stay at a hotel, you'll be required to use a credit card. This is just in case you cause damages.

Debt and Interest

Loans and credit card balances are considered debts, and they typically accrue interest. Interest rates on credit cards can vary wildly, with the average somewhere around 24 percent. That might not sound that bad, but it can get scary quickly.

Let's say you buy a new gaming console and accessories for $500 on a credit card with an average 24 percent APR. If you make your minimum monthly payment of $35, do you know how long it'd take you to pay it off?

By the time you pay it off in full with minimum payments, it will take 17 months. By the end, you'll have paid $82 in interest, adding that to the cost of the purchase. Is it worth it?

Interest is the cost of debt. It can be simple or complex, and most credit cards use compound interest, allowing it to accrue daily.

Simple Interest

Simple interest assigns the interest at the beginning of a loan at a set percentage. For example, a $100,000 loan with a 3 percent interest rate would have $3,000 in interest charged to it if the whole loan is paid off in a year. This is calculated by multiplying the principal (the amount of the loan) by the interest rate and by the number of years you'll be paying it.

Compound Interest

More commonly, especially with credit cards, you'll pay compound interest. This means that you'll pay interest on accruing interest as well as the principal. When you have to pay compound interest, you pay more over the long run because your balance owed grows while you pay it off. Some of each payment you make goes toward the principal, but the rest goes to pay off interest, meaning you're not paying it off as quickly as you'd probably think.

Chapter Summary

Credit cards might seem like a sudden windfall of fun money, but racking up debt is never a good idea. Even if you really want something, if you can't pay it off in full, you should wait until you can. Save on interest and save your credit score by using your credit wisely. This will help you to invest and plan for your future, which we'll discuss in the next chapter.

CHAPTER 7

INVESTING AND PLANNING FOR THE FUTURE

When you're just getting started in adulthood, it's easy to think that you've got plenty of time before you need to start worrying about retirement. After all, you have a whole career to build up money for your future financial security, right?

Well, the years go by much faster than you'd expect, and the sooner you start investing in yourself and your future, the more money you'll have, thanks to the very same interest you learned about in the previous chapter. When you invest and save, you can gain interest, allowing your money to work for you and grow while it sits. Having a savings account isn't enough to keep your money growing quickly enough to outpace inflation, either. Each year, your money has less buying power just because each year inflation pushes costs up. On average, the U.S. inflation rate is around 3.8 percent, though the COVID-19 pandemic caused it to increase significantly.

What that means is that your $100 one year is worth $96.20 the next, on average. If you leave your money sitting in a savings account, it loses value year after year, and the average interest rate in a savings account is around 0.39 percent. That's only 1/10 the inflation rate, meaning the longer your money sits, even in a savings account, the less spending power you'll have.

There are ways to get around this, and while I'm not delving deeply into these subjects, this will give you an overview of the options that you have. These options can help you safely build up money over time, and the sooner you set them up, the longer that interest can build. Remember this—a dollar that you save early will generate you more than a dollar saved later in life, thanks to the power of compounding interest.

For example, let's say you invest $1,000 right now in an account that has a 5% growth rate. This is how it will compound over the next 60 years:

Year	Total value of investment
0	$1,000
1	$1,050
2	$1,102.50
3	$1,157.63
4	$1,215.51
5	$1,276.28
10	$1,628.89
15	$2,078.93
20	$2,653.30

30	$4,321.94
40	$7,039.99
50	$11,467.40
60	$18,679.19

Looking at these numbers, you can see that they start to jump quickly. Look at the growth in terms of decades:

Period (years)	Growth
0–10	$628.89
10–20	$1,024.41
20–30	$1,668.64
30–40	$2,718.05
40–50	$4,427.41
50–60	$7,191.76

If you were to retire 50 years from now and invest $1,000 today, you'd have $11,467.40 with an annual compounding interest rate of 5%. If you were to wait 30 years from now and then invest $1,000, you'd only have $2,653.30 50 years from today in comparison. The initial investment would be the same, but that extra 30 years of compounding growth makes a big difference. This is why investing early is so important. The longer your money grows, the larger the growth becomes. Three of the best ways to grow your money are through life insurance (but only the right kind), investments, and retirement accounts.

Life Insurance

While life insurance is commonly seen as a way to provide for families in the event that someone dies, it's also a great way to grow money that you can use during your lifetime as well. It's a slower form of investment, but it's also the safest way to grow your money if you set up a policy correctly with the help of a licensed insurance agent.

Life insurance comes in two forms: term and permanent. Term policies are good for a set period of time and are cheaper. You pay into them, but they usually don't build cash value and they only pay out a death benefit if you die during the term you have them. This is great for families worried about making ends meet if they die while a spouse raises children because it provides a safety net while minor children are in the home.

Permanent life insurance is often more expensive, but it can also work to grow cash value that you can then borrow or withdraw while you're still alive. Because the cash value doesn't usually get added to the death benefit that pays out, the money that you invest and grow can be pulled out and used as a way to pay for retirement, investments, or other expenses. Even better, you can take that money out as a loan to avoid paying taxes on this money.

One consideration to make, though, is that if you overfund these life insurance policies, they can convert into a modified endowment contract by the IRS, which can create tax liabilities, meaning that you would owe tax on withdrawing cash value.

According to a 2023 Nerdwallet article, the types of life insurance policies that you can use to invest your cash are whole life insurance or universal life insurance policies.

Whole Life Insurance

Whole life insurance policies are pretty straightforward. They have fixed premiums (the amount you pay per month) and permanent, guaranteed death benefits to your designated beneficiaries. This means that when you die, the beneficiary listed will receive a payout equivalent to the policy value. Your cash value will grow at a fixed rate set by your policy, meaning it won't fluctuate with the market.

Universal Life Insurance

Universal life insurance is more flexible and can grow more, but the death benefit, premiums, and cash value are not guaranteed. They may change with the market, making this a slightly riskier way to grow cash value. On the other hand, you can increase or decrease premiums and death benefits within certain parameters if you realize you want to pay more or you need to reduce them.

Variable Universal Life Insurance

Variable universal life insurance is a type of universal life insurance that allows you to adjust your premiums and death benefits while also giving you control over how to invest any cash value through subaccounts. Cash value grows based on the sub account options and their performance on the market, or the insurance policy may offer a fixed interest rate based on the policy.

Indexed Universal Life Insurance

As another type of universal life insurance, indexed universal life insurance gives similar flexibility in the types of coverage and values. However, cash value earns interest differently with these policies. In this case, the growth is based on how the stock indexes perform. It's kind of like investing in the stock market, so during good market conditions, the cash value grows quicker.

Unlike the stock market, however, an indexed universal life policy typically has an interest floor, meaning cash value will never grow less than a set amount, which is often 0%. What that means is that when the stock market crashes, your cash value is protected. This also comes with interest caps, meaning that your cash value can never accrue interest at a higher rate than whatever is set, even if the stock market sees better performance.

Other types of life insurance exist as well, but these are the main ones used for their cash value. Make sure that you speak with your insurance agent before making any decisions. They will be able to help you understand the terms, answer questions you may have, and recommend the right kinds of coverage for you.

Investments and Retirement Accounts

Investing money is risky and isn't guaranteed, but it is commonly used to grow cash value. By investing smartly, you can increase your chances of seeing growth in your money. Some are tax-advantaged, meaning that they help save you money that would otherwise be spent on taxes or allow you to invest pre-tax income into them, lowering your overall tax obligation.

Types of Investment Accounts

Investing your money will help it grow, and there are plenty of options that you can choose from. Financial planners, brokers, and investment advisors can help you review your options and help you make the best decisions for you and your unique situation.

- ✧ **Annuities:** These are insurance products you can use to create regular income during retirement. Some can be tax-deferred.

- ✧ **Mutual funds:** Mutual funds are managed by a professional who pools together bonds, stocks, and other investments that then get divided into shares and sold to people who want to invest.

- ✧ **Stocks:** Stocks represent a share of ownership in a specific corporation. Their value rises and falls based on the performance of the market or the specific company.

- ✧ **Bonds:** When investing in bonds, you pay to loan money to an issuer, like the government or a business, and you receive interest payments on top of the face value.

- ✧ **ETFs:** An exchange-traded fund (ETF) is an investment that trades like a stock on an exchange but may also include sector indexes or collections of assets.

✧ **Dividend reinvestment plans:** DRIPs let you reinvest your cash dividends into more stock instead of receiving cash dividends.

✧ **Cash investments:** Certificates of deposits (CDs) and money market deposit accounts allow you to invest income short-term in low-risk settings while allowing you to receive interest.

Types of Retirement Accounts

Retirement accounts allow you to invest your income to use specifically for retirement. They can be used effectively, but there are often penalties if you try to withdraw income early. These are the most common ones you'll encounter:

✧ **Defined benefit plans:** Also referred to as pensions, these plans are funded by employers, guaranteeing specific benefits based on how much you made and how long you worked with a company. However, they're not very common if you don't work for the public sector.

✧ **401(k)s:** 401(k)s are sponsored by employers that employees pay into. The money is usually taken out of your pay automatically and then invested, and sometimes even matched up to a certain amount each year.

✧ **Traditional IRAs:** IRAs are retirement accounts that allow you to defer taxes on your contributions. This allows you to invest more upfront because you can put what would have gone to taxes toward the account. Then, when you withdraw the money in retirement, you're taxed at your income rate.

✧ **Roth IRAs:** Unlike traditional IRAs, Roth IRAs are not tax deductible. However, other than that, they work the same as a traditional IRA (Folger, 2022).

Especially if you have an offer from an employer to match your contributions into these retirement accounts, you should try to max them out each year as often as possible to get the most out of them.

Chapter Summary

Investing now will set you up in the future. The sooner you start, the more your money can grow into what you will eventually need. It's never too soon to start thinking about retirement, and when you free yourself from financial stress, you can start thinking about other things, like your relationships.

PART 3

RELATIONSHIPS AND COMMUNICATION

Communication to a relationship is like oxygen is to life. Without it, it dies.

–Tony A. Gaskins Jr.

CHAPTER 8

DIFFERENT RELATIONSHIPS, SAME FOUNDATIONS

We all crave relationships in our lives. Friendships, familial relationships, romantic partners, and even workplace relationships help meet our social needs and can make us feel fulfilled and confident in ourselves. I don't know where I'd be in life without my family or friends, and I'm sure you feel the same way.

But relationships aren't easy to maintain, and knowing how to spot and leave a bad relationship can be even harder. Knowing how to navigate relationships is one of the most important skills you can learn. Part of being able to navigate is knowing how to communicate, which we'll discuss in the next chapter. Part of it is also knowing what goes into fostering and maintaining those connections. After all, they're two-way streets.

No matter what kind of relationship you're talking about, they all should be based on mutual trust, honesty, open communication, and respect. Remember that you deserve to be treated well, and respect is a basic human decency, not something that needs to be earned.

Relationships should make you feel good. They should make you feel heard and seen, and you should feel like you can be yourself in them. Those that don't make you feel good or those that show signs of red flags can be harmful to your mental health. I've had toxic friendships and I know how much they can mess with your mind. I know what it's like to feel like I was the problem and that if I changed, I could enjoy the relationship that I wanted with the other person. The truth was, the foundation for a healthy relationship just wasn't there with them.

The Foundation of a Healthy Relationship

Relationships of all kinds are hard work. Yes, it seems like this is something that should be simple, but the reality is they aren't. They take a lot of effort to maintain, but in the end, the effort is worth it. There will be times that you fight with those you care about, and we'll talk about solving those conflicts in a healthy manner in the next chapter. No matter what is going on in your relationship, however, these four factors should be present. You should always feel like there is a foundation of honesty, trust, open communication, and respect, even in conflicts.

Honesty

Honesty is where transparency and authenticity shine through. It is what allows you to tell the other person anything without fear of judgment or backlash and what allows the other person to come to you as well. It's easy to feel tempted to slip into dishonesty to avoid hurting someone's feelings, but this isn't a good way to approach the situation. It can be harmful to the relationship because you aren't being straightforward.

Honesty involves being able to share what you feel and trust the other person with that information, building intimacy. Intimacy isn't limited to just romantic relationships, either. To be intimate with someone is to be *close* to them. It's to be connected and supported and comfortable with the other person, and it's present in most personal relationships to various degrees. Yes, you're usually the most intimate with your romantic partner if you have one, but sharing your thoughts and secrets with your best friend or a parent is another way to be intimate.

Trust

Trust in relationships allows you to feel safe and confident with the other person. You know that they will not hurt or betray you. As a result, you can be vulnerable and honest with that other person. Friends, family members, and romantic partners can all be some of our most valued confidantes, allowing us to connect and show our truest selves to them.

Trust brings so much to our relationships. It fosters positivity, forgiveness, and closeness. It helps us to navigate and reduce conflict because when you trust someone, you feel more compelled to find solutions and common ground or to give them the benefit of the doubt when (not if!) they mess up.

Trust is a beautiful thing, but it's also something that has to be built and fostered. It's fragile and easy to destroy, and once you damage trust, rebuilding it is even harder. To foster it, you need to communicate honestly and be on the same page with the other person.

Without trust, you can harm your relationship, eroding it with secrecy and pushing away your loved one. Trust can be hurt by insecurity, which can make you even more insecure in your relationship with the other person.

Open Communication

Open communication builds upon the previous two foundations, helping to secure the relationship by discussing anything that may get in the way of it. Problems and fights happen. In fact, according to John Gottman, a relationship researcher, the magic ratio between positive and negative interactions is 5:1, meaning that for every one negative interaction, there should be five positive ones. That sounds like a lot more negative interactions between people than would be expected, but it just goes to show how common conflict really is.

That's why it's so important to have open communication. Not only will it build trust in a relationship, but it will also help solve those conflicts in a constructive manner, which will help you to strengthen your connection with the other person.

Respect

The problem with respect is that so many people see it differently. You've got a whole group of people who believe that respecting someone is listening to them, while other people say respect is treating someone with basic human decency. The respect you need in any relationship is the kind where you regard them with kindness. You treat them well like you'd want to be treated.

Mutual respect forms the foundation of relationships of all kinds and is shown through giving consideration to the other person's feelings, thoughts, and boundaries. To respect someone is to show you care about them through how you act and speak toward them. It can also involve being accountable for your actions when you make a mistake or hurt someone's feelings. No relationship is perfect, but respecting the other person should be a common pattern.

Relationship Red Flags

Red flags can pop up in just about any relationship, from romantic partners to coworkers. When you see red flags waving, it's your sign to run like the wind, or at least consider the relationship heavily because there's something toxic going on. Some of these red flags may not be obvious if you're not looking for them, but they are a sign that the other person isn't likely to be in a healthy relationship of any kind.

Violent Or Abusive Actions

While violence is straightforward, abuse can take several different forms, all of which are red flags. You can experience abuse in more than just romantic relationships too. Friends, family, and coworkers can be abusive. Some types of abuse include:

✧ **Physical abuse:** This is any type of physical violence or threats used to keep control of a situation. It includes throwing, breaking, or destroying objects.

✧ **Emotional abuse:** Emotional abuse is a lot harder to identify because it's non-physical. It's any behavior designed to isolate, control, or scare you, like name-calling, insults, possessiveness, trying to get you to cut off your friends or family, monitoring your behaviors, humiliating you in front of others, gaslighting, and blaming you for their abusive actions. It could also include threatening you or damaging your belongings.

✧ **Financial abuse:** When a partner limits access to finances or actively hinders your ability to earn money, they are financially abusive. This isn't the same as expecting adherence to a budget—it involves actively preventing access to funds, maxing out your credit cards, a refusal to contribute while expecting you to work for everything, or refusing money for necessary expenses.

✧ **Sexual abuse:** Sexual abuse happens when a partner or other person takes control of physical and sexual intimacy without consent. It includes manipulating or guilting into having sex, nonconsensual sexual actions, ignoring how you feel about sex, or intentionally attempting to give you a sexually transmitted infection. Sexual abuse can be present in any kind of relationship or even without a relationship with the other person.

✧ **Digital abuse:** Digital abuse uses the internet to bully, intimidate, or control a partner, often through emotional abuse.

✧ **Stalking:** Stalkers follow, harass, or watch their target despite being told to stop, causing them to feel uncomfortable, unsafe, or afraid.

Mismatch in Goals

This is more of a romantic relationship red flag than any other kind. When you and your partner want vastly different things, it's a red flag for the relationship because it means someone will have to give up their wants for the other party. For example, if you want children but your romantic partner doesn't, you have to grapple with whether you're willing to forego having kids to keep your partner or if you're both simply too incompatible for each other. It could also involve career goals, how to handle finances, or irreconcilable political or religious differences.

Jealousy

When someone is constantly jealous when you spend time with other people, regardless of what your relationship with them is, it's a sign of insecurity. That insecurity can be incredibly damaging to your relationship and cause issues down the road. It can also be a sign of possessiveness.

Lack of Trust

Trust is the foundation of all relationships, and without it, there's no real healthy relationship.

Lying or Infidelity

Both lying and infidelity involve dishonest behaviors and can be major red flags in any relationship. People comfortable with lying to you often continue to lie, and without being able to trust the other person, it's hard to maintain any kind of relationship.

Controlling

People who attempt to control you by limiting access to other people, telling you what to do, or otherwise attempting to monitor your behavior are usually not respectful of your autonomy. While, especially at work, there's some expectation that your supervisors will tell you what to do, it shouldn't get to the point where it's controlling you outside of work as well.

Stories of "Crazy Exes"

This goes for friends, bosses, coworkers, and romantic partners. If the person you are speaking to has a bunch of stories about how other people are all problematic for a bunch of reasons, there's a good chance that you're not getting the whole picture. For example, if your new romantic partner has a whole slew of exes that all are terrible, dishonest, and controlling, there's a chance that your partner actually has unresolved issues that will make it difficult to have a meaningful, healthy relationship with them and they perceive healthy boundaries, conversations, and expectations as wrong.

Inability to Maintain Friendships

People who have no friends or struggle to maintain friends or relationships often have a reason for it. This is especially true if you hear a lot of deflection and refusal to take personal accountability for any part in their situation.

Gaslighting

Gaslighting can be a huge problem in many relationships, causing you to think that you are wrong. It happens when someone says or does things that make you question your own perception of what happened. For example, they might say they don't know what you did with your phone when you notice that it's not on the counter anymore and mention how you often lose it when, in fact, they have it in their pocket. They can use other tactics to manipulate you and make you feel like you're the problem instead in an attempt to control you and your behavior.

Love Bombing

Love bombing is the attempt to gain love and trust quickly by showering someone with praise and affection. They may tell you how much they love you, how you're different from everyone they've ever known, or give you plenty of gifts in an attempt to make you feel good. By making you feel good, adored, and desired, they essentially create an addiction to those feelings, but it usually fades over time. Once you're hooked, you get less affection and adoration, so you chase after getting back to that pedestal, which is how the person love bombing gets control.

Breadcrumbing

Breadcrumbing is another way to play with your feelings by giving you just enough affection or encouragement to keep you hooked on the relationship. However, as you try to get closer, they'll pull back. If you start to lose interest, they'll give you more. There's no commitment with this type of hot-and-cold behavior.

Chapter Summary

While you're not defined by the people around you, they do influence you. Healthy relationships of all kinds need healthy foundations, and as you gain more experience in life, you'll learn to spot the red flags and know when something isn't quite right. This will help you to communicate better in your relationships, too, because you'll be able to articulate what you see that's wrong and make moves to fix the problems. The next chapter is all about learning healthy, effective communication techniques.

CHAPTER 9

DEVELOPING HEALTHY COMMUNICATION SKILLS

C ommunication can be *hard.* You can say one thing and the other person can hear something completely different from what you intended to convey. Back when I was dating my husband, I remember a conversation we had when we just weren't on the same page. We had an argument that was so unimportant I can't even remember what it was about. I just remember feeling frustrated, unheard, and unloved. We weren't on the same page, and I really thought it'd be the end of our relationship.

Nowadays, we have much better skills regarding our communication. We're capable of talking through our issues and finding common ground that will help us to get past our conflicts. Don't get me wrong, those arguments still suck. It's never fun to fight with someone you care about, but it's much easier to get back on the same page and keep moving forward when you have the right tools in your toolbox.

Communicating Effectively

The best thing you can do for your relationships of all kinds is learn how to communicate clearly and effectively. These are strategies that I've implemented and dedicated myself to teaching my own children to better prepare them for adulthood and I think that anyone could benefit from them. If you put these tools to the test, especially if your loved ones do them with you (remember, communication is a two-way street, after all!), then you'll probably see improvements in how you interact and get along with each other too. It all begins with learning how to listen actively, and then begin putting these strategies to good use.

Active Listening

When you listen actively, you do more than just hear the words the other person has to say. It's about really understanding the meaning of the words being told to you before you ever begin formatting a response. All too often, people get so caught up in trying to respond as quickly as they can or thinking of how they'll respond instead of paying attention to what's being conveyed.

To listen actively, you need to:

- ✧ Be present in the conversation, giving it your complete focus.
- ✧ Hold eye contact and open body language to convey interest in the conversation.
- ✧ Pay attention to body language cues.

✧ Instead of responding, ask open-ended questions to encourage the other person to elaborate.

✧ Before responding, paraphrase what you have heard to make sure that you're both on the same page.

✧ Listen without judgment or without giving advice unless it's asked for.

How to Communicate Effectively

Being able to listen only helps with half of the communication. After all, it takes two to communicate; otherwise, it's just a lecture. Communicating effectively requires you to be comfortable with not only listening but also with responding.

Choosing to speak concisely is a great way to help improve communication skills. Stick to the basics, especially when emotions run high. I've experienced arguments that quickly devolve because we get stuck on tangents instead of focusing on what matters the most, and it's never fun. To avoid this, if you have to have a heavy conversation, try planning it ahead of time.

While sometimes, these conversations pop up when you least expect them, there's nothing wrong with stopping in the moment, saying you need some time to think, and coming back to the conversation when you and the other person are calmer and able to tackle it on with a level-headed approach. Some other great ways to keep your communication clear include:

✧ **Pay attention to body language:** Your body speaks just as much as your mouth does, and if you're not careful, you may send off cues that disrupt what you actually want to say. For example, if your body language comes off as angry, the other person may get defensive, which will shut down any effective communication.

✧ **Be careful with your tone:** Like body language, how you speak and your tone of voice will also influence what you're trying to say. Would you want to listen to someone tell you how to be confident if they stuttered and stumbled over their words in the most timid voice you've ever heard? Probably not! Speak calmly, especially during important conversations.

✧ **Avoid judgment:** You don't necessarily have to agree with what the other person has to say, but you should hold off on judgment. When you communicate with someone, you need to be open to what they have to say and hear them out to truly understand what they're saying.

✧ **Pause before you speak:** This goes back to taking the time to communicate clearly. While you don't necessarily have to take a break mid-conversation, you should take a moment to breathe before responding to make sure you've thought out what you want to say.

✧ **Use "I" statements:** Especially when emotions are high, you should stick to "I" statements. For example, "I feel like you don't have time for me" is a much more effective phrase compared to "You never make time for me." Instead of making it an attack or a judgment, you're discussing your feelings instead.

This stops defensiveness or arguing over whether that's actually the case or just your perspective on it (which is valid, too!).

By learning to communicate better, you can help avoid conflicts, but not all of them can be dodged. It's only natural for there to be disagreements sometimes, and that's okay! You and the other person, no matter who they are to you, don't have to see eye to eye on every single thing. You're both unique people with your own thoughts, feelings, and experiences guiding you.

Conflict Resolution

As natural as conflict is in every relationship, it's still a big drag, and it can be something that a lot of us try to run away from. Running from conflicts and constantly people-pleasing to avoid them can both be huge detriments to your relationships and your mental health. As tempting as it can be to ignore them, all this does is let them continue to fester and worsen, and when they finally explode, the results can be disastrous. But conflicts are also opportunities for growth and bettering your relationships with other people. They let you build trust and feel secure that you and the other person can work through your disagreements.

Because conflict triggers such strong emotions that can get the best of us sometimes, it's important to stay ahead of your stress level when you face one. To handle a conflict healthily, sometimes you need to put a pin in it for later to calm down, which is absolutely valid, as long as you come back to it later instead of ignoring it.

Solving your conflicts will require you to:

- ✧ manage your stress without getting distracted.
- ✧ stay grounded and control your behavior while managing your emotions.
- ✧ listen to the other person's feelings.
- ✧ respect your differences.

Sounds easy enough, right? Well, like all things worth doing well, it's easier said than done. Try implementing some of these strategies to help defuse your conflicts.

No Interruptions

Take turns speaking instead of constantly trying to butt in. Let one person have the floor to speak their mind while the other listens actively. Once you confirm you understand what the other person is saying, you can formulate your response.

Discuss From a Place of Curiosity

A lot of times, conflicts arise because you and the other person aren't on the same page. Approaching the conversation from a place of curiosity and without judgment allows both of you to better understand each other. You may learn something new about the other person, which can be useful in avoiding future conflicts over the same issue.

Use Repair Attempts

Repair attempts are ways that we try to reconnect with someone after a conflict arises. They can help assure the other person that you see that there's a problem and that you want to de-escalate. Some people turn to humor (but make sure the other person won't get more upset!), say you understand, and show positive, open body language. You could even offer a hug or hold their hand to show that you care and don't want to continue fighting.

Apologize—The Right Way

Genuine apologies are more than just saying, "I'm sorry." They should also say what you did wrong, why it was wrong, and what you'll do in the future to avoid the problem. They should also include some sort of restitution—an offer to make it right. Apologies should never be followed by "but" or other words that immediately imply you're going to deflect or justify your actions.

For example, "I'm sorry I broke your laptop. I really wasn't paying attention to where I was walking, and I didn't mean to knock it off the desk. I'll be sure to pay more attention in the future to avoid this. Is there anything I can do to make it up to you?"

Ask What They Need

This is a point that should go both ways. You should tell the other person what you need while also asking them what they need to find some sort of resolution. Don't be afraid to vocalize what you need from them to prevent this from being an issue again in the future. They aren't mind readers, and neither are you. This helps boost communication and keep you both on the same page.

Find a Compromise

In many conflicts, a compromise can be a great way to put an end to the argument. While it's not always right (or fair) to expect a compromise, such as if you have a roommate who never cleans up after themselves (been there, done that!) and you're sick of playing maid, in many cases, compromise can be one of your most valuable tools.

For example, imagine that you and your best friend both have vastly different ideas for a fun night. Your friend wants to go out to the club or hang out at a party while you prefer staying in. A valid compromise is that you go out one night and stay in the next. Or, let's say you like to sleep with a TV on but your college dorm roommate prefers to sleep in the dark and silence. A good compromise here could be you watching videos on your phone with the screen dimmed and a set of headphones so you both mostly get what you want.

Sometimes, compromises may seem unreasonable to you, especially if they push you past certain boundaries that you have. It's okay, and even healthy, to have boundaries, and that means you also need to know how to enforce them.

Boundary Setting

Boundaries are the lines you draw in relationships that you do not tolerate being crossed. It could be something like don't take food off your plate or that you want to be called a certain name. Your boundaries are a form of self-care that help you to feel safe and secure in your relationship. They should be communicated clearly and protected as long as they're healthy.

Unhealthy boundaries can be dangerous and tend to either harm or hold you back or attempt to exert control over someone else. Some common unhealthy boundaries (which are also red flags in relationships!) are:

✧ putting yourself down or letting someone else put you down.

✧ attempts to control someone else's behavior, such as saying that the other person can't have any friends other than you.

✧ attempts to change someone else, telling them how to act or what to do.

The boundaries you'll enforce in your life will be related to you and your wishes. Healthy ones create a sort of reflection of your lifestyle, showcasing the rules, principles, and guidelines that you have for your relationships. Some common healthy boundaries you may choose include:

✧ refusing to be manipulated or blamed for someone else's actions.

✧ expecting to be treated with respect and kindness.

✧ asking for space when you need it and expecting the request to be respected.

✧ communicating what makes you uncomfortable and expecting the request to be respected.

✧ expecting a certain degree of privacy with journals, passwords, or certain feelings or events.

✧ expecting your time to be respected.

✧ expressing sexual boundaries and expecting them to be respected.

✧ expecting your religion (or lack thereof) to be respected.

✧ protecting your material possessions and what will and won't be shared.

Your exact boundaries may deviate from these, such as saying that if someone leaves you hanging and doesn't respect your time, then you'll stop waiting for them. It's okay to protect your boundaries, and although it might feel like you're retaliating against the person who broke them, you aren't. If your boundaries are broken, especially repeatedly and after many attempts at communicating them clearly, then you are well within your rights to remove yourself from the situation.

Setting Your Boundaries

Establishing your boundaries shouldn't be difficult in a healthy relationship, especially if you put your good communication skills to the test. It's all about communicating them and it's often best to do so in a moment of calmness. After a boundary has been crossed, handle the natural anger you feel first and then write down what's bothering you so you won't forget it.

When you've calmed down, you can go to the other person and calmly and clearly state what happened and how it made you feel. You can then assert your boundary, stating exactly what that boundary is, that you will not tolerate it being crossed or ignored, and why it's a problem.

This should come from a place of love and kindness, explaining that you trust the other person not to violate your boundaries, and you should follow up by asking the other person if there are any boundaries that they need enforcing. They should have some things that they state are their non-negotiable points. You can model good boundary respecting as well by following theirs and apologizing whenever you make a mistake.

Setting and enforcing your boundaries is part of keeping yourself healthy. Your mental health and self-care are just as important as feeding yourself or sleeping. Remember that your boundaries are what allow you to feel safe and secure, and in healthy relationships of all kinds, people respect those boundaries.

Chapter Summary

Healthy communication will take you far in life. It'll help you to relate to others, express your own boundaries, and solve conflicts. Skills like active listening and learning not to interrupt others can all help you to be more successful in your communication, and when you can communicate well, you can work better with the people that surround you, whether they're coworkers, classmates, or your friends and family, reducing stress, and increasing positive feelings. All of this can have an overall impact on your general health too.

Moving into the next section of the book, we're taking a closer look at your physical and mental health, which go hand in hand.

PART 4

HEALTH AND WELLNESS

Self-care is not selfish. You cannot serve from an empty vessel.

–Eleanor Brown

CHAPTER 10

PHYSICAL AND MENTAL HEALTH GO HAND-IN-HAND

Your body and mind might seem like two separate things, but the truth is, they're more connected than most people would think. From the gut-brain axis influencing the neurotransmitters that make you think and feel to exercise being a fantastic way to boost energy levels and mental health, the two are highly linked. The best way to take care of your mind is to take care of your body and vice versa. After all, how good will you feel mentally if your body aches or is too tired to do anything? Or how good do you think you'd feel physically if you're stuck in anxiety or depression?

By taking care of both your body and mind, you'll feel your best. That means getting enough sleep, eating healthily, and keeping hydrated. It also means being able to guard your mental health with healthy boundaries and good mindsets. When both your body and mind are healthy, you have more energy and mental bandwidth to take care of the things you need to do, like work, keep stress levels down, or maintain good relationships.

The Connection Between Physical and Mental Health

Our bodies react to our perceptions of the world around us that our minds generate. When you think something is scary, your body responds in kind, entering the fight, flight, or freeze response. While your college final is a far stretch from being as dangerous as a lion staring you down, your body still reacts the same way to stress-inducing events, regardless of the actual threat level they may pose.

Now, imagine that you constantly live with stress. You're busy with school and work, and you want to spend time with friends. Or you're having a hard time somewhere. What do you think your body does? Those stress hormones prepare your body to fend off the potential threat, causing your heart to race, inducing anxiety, and building up cortisol. This redirects your body's energy and efforts to survival instead of maintenance processes that usually happen at rest.

While short bursts of these hormones aren't a big deal for your body; when you live under a constant state of stress, cortisol, a stress hormone, can cause inflammation throughout your body. Extended periods of exposure to this can lead to depression and constant feelings of fatigue while also weakening your immune system. In other words, people who are stressed often get or feel sick, and it can also increase their risk of several diseases.

Much of what you need to do to stay healthy uses this connection between body and mind. Exercise, for example, is great for you and boosts your mood. Eating healthy foods encourages a healthy gut biome, which also leads to having more energy and feeling better overall.

Maintaining a Healthy Body and Mind

Your body is the only one you get, so taking care of it is important. Yeah, you're young and your body can bounce back from a lot more than mine can. You can probably eat that extra slice of pizza without a care in the world, whereas I have indigestion if I so much as think about indulging. Just because you're young doesn't mean that you should neglect your health, even if your body can take it.

When I was in college, I lived off cheap ramen, pizza, and microwave meals. Let me tell you, if I tried to make that my diet today, it wouldn't be a fun time. I also rarely bothered with exercise and lived by the motto of "Sleep is for the weak! I'll sleep when I'm dead." It's a wonder my body never gave out on me from the years of abuse in my young adult years.

Nowadays, I make sure I walk the dogs for at least an hour most days. I eat healthy, well-balanced meals. I'm that boring old lady that goes to sleep at 10 each night when before, I'd still be getting ready for that night out. And you know what? My body feels so much better for it. I've noticed the slip in my mood and energy levels when I'm not taking care of myself the way I should be.

Taking care of yourself might feel like a huge time sink, but like saving for the future, it's an investment in yourself and your long-term health.

Sleep

While teens need an average of 8–10 hours of sleep per day, including potential naps, adults need around 7. I know, I know. If you're in college and have a job and a semi-healthy social life, it's more likely that you'll live off of copious amounts of coffee, energy drinks, and the occasional quick nap between classes in the library. Here in Seattle, I've walked through the campus at the University of Washington to enjoy the cherry blossom blooming and have seen students sleeping in the grass under the trees!

When we're busy, it's easy to make sleep the first thing we cut, but your body needs it consistently. Getting those 7 hours of sleep each day should be a major priority for you whenever possible. This is best done by consistently sleeping and waking at the same time. Of course, young adults have lives to live and people to see, but your sleep quality will have a major impact on your overall health and well-being.

Try keeping your room dark, comfortable, and relaxing. If you're able to, avoid electronics from the bedroom and try to skip large meals, caffeine, or alcohol before bed. All of this helps foster healthier sleep, which can leave you feeling better overall. Exercise can also help you sleep easier at night.

Exercise

Exercise helps you to maintain a healthy weight, but it also does more than that. It can improve your mood, brain health and keep you energetic, as well as strengthen your body and reduce the risk of many diseases. Ideally, you'd be active at least 150 minutes per week, which sounds like a lot but it is really just 30 minutes five days per week. Part of getting your exercise in for the day should include two days of strength training, making sure to focus on all major muscle groups at least once.

If this is tough to schedule in, there are plenty of ways to change up your daily schedule to stay active and still reap the benefits. Try implementing some of these:

- ✧ If you work at a desk often, use a standing desk.
- ✧ Walk to work, class, or on errands instead of driving if possible.
- ✧ Park in the back of parking lots and walk inside instead of parking as close to the store as possible.
- ✧ Take the stairs instead of the elevators.
- ✧ Implement a daily walk after work to decompress.
- ✧ Wake up 30 minutes early to get a quick workout in from home.
- ✧ Use an under-desk bicycle for some extra exercise.
- ✧ When you're watching TV, get a quick bit of exercise in during commercials.
- ✧ Have some basic small exercise equipment at home or easily available for at-home workouts.
- ✧ Use the weekend to catch up on missed exercise during the work or school week.

The more consistently you exercise, the easier it will become, and soon, you may find that you feel much better than you did before.

Diet

Eating healthily can be a challenge. From healthy whole foods often being more expensive than processed foods to needing to find time to meal plan and prep, it can be tough to squeeze it in. We've already addressed plenty of ways to implement a good, healthy meal plan, but now's the time to dive into what makes a healthy meal and how it'll benefit you.

Eating healthy meals can improve overall wellness by providing everything your body needs to thrive. It's associated with benefits such as longer lives, healthy skin, teeth, and eyes, and a lower risk of heart disease, type 2 diabetes, and cancer. It's also a major component in maintaining a healthy weight.

On the mental health frontier, a healthy diet full of nutrient-rich foods decreases mood swings and improves your ability to focus for longer periods. Some studies also suggest that clean diets can improve the symptoms of depression and anxiety, as opposed to unhealthy diets being associated with an increased risk of dementia or stroke.

Healthy diets often are fiber-rich, which helps keep your blood sugar (and energy) steady to avoid sugar crashes. Antioxidants in healthy foods fight inflammation, which can help counteract the effect of long-term stress. Probiotic-rich fermented foods improve your gut bacteria biome, which can leave you feeling better as well. Folate, a B vitamin, manages dopamine production, while vitamin D, which you get from sunlight and foods like mushrooms, can boost serotonin and moods. Magnesium is crucial for nerve and muscle function while also keeping your gut bacteria healthy. Mineral deficiencies can set your biome off-kilter, which can lead to anxiety and depression symptoms.

Implementing a wide range of whole foods is one of the easiest ways to get everything your body needs. It can be tempting to just pop multivitamin supplements, but keep in mind that the nutrients in food are often much more bioavailable than in supplement form, meaning that your body can better benefit from them in food sources.

I know how hard it is to get a rainbow on your plate every day, a way that many people rely on to get a range of vitamins in their diet. However, there are little changes you can make that will taste great and help keep your body healthy. This is what I do to make sure I get most of what I need in my diet.

Add More Fiber

Fiber keeps you full and your blood sugar stable. I keep prepped veggies available in my fridge to grab whenever I need a quick snack. Celery and carrots do great in jars of water! They last much longer than if you just left them in a bag. Reach for whole grains, beans, and lentils when you really need some staying power in your diet.

Vitamin D and Calcium Go Hand in Hand

When eaten together, vitamin D and calcium have a synergizing effect. Many foods are fortified with these nutrients to boost their bioavailability. Foods like milk, salmon, and dark, leafy greens will give you the boost you need. Remember, we get a lot of our vitamin D from sunlight, so don't forget to get outdoors!

Skip the Added Sugars

Added sugar may taste good, but all it does is prepare you for some serious sugar crashes. Instead of soda, opt for water with fruit slices, or use fresh fruit to sweeten your yogurt instead of buying the sweetened stuff.

Healthy Fats

We need fats to function, but only if they're the right kind. Ditch the saturated fats for unsaturated ones, like olive oil, instead of canola oil or margarine. Limit red meats in favor of seafood or vegetarian meals, and when you do choose pork or beef, try to choose leaner cuts.

Be Careful With Salts

We need both salt and potassium in balance with each other for our nerves to work. However, it's really easy to get too much salt and not enough potassium, which can leave you feeling unwell and raise your blood pressure. Cut out food from restaurants and processed sources and make your own food and rely on herbs and seasonings instead of salt.

An ideal plate will be half fruits and veggies (ideally of different colors), a quarter whole grains, and a quarter protein. Especially if you live in the United States, you probably have the idea that your meal is built around protein, but really, it should be built around the plant-based foods you choose.

Food is expensive, but it's also an important way to keep your body healthy. It's another way of self-care. Another way to look at it is that if you eat healthy foods, you may save money on medical expenses.

Chapter Summary

Your health is one of the biggest investments you'll ever make in yourself. Yes, it can be expensive to take care of yourself well with rising food costs, but this is one where you shouldn't skimp if you don't have to. You can still be mindful of expenses and eat well if you put together good meal plans and keep a healthy diet, and having a healthy body is one of the best ways to make sure that you have a healthy mind as well. In the next chapter, we're going to discuss just how important self-care is and what you need to do to keep your mental health in good shape.

CHAPTER 11

SELF-CARE AND HEALTHY HABITS

S kipping out on self-care is another thing we tend to do to maintain our busy schedules. Why take that mental health time when you have to study and write that paper or you have overtime for the week and still have chores to do? Well, the answer is simple: You can't be on the go constantly and worrying about everything but yourself. Taking time to implement self-care can be one of the best ways to avoid burnout and improve your mental health. Some aspects of self-care are meeting your basic physical needs, like we talked about in the last chapter. Eating good foods, sleeping well, and keeping your body in shape with exercise are all forms of self-care.

I've been hit by burnout before, exhausted and feeling like I didn't have the mental energy to do *anything*. I didn't want to do chores and they piled up. I could barely drag myself out of bed to work or get to class. I had chosen a particularly heavy course load for the quarter and was maxing out the number of credits I could take as a full-time student. I also worked to pay my bills and support myself at the time. I was up at 6 a.m. to get ready for school, had classes from 8–3 most days, with small breaks between them that I spent working on homework and studying. I worked from 6–10 p.m. most days, got home at 10:30 p.m., and did homework til close to 2–3 a.m. most days. I threw out exercise, time with friends, and my hobbies, telling myself it was temporary and I'd be fine.

Halfway through the quarter, midterms came around, and I had two long research papers and two exams to study for, plus my usual work. Of course, most of my coworkers were also college students and had asked for extra time off, which led to me being scheduled for longer shifts than usual. I was eating nothing but processed garbage when I could spare a few minutes and awake through the magic of caffeine.

One evening, on my way to work, I found myself feeling completely drained. I drank another energy drink and went on my way, only to start feeling jittery and lightheaded, like I'd pass out if I didn't sit down. Long story short, I got sent home from work by my manager because he was afraid I'd genuinely pass out at work and had the longest sleep I had for weeks.

My dear husband, who was my long-term boyfriend at the time, fussed over me and babied me for the rest of the evening, giving me that "I told you so" look without actually saying the words out loud. And sure enough, he *had* told me so. He'd tried to discourage me from taking so many classes or accepting so many hours. He'd encouraged me to ask for time off that week well in advance, but I was convinced we needed the money. He'd begged me to take time to myself to rest and relax when he'd catch me dozing off on my textbooks at my desk, but I told him I couldn't. Long story short, he was right. He loved me and wanted me to take care of myself. I had assumed that I'd have time to rest later.

Why Self-Care Matters

Self-care matters because it keeps us from burning out, it relieves the pressures of daily life, and lets us rest. Without rest, it's hard to maintain high levels of productivity for long. You might get a quick burst out of foregoing the self-care, but it's not sustainable, and you can very quickly end up like me, exhausted and feeling like utter garbage. I burnt the proverbial candle from both ends and by the time it was completely gone, I was in need of some serious rest.

I could have completely avoided the problem with self-care, which is proven to reduce anxiety, depression, and stress. As a result, it makes us more able to concentrate, feel happier, and have more energy. Speaking purely physically, self-care has been shown to reduce heart disease, cancer, and stroke. It can also greatly improve our quality of life by encouraging us to follow our passions and remain rooted in what we want and need the most in life.

Types of Self-Care

Self-care can take many different forms, from taking care of our bodies to finding things we love to do and making time for them. I like to break down self-care into three categories, depending on what it does for us at the time: physical, emotional, and spiritual.

Physical Self-Care

Physical self-care is all about taking care of your body and involves most of what we talked about in the previous chapter.

Emotional Self-Care

Emotional self-care emphasizes how we take care of our mental health. It can involve our self-talk, setting boundaries to protect us from unnecessary stress, or taking time to ourselves to rest and enjoy ourselves. Try setting up a coffee date with a friend or a weekly movie or game night that you can count on to unwind. Remember, you have permission to unwind and rest. Protect that. You work to live, you don't live to work, and that's a lesson I learned far too late in life.

Emotional self-care comes in several forms, with my favorites being:

- ✧ accepting and allowing yourself to feel what you feel
- ✧ learning your emotional triggers and how to work with them

✧ putting your needs first and tending to them

✧ maintaining your boundaries

✧ avoiding negative people and places

✧ using self-compassion and not being too hard on yourself

✧ asking for help when you need it

✧ resting when you need it

✧ finding time each day to do something you love

Spiritual Self-Care

Spiritual self-care is very personal. For some, it's focusing on their religion. For others, it's finding ways to care for themselves deeply through meditation or regular acts of kindness, or a gratitude journal. It's all about developing a deeper sense of meaning within yourself, fostering and nurturing a sense of your beliefs and values. Some ways I practice spiritual self-care include:

✧ practicing yoga

✧ meditating

✧ finding ways to connect to the greater community, such as joining clubs or volunteering

✧ taking time to get into nature

✧ practicing forgiveness and letting go of grudges or negative emotions

Starting a Self-Care Routine

Building a self-care routine can be tough if you've gotten into the habit of putting your needs last or ignoring them. It can feel selfish or like you're putting too much time into yourself when there are other things you could spend your time on. It can also be tough to get into the habit of taking the time for yourself. Making self-care your habit is one of the best ways you can support yourself. Getting into the habit can be broken down into several steps that can make it easier to implement.

Identify What Makes You Feel Centered

As much as everyone needs self-care, it also looks different for everyone. While you might think spending an hour at the gym lifting weights is a great way to spend your time, someone else might think it's brutal. Self-care is all about what you can do to feel centered and good about yourself.

Make a list of the things that you love that make you feel centered and fulfilled. Maybe you like to read and write or ride horses. Or, you could be the kind of person who loves cooking or gardening.

Think of How to Implement These Into Your Life

Once you have your list of things that help you feel centered, you need to start implementing them. Let's say your list is:

- ✧ listening to music
- ✧ writing

✧ jogging

✧ yoga

✧ spending time with friends

Now, it's time to slide those into your regular schedule. Listening to music is easy—you can pop in a pair of headphones or listen to music on your commute or while doing chores. Jogging and yoga can fit into your exercise regimen. The hard part would be fitting in writing and spending time with friends into your life, but it's important to do so. Maybe you opt to write for ten minutes before bed each night and schedule a regular weekly meetup with your friends.

Set Goals for Daily Self-Care

In two chapters, we'll be diving into how to set goals so you can achieve them, so we'll hold off on going in depth here. Setting goals to meet your self-care daily is a great way to prioritize that care, as long as you choose SMART goals. These are goals that are specific, measurable, achievable, relevant, and timely (Boogaard, 2021). Maybe you set goals to go to bed at a set time, eat a healthy diet, and get your exercise time in.

It's okay to work your goals in slowly, starting with one or two easier ones until they develop into habits. Then, you can start implementing more self-care and better address your needs.

Create a Support System

One of my favorite ways to stick to my goals, especially in self-care, is to set up a support system. This is more than just having people who cheer you on and encourage you. It's also a good idea to have people who use the same self-care activities for themselves, allowing you to both work together. If you want to exercise more to care for yourself, you can have accountability buddies that you jog or go to the gym with. Writers can write concurrently with their buddies to keep going even when they feel like writer's block is overwhelming.

Having a support system of people who self-care like you do means that you can talk together and work together to meet your goals. They'll understand your struggles and be able to talk through problems. Plus, it's always satisfying to do something with someone else and get that social interaction in too!

Take the Trial and Error Approach

The most important part about putting together your self-care routine is to remember that it's all about trial and error. What works for someone else may not work for you, and vice versa. You might also try to set up a routine that just isn't working for you. Instead of trying to browbeat yourself into being able to do it and creating negative associations, remember that it's totally valid to take a new approach.

Your needs will change over time. Your schedule will, too. That means that self-care has to be flexible to fit into your schedule. After all, you wouldn't forego a great job that overlaps with your scheduled gym time—you'd probably shift your gym time to accommodate your work schedule. Other self-care practices can be shifted around too.

Don't be afraid to mix things up if you need to find a better schedule for you. What's most important here is that you get your time for self-care and make it enjoyable.

Self-Care and Stress Relief Tips

A lot of what we've already talked about throughout the book falls into self-care. Eating well, staying hydrated, sleeping, and exercising all help your body. Setting goals and priorities can help too. There's more to self-care than just that, and many stress relief tips can also help with your practice. Here are some of my tried and true stress relief and self-care tips and tricks.

Set Up a Gratitude Journal

Gratitude journals remind you of the positives in your life and improve your mindset to be more positive. Each night before bed, I stop and write down at least three things that I'm grateful for. Even on the worst of days, there's always something I can appreciate. Some days, I've written that my husband, children, and I are alive and mostly well. Others, I've written about a sweet thing someone did for me or about the beautiful view I saw.

This helps to reframe your mindset to be something more positive just because it has you thinking about good things that happened throughout your day.

Pick Up a Self-Care Book

There are so many good books out there about self-care. We've touched upon some subjects, but this is really just an overview. Especially if you like to read, picking up a dedicated self-care book may be just what you need to get inspired and fix up your routine. They can also offer insight into areas you struggle and how to overcome them. If you're busy, you can choose an audiobook to listen to during commutes or chore time.

Enjoy a Pet Companion

Did you know that pets, particularly dogs, can reduce stress and anxiety and even lower blood pressure? There's a reason they're used as emotional support animals and service animals for people with disorders like PTSD—they're great at it. You might not be able to get a pet of your own, especially if you're still in college or you live somewhere that isn't pet-friendly, but there are still ways you can take advantage of this. Volunteering at a pet shelter, choosing to moonlight as a pet sitter on the weekends, or spending time with friends or family members with dogs can all help you reap the benefits of a quick puppy snuggle and assuage your frayed nerves.

Get Outside

Being outside is so good for us. Remember, we evolved to be outside, working, hunting, and farming. Nowadays, we spend so much of our time indoors, at school, or sitting at a desk at work, and it can really be draining. Getting outside can improve energy levels and help with burnout while also improving sleep quality. Your circadian rhythm, which regulates your sleep and wake cycles, relies on natural sunlight to manage your hormone levels, so getting out there is a great way to reset them. Go hiking, plant a garden, or just take a nice walk and bust that stress.

Breathing and Grounding

Having tools and tricks that can ground you help when your emotions run haywire. There are always times when we feel overwhelmed. Even the most organized of us, the ones who seem the most put together, have times when something seems impossible, or they're blinded with anger or burnt out so much that they just want to give up.

Various grounding techniques exist, from mindful meditation to yoga. One of my favorites is a trick that's easy to implement anywhere you go. It's called square breathing and you can do it in a meeting, driving your car, or just about anywhere else. All you have to do is a few quick deep breathing exercises and feel the benefits. It's discreet and suitable for those moments when you're out and about and just need to reset your mind.

To begin, you breathe deeply through your nose for four seconds. You hold your breath for four seconds, then exhale through your mouth for four seconds. Finally, hold it for four more seconds before starting over. It's called square breathing because it's paced out with four seconds per step. As you do this, you activate your parasympathetic nervous system, which is the part that controls your fight-or-flight response. By breathing calmly, you send messages to that part of your nervous system that says there's no danger here and it calms you down.

Chapter Summary

Being in control of yourself and your mind can be difficult at times, and without self-care, you can find yourself quickly burning out. Implementing a solid self-care routine is one of the best ways you can keep yourself grounded and feeling good about yourself. Grounding techniques, in particular, like deep breathing exercises, can help you when emotions run high and you find yourself feeling out of control. These can be particularly useful when you find yourself in stressful situations, like when you go to a doctor's office.

The next chapter focuses on handling medical matters of all kinds, including what to expect with health insurance, how to set up doctors' appointments, and when you need to be seen.

CHAPTER 12

MEDICAL MATTERS

One of the biggest changes that happen when you reach adulthood is that suddenly, you're responsible for your own health. You have to consent to treatments, you have medical privacy from your parents, and you get to make all the decisions. Depending on your agreement with your parents, you may also be responsible for paying for your care. This can feel like a pretty big responsibility, especially if your parents handled everything before.

When I turned 18, the revelation that I had to schedule my own appointments *terrified* me. Looking back on it, I'm not sure why it was such a problem for me, but I think a part of it was that I was intimidated by having to make the phone call, get myself to the appointment, and then be on my own for the appointment. While it had been years since my parents went into the room with me for most of my annual checkups, they still were present and could handle if any treatment was needed. It was far easier to pretend that I was healthy and therefore didn't need the appointments.

There's a problem with this line of thinking, though—when you don't get regular screenings and checkups, you can miss something important that would have otherwise been detected earlier. There are all sorts of symptoms that you might not be conscious of that can be detected in a blood test or physical exam. Missing preventative care can mean dealing with costlier care in the future.

Health Insurance

In the US, young adults can remain on their parent's health care plans until they turn 26, meaning that even if you're an adult and responsible for yourself financially, your parents can still keep you on their own insurance plans through work or that they pay for themselves. This is good news, too, because health insurance can be expensive. Even being on their plans, you still have to deal with deductibles, copays, and other costs associated with them.

In other areas of the world, health insurance may look different. Many countries have a nationalized health system where the cost of care is covered by the country. In Canada and several European countries, for example, public health care is free to everyone. The same goes for Australia and Brazil.

Important Terms in Health Insurance

Whether you have your own health insurance plan or rely on your parents', there are some terms you'll want to know in advance:

- ✦ **Deductible:** A deductible is an amount you have to cover for your health care before your insurance plan begins to pay. For example, if your plan has a $2,000 annual deductible, your health insurance won't start paying out on treatment until you've already spent and paid $2,000 out of pocket.

✧ **Copayment:** Even when insurance is covering the bill for your appointment, you may have a copayment (copay). This is the amount you pay as your portion of the bill. They can vary based on your plan.

✧ **Coinsurance:** Coinsurance refers to the share of the cost for covered services that you are responsible for. It's usually a set percentage in your plan.

✧ **Premium:** Each month, you or the policyholder have a premium. This is the amount you pay to keep your plan active.

✧ **Network:** Not all medical facilities accept all insurance, especially if you're in the United States. When a facility or doctor is in network, they accept your insurance.

✧ **Out-of-pocket maximum:** This is the most you'll pay out of pocket for your care for a calendar year. Once you reach the out-of-pocket maximum, your health insurance will cover the rest of the bills until the end of the year. You'll still owe your regular premium, but anything else should be covered if it's in network.

What if I Don't Have Health Insurance?

If, for whatever reason, you don't have health insurance, you can still go to the doctor if you need to be seen. However, you'll have to pay the office yourself for the services. This can be especially stressful for young adults who usually don't have a lot of money and can be a big reason for not going in for routine care. If you don't have insurance, you can be seen in the emergency room. You can't be turned away due to a lack of money if you truly need care.

Another consideration, if you don't currently have insurance, is looking into your state's Medicaid program or seeing what the cost for sliding scale insurance looks like. You might be able to get assistance with health care coverage this way.

Making a Doctor's Appointment

If you move for college, you may need to set up new health care local to you. Many college campuses have on-site health care available, or you can set up appointments around the area. When it's time to make a new appointment, find a doctor that accepts your insurance and meets your personal preferences. For example, if you're a woman and would prefer a woman treating you, or vice versa, for men, you can do that.

Then, you just follow some simple steps:

1. Call the office and inform them if you're a new patient. You may have to wait a week or two for a new patient appointment. If you're requesting care with a specific doctor, this is the time to bring it up.

2. Let the receptionist know why you need the appointment. It could be a checkup due to specific concerns like an illness or to have tests run.

3. Provide your insurance information.

4. Ask if you need to bring anything to the appointment, like records or a list of your prescriptions.

Sometimes, you'll have an appointment scheduled within a day or two, or it could be weeks or months, depending on the reason for the appointment and the doctor's availability. However, not all conditions can wait.

What to Do if the Problem Can't Wait for an Appointment

If you have to wait for a new patient appointment but have a pressing medical concern, you've got other options. Urgent care offices often allow you to be seen on the same day, which can be a great help if you think you have a minor infection or need antibiotics. Some common reasons people go to urgent care include:

✧ urinary tract infections

✧ a persistent cold or flu

✧ a minor injury like a sprain or strain

✧ stomach bugs or food poisoning

✧ sudden rashes or insect bites

✧ burns, cuts, or scrapes that need treatment but don't warrant going to the emergency room

Sometimes, going to the emergency room is the right answer for more serious conditions or injuries:

✧ sudden severe pain

✧ uncontrollable bleeding

✧ vision changes

✧ pain or pressure in the chest or upper abdomen

✧ altered consciousness, confusion, or disorientation, especially after a head injury

- ✧ vomiting or coughing up blood
- ✧ bright red blood in bowel movements
- ✧ shortness of breath or difficulty breathing
- ✧ severe headaches, especially with slurred speech or difficulty speaking
- ✧ dizziness, fainting, or weakness in half the body
- ✧ having a seizure for the first time, or for people who are known to have seizures, one that lasts longer than five minutes
- ✧ feeling like you want to hurt yourself or others
- ✧ severe injuries, including broken bones, head injuries, deep cuts, and severe burns
- ✧ severe, persistent vomiting or diarrhea

If you're not sure if something is ER-worthy, the best thing to do is call the hospital. They often have triage nurses available to speak to about whether you need to be seen immediately or if you can wait for an appointment.

Attending a Doctor's Appointment Alone

When appointment day rolls around, you might be nervous if you've never been responsible for getting yourself there alone before. With a bit of preparation and planning out what to expect and what to do, it's not so bad! It gets easier after the first few times, especially if you're prepared.

Be Early and Prepared

Make sure that you arrive at the office 10–15 minutes before your scheduled appointment time. You may need to fill out intake paperwork or you might get lost trying to get there. This 15-minute buffer helps in case of traffic or you get lost. Bring your ID, insurance card, and anything else the receptionist said that you needed when you scheduled your appointment, too.

Have Questions Ready

If you have any particular concerns before your appointment, write them down, along with any questions you may have. The appointment probably won't be very long, so you'll want to be able to efficiently go down the list and address all concerns.

Be Specific

When you describe symptoms and concerns to your doctor or nurse, be as specific as possible. It's best if you're able to tell them when the symptoms started, where the pain is, and anything you've done to try to alleviate them.

Chapter Summary

When you become an adult, you also inherit the responsibility for your health and well-being, something that, before this point, your parents were responsible for. As scary as it can be the first few times, it gets easier with practice! This is true of many things in life as you learn to readjust your expectations and keep pushing yourself out of your comfort zone.

The next section of this book focuses on personal development, including being able to learn and grow as a person. Personal development is all about learning, resilience, and recognizing that it's okay to be uncomfortable sometimes.

PART 5

PERSONAL DEVELOPMENT

Everyone thinks you make mistakes when you're young. But I don't think we make any fewer when we're grown up.

–Jodi Picoult

CHAPTER 13

TIME MANAGEMENT AND GOAL SETTING

W e never get our time back. Once it's gone, it's gone for good. If you waste that time endlessly scrolling through TikTok or Facebook, that's time squandered that you may one day wish you had spent differently. Did you know that the average person uses social media for 2 hours and 31 minutes per day? How much is that in a year? Well, it's nearly 919 hours annually or the equivalent of 38.3 days around the clock. If we count just waking hours, averaging 16 per day, that number nearly doubles to 57 days. That's right, nearly two months of time each year is spent on social media on average.

What would you do with all that time if you had it? That's enough time to spend on hobbies, studies, or passions, and instead, it's wasted scrolling through things that you probably won't remember a few days later.

Social media, silly videos on the internet, and other time wasters sap away at what time we have, wasting it away. Wouldn't you rather do something productive with it instead?

Learning to balance your time is one of the most important parts of being an adult. As kids, we had our parents there to tell us what to do and when to do it. They could limit screen time and wasted hours by setting rules, but as soon as you enter adulthood, your time is your own and no one else's. What will you do with it?

Time is Money—Don't Waste It!

We've all heard people say that time is money, but it's actually quite true. Every hour you have is one that you can use to potentially earn or save money. A freed-up hour can be used to cook yourself a nutritious meal, saving money on eating out. An hour could be spent doing chores instead of outsourcing or working on your passion projects that could one day become your livelihood.

The worst thing you can do to yourself is waste your time. Sure, you can have fun and do things that you enjoy, but when you're constantly letting the little things eat away at your time, you're quite literally wasting your life away. The good news is that you can reclaim your time. You can put down the phone and stop doom-scrolling and instead direct your efforts to things that will be more productive.

Time Sinks to Avoid

Ready to figure out how much time you waste? We're going to go over a list of the most common time-wasters people in college tend to fall into. How many of them apply to you? How much time do you spend each day doing each of these activities? One or two little time wasters might not seem like a big deal, but if you're not careful, you can build habits that waste more time than you use to be productive. That's not to say that you have to be active and productive all the time—you need downtime to rest, too! But as they say, everything in moderation. Check out these common time wasters:

Binging TV Shows or Online Videos

Watching an episode of your favorite show is a great way to unwind after a long day. Watching hours of it while you try to do other things, on the other hand, can really just distract you. This is especially true if you're trying to study while watching a show. Stick to playing instrumental background music if you don't want to study in silence.

Studying Without a Plan

If you study without some sort of plan, you can find yourself wasting a lot of time. It's not enough to just read the textbook from start to finish, and when you have several classes to study for, you have to be intentional with your time.

Develop a study plan that outlines what you will do and when so you'll know how to tackle it all and best spend your time. For example:

- ✧ Take notes on the assigned chapter for psychology for 45 minutes.
- ✧ Study for the upcoming chemistry midterm for an hour.
- ✧ Spend half an hour working on a philosophy paper.

When you study with an intentional plan, it's much easier to make good progress.

Social Media

With so many social media platforms to browse, it can be easy to underestimate how much time you're actually spending on them. You might spend 20 minutes on Facebook, 30 minutes on Instagram, and another 30 minutes scrolling through TikTok and not realize just how much time you're spending. Then, add in notifications popping up and sucking you back in, or the time that you spend chatting with people on the platform and the amount of time balloons up pretty quickly.

Instead of using social media all day, disable the notifications and set specific times when you'll use the apps. You don't have to cut social media out cold turkey and it can be a great way to stay in touch with friends, but you shouldn't let it consume your life.

Procrastination

We all procrastinate from time to time, but if it's a habit for you to say that you'll do something later or tomorrow, you're probably wasting a lot of time while also putting some pretty stressful time crunches onto yourself as well. If you say you'll study later, you lose out on study time that you might have now and you may find yourself staying up later to get to it all. Or, if you say you'll do the dishes after work instead of before like you normally do, you may find yourself in a position where you don't have anything clean to make dinner with. Beating procrastination can be tough, but learning to do so is one of the most valuable tools you can teach yourself. If you have to do something that will take less than five minutes, do it immediately instead of putting it off.

Schedules, tools like the Pomodoro method (more on this later!), and breaking down tasks into smaller steps so they don't feel so overwhelming can all help you beat procrastination.

Overplanning

Are you an overplanner? A lot of us are—we spend inordinate amounts of time trying to make sure that every last detail of our plans are going to go off without a hitch that we run out of time to actually properly execute it. Or, all that overplanning can lead us to give up when whatever it was doesn't go exactly according to plan.

Trying to Make Things Perfect

If that last point resonated with you, you might also spend a lot of time agonizing over the tiniest details of whatever you're doing. If it's not exactly right, you might focus endlessly on a small detail that really isn't very important.

There's no such thing as perfection, meaning it's useless to waste your time trying to achieve it. Instead, focus on setting realistic standards and let go of the small details. No one cares if the sandwich you make doesn't look perfect if it still tastes good.

Unclear Goals

Setting goals that aren't efficient is another way that a lot of people waste their time. We'll be talking about setting effective goals later in this chapter. When your goals are unnecessarily vague, like "I want to lose weight" or "I want to eat more vegetables," you don't really give yourself something concrete to work toward, and we'll talk about addressing that shortly.

Multitasking

We often think that multitasking is the perfect way to squeeze more into a short period of time, but the truth is this is incredibly inefficient. Your brain can only really focus on one thing at a time, which means when you're multitasking, you are constantly forcing your brain to shift gears, which can quickly draw things out and cost you time.

It's better to focus on one task at a time, giving it your full attention, rather than trying to do several things at once. If you're in a position where you feel like you have to multitask, try breaking down the task into something more manageable. The more you streamline your process, the quicker you'll get things done, and the more time you'll save!

How to Manage Your Time

As you start saving time, you'll better be able to manage it. For most young adults, college is the first real test they get at managing their time by themselves, and that freedom can be addictive. There's no one telling you what to do, when to study, or how to live. The problem is, if you've never had the experience of managing your time yourself or facing the consequences of poor time management, you're at risk of completely dropping the ball.

It took me a solid two weeks after I moved into my dorm to realize that my time management was *horrible*. I'd put off my studying or homework assignments until the last minute, which meant my first few grades in my classes were much lower than what I was used to. I'd prioritize having fun and making friends rather than getting to the tasks I needed to handle. By the end of my second week, I was exhausted and staring at a whole mess of studying, chores, and other responsibilities.

Part of the reason I struggled so much was that when I lived with my parents, they had me on a structured schedule. I had to complete my homework before I could go out with friends. I had to do my chores beforehand, too. All the structure they built into my life felt like a big drag when I was a teen, but once I got to college, I realized that they were really just trying to help me out and set me up for success.

While my first semester of college ended with grades lower than I was used to, it also gave me a solid understanding of what it's like to be an adult. I needed to manage my time because no one else would do it for me. I had to take responsibility for those lower grades, and by the time the second semester rolled around, I had the solid schedule and foundation I needed to succeed.

My recommendation for time management is to have a predictable schedule and stick to it. Anything that you need to do should be prioritized in the level of importance to you, which means that you'll have to make those major decisions for yourself.

For example, you might really want to go to that party, but you have to be up early the next morning for your weekend job. What's more important to you? You may decide that you still want to go to the party, but you also don't want to be exhausted, so you decide to go home early instead of partying into the wee hours of the morning.

Prioritize Your Work

Prioritizing your work is all about figuring out what needs to be done immediately and what can wait or be eliminated entirely. When it feels like you're drowning in work, make a list of all the tasks you're trying to squeeze in. Then, start rating them by their urgency.

Unimportant tasks, like endless time scrolling through social media, can be put off or don't matter to you.

Important tasks matter to you or need to be done. These could be your hobbies, studying, working, or completing your chores. They need to be scheduled somewhere during your day and completed in a timely manner.

Urgent tasks are things that have to be done to avoid issues. This could be completing an assignment for school, studying for an impending test, or getting car maintenance done to keep your car running. Many of these tasks could be things that were once important that you decided to push off until you couldn't any longer.

One of the best solutions to having a buildup of tasks is to avoid procrastinating. We'll have some tips for time management and beating procrastination shortly.

Don't Overcommit

Saying no when you're asked to do something can be difficult, especially if you fall into people-pleasing habits. The problem with this comes when you start getting overwhelmed with commitments. Life is busy enough on its own, with work, school, and maintaining a social life. There's no need to make it worse by taking on every little favor that people ask you to do.

Or, maybe you're already overcommitted because you thought you'd have the time to do everything, only to find out that it all piled up on you. I get it—as a busy parent, I'm constantly inundated with all the things needed from me for work, my children, and my husband. There's always laundry to do, homework to complete, extracurriculars to drive to, and more. In college, it seemed like there was just as much going on. I had to study, work, and still find time for my friends.

It's okay to say no to things that you don't have the time or bandwidth to complete. Let go of the things that don't matter to you or that you simply can't dedicate your time to. Yes, this might mean letting go of some things that are important, like foregoing a favorite club on campus to go to work sometimes or not going out with friends every night, but it'll help you to balance your schedule.

By avoiding the trap of overcommitting, you free up time that can better be utilized doing important and urgent things on your list. All you'll need to do is use that time wisely and efficiently.

Pomodoro Technique

One of my absolute favorite ways of being efficient with time is using the Pomodoro Technique to manage my time without feeling like I'm overwhelmed or like I don't have time to relax. As a fun aside, the technique got its name from the Italian word for tomato because the person who mainstreamed it used a kitchen timer shaped like a tomato to break up his time.

With this technique, you are breaking up your time into 25-minute stretches of working on something with a 5-minute break. After four intervals, you get a 15- or 30-minute break to unwind.

This helps by breaking down what otherwise feels like a long, unbearable task and turning it into smaller chunks that feel more manageable. That means less time dwelling on how long it will take, feeling overwhelmed and procrastinating, and more time doing what you need to do.

Get started by choosing a task you need to complete, like a paper, or choosing to study something or a chore. Set a timer for 25 minutes and work the whole time. Don't get distracted, leave your phone somewhere you won't be tempted by it, and get going. When the timer goes off, give yourself that quick break. I like to write down my progress as I go so I can see how productive I've been while I use this method. If I'm reading or writing, I jot down my word count or how many pages I got through and then unwind. After your short break is over, set up the timer and start again. I'd bet this will help save time by keeping you on task!

Time-Saving Tips

Still feel tight on time after implementing these changes? These are some of my favorite tips I used in college and still use today to make the most out of my time:

✧ **Pay attention to your time:** I like to keep track of my time by making sure I'm conscious of how long I spend on my biggest time wasters. For me, checking my phone is absolutely one of the worst. When I feel like my time is getting out of control, I take a look at my phone's apps to see just how long I spend on it. The number can be pretty scary sometimes and it reminds me to set it down and focus on what's going on around me instead.

✧ **Use downtime to your advantage:** Do you commute to work or school? Whether you walk, ride a bus, or drive, you can always boost your productivity with audiobooks. Or, if you take the bus or carpool, you can use the time you spend traveling to study, catch up on work, or tend to some of your planning for the week. Instead of just waiting around, get productive instead!

✧ **Separate work and pleasure:** We associate our spaces with what we do most in them, so separating where you work from where you sleep or enjoy yourself can help put you into the productive mindset by association. This could be tough if you have a dorm, but you could choose to do most of your studying in the library on campus. Dedicate a set office for yourself in your home if you've got the luxury to do so.

✧ **Outsource if you can:** This might be kind of hard, depending on where you are in your life. Some things can be outsourced, and if you have the ability to do so, you should. For students, a major source of outsourcing is eating in the school dining halls. You don't have to cook or clean up after yourself.

✧ **Find tools to help you:** Let me tell you—when I first heard about robot vacuums, I thought it was a ridiculous luxury and a waste of time and money. Now, with children and pets? I couldn't imagine it any other way. These tools are my livelihood and keep me grounded. If there are tools that will boost your productivity and they're affordable to you, they're probably worth the investment.

As you implement these tools, you can remain focused on what matters the most. Then, you just have to make sure you have the goals to roadmap your plan forward.

SMART Goals Keep You Focused

We already introduced the topic of SMART goals earlier when talking about self-care, but now it's time to go in-depth with them. As stated earlier, SMART goals are specific, measurable, achievable, relevant, and timely.

The reason I like these goals is that it keeps me focused. When writing goals in this format, it's much easier to see exactly what needs to be done by which date or time to stay on track. As a result, I'm able to focus so much more on what needs to be done without getting stuck with tasks that suddenly become urgent or necessary to complete quickly to meet requirements.

✧ **Specific:** Goals should be very specific. For example, if your goal is to get good grades in college, you don't really have a metric that tells you what you're aiming for. What's a good grade to you?

✧ **Measurable:** By making your goal measurable, you give yourself something that has a definitive ending. This could be getting a 3.5 GPA or not getting below an 80% on an assignment for the semester.

✧ **Achievable:** Goals need to be achievable, too. You can't, for example, say you want to graduate with a 4.0 GPA when you already have below that, or you want to run a marathon in a week when you're currently living a relatively inactive life. Make sure you're realistic about what you can and can't do when you set your goal. It should be something that's a bit of a stretch and makes you work for it, but not something you can never do. How will you achieve it? If you want to get that 3.5 GPA, what's your study plan? How many classes will you take at once?

✧ **Relevant:** Your goal also needs to be relevant to you. Is it something you'd willingly do? Do you have an interest in doing it? If you genuinely don't care about college, for example, because you plan on going into a career that doesn't require a degree, are you really going to give it your all?

✧ **Timely:** Finally, your goal needs to have some sort of finality to it. There has to be a deadline on it so you know whether you've succeeded or failed. This could be graduation if you want that high GPA or an arbitrary date you've set. This will help keep you accountable and working toward your goal.

When you set up your goal, start by writing down each step. What do you want? How will you achieve it? Why does it matter to you? When do you need to be done with your work toward it? These things matter, and writing them all down will help paint a clearer picture of what you'll need to do and how to schedule it all into your plan.

Chapter Summary

A major part of personal development is being able to stick to schedules and manage your time wisely. When you can mitigate time sinks and focus on SMART goals, you can push yourself forward, learning more and working toward being more successful. From there, it's all about resilience and remembering that it's okay to be a work in progress. It's okay to not be able to do everything right the first time, and developing a growth mindset, which we'll introduce in the next chapter, is all about getting back up when we fall.

CHAPTER 14

GROWTH MINDSET, SELF-CONFIDENCE, AND RESILIENCE

With tools for managing your time in place, you can start tackling your goals and bringing them to fruition. It's so fulfilling to see all your hard work bear fruitful results! As you achieve your goals, you'll likely find yourself feeling more confident and capable in your life. The key here, though, is recognizing that when you do fail at something (and it will happen, I promise!), you can keep moving forward.

One of the hardest things in life to learn is to be resilient. Resilience requires you to be confident and recognize that failing at something isn't the worst thing in the world. In fact, failure is what propels growth. If you didn't fail at something, how do you know that what you were doing wasn't too easy for you?

Something I had to learn with my kids is that praising them for every single thing they did right wasn't the right path to building confidence. In fact, the more I praised them for getting things done correctly, the more resistant they were to try new things. When I talked to them about it, what they said surprised me: They were afraid that if they messed up, I wouldn't give them the praise, and I'd be disappointed in them. In other words, they were afraid of failure and what I'd do if they struggled, so they resisted trying new things and challenging themselves. Instead of teaching them to be confident, bold children who wanted to tackle everything life had to offer, they wanted to stay firmly in their comfort zone.

Your Brain Never Stops Growing

If staying in your comfort zone resonates with you, you're not alone. Looking back on it, I was the same way when I was younger. I was afraid of making mistakes because mistakes meant I was wrong, and being wrong meant I wasn't right and I hated not being right. It was a dangerous thought spiral. I thought that if I just didn't try, I couldn't fail, but this is the wrong way to look at it. You don't fail at something until you give up on it. By never being willing to try something, I was inadvertently failing by default, but somehow convinced myself it wasn't the same thing.

Developing a Growth Mindset

Part of what builds resilience is to develop a growth mindset. Resilience is the ability to bounce back from failure and keep moving toward your goal. It's okay to be disappointed that you didn't succeed, but what's more important is recognizing that you can keep working in the future to see better results.

In other words, just because you didn't succeed today doesn't mean that you won't succeed in the future. This is because your brain never stops growing. It's like a muscle in the sense that the more that you work it, the stronger it becomes. It's never too late to learn a new skill or achieve new goals, and it's only natural not to be very good at something when you first start.

Imagine if we all gave up the first time we tried and failed something. Babies would never crawl or walk. We'd never talk or read or write because all of these are learned skills that have a lot of failure at the beginning. Doctors would never perform surgery or help heal people. Lawyers would give up in law school the first time they misremembered something.

We all fail from time to time. We all get things wrong every now and then. And that's okay.

When we focus on a growth mindset, we don't look at the results as much as we look at the effort put into it. After all, it's the effort that really deserves the praise—it's all the hard work you put into getting to that end goal that really matters. Yes, it's great that you succeeded, but that success is meaningful and satisfying because you worked for it.

If you shift your mindset to focus on the effort you put into a situation instead of the end result, you find that it's easier to bounce back after getting an undesired result. Instead of thinking that where you're at in that moment in terms of skill level is it, you'll see that you can keep learning and growing. In other words, you become resilient, and that resilience will help keep you moving forward with your life.

Tips to Develop a Growth Mindset for Resilience

If you're the kind of person to crumble at the thought of failure, don't worry—you can change your mindset. After all, that's what this is all about, right? Developing a growth mindset both requires and develops resilience. The more you practice, the easier it will become, just like with any other type of exercise. Only this time, you're exercising your brain.

Embrace Your Imperfections

You don't have to be perfect. In fact, your imperfections are valuable parts of who you are and how much room you still have to grow. When you get something wrong, it's not a ding against who you are as a person. It's not a sign that you're useless or stupid. It's just a sign that you don't know that information or skill *yet*. You see, the "yet" is important here.

Just because you don't know something today doesn't mean you won't know it in the future. Remind yourself of this when you make mistakes. Instead of beating yourself up, say, "I don't know this yet, but I can learn."

See Challenges as Opportunities

When something is difficult, it's not a sign of you being inadequate, either. It's actually a really good opportunity for you to begin learning and for you to grow. Every challenge, every mishap along the way, is a way you can move forward and develop as a person. I'll bet you didn't know algebra when you stepped into class for the first time, but by the time you left, your skills had grown dramatically. Everything is like that. It's not raw talent that makes us successful—it's how we handle the challenges and use them to grow along the way.

Focus on Positive Language

So much of what makes up our mindsets is how we speak, both about ourselves and about the world around us. When you use negative language, like "I'm never going to figure this out," you're putting yourself in a precarious position. How much effort do you think you'll really put into figuring out whatever it is if you don't think you can actually do it? You might make a halfhearted attempt, but to really put your all into something, you have to believe that you can do it.

Get rid of absolutes in your language. There's no "always" or "never" or black and white. The world is more than shades of gray, too. We live in a vibrant world filled with spectrums of color, just like we ourselves have spectrums of abilities. You add or take away a little light to a color and what you're left with changes. Likewise, your abilities are the same way. They aren't stagnant and they can change based on what you put into them.

The more you make yourself comfortable with positive language, the better you will feel. Even better, the more confident you can grow. Growth mindsets and positive mindsets leave us feeling better about ourselves, granting us the key to success.

Self-Confidence and Success

Self-confidence is what gives you faith that you can succeed. It's what allows you to keep on trudging through the hard times and to trust yourself enough to know that you'll make the choices that are right for you. It also assures you that even if you don't have the answers now, you'll be able to come up with the answers with a little bit of effort.

In other words, self-confidence is having trust in yourself. It's not the same thing as being overconfident, where you overestimate your abilities. Rather, when you're self-confident, you're well aware of what you can do. This comes with all sorts of benefits that will help you through your life and take you on the pathway to success.

Self-confidence shows in how we present ourselves to others, how we hold our bodies, and how we approach problems. That inner confidence tells people they can put their confidence in you too. The result? People with self-confidence are more likely to get raises and promotions when they interview. They're also, as a result, more likely to be successful.

The good news here is that self-confidence is something we learn. Some people might be naturally more self-confident than others, but that doesn't mean that you can't grow it too. Growth mindset, remember?

Trial and Error and Trial Some More

Self-confidence is all about being able to pick yourself back up again when you fall. It's being able to trust your abilities. That doesn't mean that you trust that you're perfect already—it's about being aware of what they truly are and what you can do to continue learning and growing.

If you're not confident yet, all you need to do is to keep on trying, even in the face of challenges. This is a cycle of trial and error. Each error brings you another step closer to finding your solution. It's like being a scientist—you know what you want to do, and then you have to experiment to find the answer. Every time you try something that doesn't work, you know that it's time to try something different. Eventually, you'll get it right.

The more you work at this, remembering that you have a growth mindset and that you can continue to learn as long as you live and keep trying, the more confident you'll become. You'll become comfortable with making mistakes or failing, recognizing the silver lining of learning that comes with it. As you become more comfortable, you'll also be able to explore more, opening up doors that you never knew existed in your future.

Step Out of Your Comfort Zone

Self-confidence helps us step out of our comfort zone because we know we can trust ourselves to navigate through it, no matter what happens. It's the ability to trust that there are more things to learn and that sometimes, the learning and growing process is uncomfortable. However, resilience helps us through.

I've had to step out of my comfort zone countless times throughout life, applying for jobs, deciding to have children, making moves across the country... It can be intimidating or even terrifying when you face the unknown. But, it's only unknown for as long as you let it be.

The funny thing about stepping out of your comfort zone is that the more you do it, the easier it becomes and the more confident you feel. That's why I like to try new things all the time. I might try cooking a new meal with a technique I've never tried before or going to a new activity. There's something awe-inspiring about facing something brand new and slowly but surely learning how to actually do it. It's like being a child again, growing and learning.

Just because your body finishes growing doesn't mean your mind has to, and the more you try new things and stick to them, even when they're hard, the more likely you are to succeed. After all, you miss 100% of the shots you don't take. Your chances are infinitely higher just by trying, even if they're still low. And the more you practice, the easier those shots will get over time.

Chapter Summary

Developing a growth mindset and having the self-confidence and resilience to continue in the face of failure are the keys to success. When you learn to pick yourself up after you fall, you grow as a person, and that growth is priceless. You'll be able to step out of your comfort zone and thrive. Remember that failure isn't concrete until you give up. Until then, any mistakes and mishaps along the way are just speed bumps on your path to success.

CONCLUSION

> *Relax. You will become an adult. You will figure out your career. You will find someone who loves you. You have a whole lifetime; time takes time. The only way to fail at life is to abstain.*
>
> *–Johanna de Silentio*

The thing no one ever tells you about growing up is that it's not about knowing everything there is to know or being right all the time. There's never going to be a time when you feel perfectly equipped to take on everything the world has to throw your way. No—growing up is learning how to navigate through it all, even when you don't have the solutions. It's about learning to stand on your own two feet as an independent adult, but that doesn't mean that you have to face the world alone.

Rely on your loved ones. Build a social safety net of people you trust. Keep on learning, even when things are tough at first. Foster that growth mindset until the idea of failing isn't scary anymore. Put all these skills to the test and keep on practicing them.

You'll make mistakes. You'll probably miss a bill or two by accident (but I really hope you don't!). Things won't always work out as planned, but that's life. As you work on yourself and your skills, you'll keep learning. You'll grow. You'll *thrive*. All you have to do is remember not to give up.

Adulthood can be scary. After all, there's a lot riding on you that you'll have to figure out. However, I know that you can do it. We all can. Keep up the good work. Don't be afraid to ask questions or for help. And most importantly, have the confidence in yourself that you can, and will, succeed in this life, no matter where it takes you. Whether you enter the workforce immediately, decide to run your own business, go to college, or pursue a trade, you can do it. You just have to remember to pick yourself back up again when you fall. If you can do that, you're already halfway there. Good luck and happy adulting!

MONEY SKILLS

FOR TEENS

*These Are The Things
About Money Management
and Personal Finance
You Must Know But They
Didn't Teach You in School*

EMILY CARTER

INTRODUCTION

You are at a stage in your life where you need to learn as much as you can and prepare yourself for what is coming. Finances and financial literacy, in general, are very important parts of being an adult, and making the right financial decisions can set you up for a great life. Being financially literate will teach you important lessons that many adults only learn later in life after they've already made a few mistakes. This is not to say that these mistakes cannot be reversed, but they take time and effort, and you certainly want your adult life to go as smoothly as you possibly can. While there are many different aspects of life that we can't control, finances aren't one of them. We can act on them and turn things around.

By understanding finances, you can learn the differences between your needs and your wants, the real value of money, how money can work in your favor, and how you can avoid crippling debt. Your future and your financial independence are coming, and it's always best to be prepared for them.

The main goal of this book is to encourage you to take control of your finances from the very start so you can build enough wealth to live a peaceful life (at least when it comes to your finances) and to prepare you for what's coming. This book is structured in a way to make you understand the very basics first, such as what money is or how to make money as a teenager. Then, once you know the basics, I'll move on to more complex subjects such as banking and financial services; what is budgeting and how can it help; what is credit or debt management; the intricacies of insurance and how it can provide security for you, and your loved ones; and how caring about retirement now can help you later in life.

This is the beginning of your journey, but if you make good decisions now, you will have a much easier life in the future.

CHAPTER 1

UNDERSTANDING MONEY

> *A wise person should have money in their head, but not in their heart.*
>
> *–Jonathan Swift*

When we think about money, we think about notes and coins and, more recently, numbers in our banking apps that allow us to pay for products or services that we want or need. But in a sober way, money is a system of exchange that allows us to get services or goods for a certain value in money. The monetary system was created to replace another, older system that you might have heard about called barter trading, which was used thousands of years ago. In this system, money wasn't involved, so if you wanted a service or good, you'd have to exchange it for another service or good. Let's say you lived during those times and you wanted someone to come fix your fence; in return, you'd give him goods, which at the time could be eggs, a cow, or milk. Or, if you could perform a service such as shoemaking, maybe you'd fix or even make new shoes for the person fixing your fence.

So, in other words, money is an asset, in this case, a liquid asset (because it can easily be transformed into cash; for instance, if you withdraw $10 from an ATM, you're turning money into cash), that allows us to make transfers of value in an easy way between two people or organizations.

In this chapter, we are going to understand the role of money in our lives, what exactly the value of money is and its impact on our personal finance decisions, and how we can develop a healthy money mindset and set attainable financial goals.

The Role of Money in Our Lives

In our lives, money is important because it allows us to have a better quality of life by enabling us to have options in the things we do in our day-to-day activities, both short- and long-term. Having enough money allows us to have more security and freedom. It's safe to say that the amount of money we have can dictate our lifestyle.

It's also true that money, at times, can have negative effects on people, but it largely depends on their actions. In fact, our actions regarding the money we collect are crucial; whether it is how we spend it, save it, or invest it, these actions have an impact on our lives. The store value of money is crucial, allowing us to keep it and use it later on. This ability allows people and businesses to plan for the future, such as retirement, purchasing a property, or buying a car. Money can also be used as a medium to account for and give value to services and goods. If a pair of shoes costs $100, this is money being used as a unit of account to allow us to understand the value of the pair of shoes compared to other things. It's extremely easy for us to compare different items and services and make financial decisions.

Besides that, money can also be used in more complex contexts, such as a vital part of financial markets or financial institutions such as banks. In the case of banks, their business is solely based on money, especially the loan and the store of money, while investors use the money to purchase financial instruments such as bonds or stocks.

Money allows us to pay for the most basic things, such as healthcare, food, and housing. But it can also be a source of stress, happiness, status, or power. Whether we like it or not, even though we often hear that money is not everything (and it certainly isn't), it's a crucial part of our lives and our society, and without it, the world would be a completely different place.

Moreover, money can also have an impact on emotional, mental, and even physical well-being. This often stems from a lack of it rather than an abundance. Stress-related money issues can come from difficulties in paying bills or providing basic needs to us or our families, which can lead to anxiety, stress, and even depression. The constant pursuit of money can have an effect on our happiness, even if we have enough of it. It comes down to a never-ending cycle of permanent desire and chasing material things. And so having a good balance between what we want and what we have is essential for our own health. At the end of the day, money is simply a tool; it can't buy happiness or fulfillment, and it can only fulfill these momentarily. While the scope of this book is about money and all the things we can accomplish with it, it's important to understand that there's more to life.

How to Develop a Healthy Money Mindset and Set Up Your Financial Goals

Now that this is out of the way let's get down to what this book is about. Developing a healthy money mindset and setting financial goals is the first step to understanding money and being able to manage it.

Did you know that one in five people says they are overwhelmed by debt? This is according to a survey done by the Money Advice Service, which can have a negative impact on people's health. This comes from the constant worry that occupies our minds, which in turn can inflate the issue, making it look like it's impossible to resolve (FarmWell, n.d.). Ignoring the problem is probably our first reaction. I know it was mine before I learned the hard way that we shouldn't simply ignore these issues, as oftentimes, they simply don't go away and come back way worse than before. As hard as it might seem, we need to look the problem in the eye and try to understand what we can do to overcome it. What are the steps that you need to take to make this problem go away? Everybody's different, and so we have different issues, but by developing a healthy money mindset, you become a lot less scared of these problems, and you will have a clear head on what you need to do next.

Some of the most common barriers when it comes to developing this mindset are how to properly manage money. This can stem from a lack of knowledge, a lack of confidence, or even debt. Although all of these can be worked out. One other problem when establishing a healthy money mindset is the too-often limiting thought about money and finance in general. The problem here is that these thoughts often limit the things we can do. You might not even realize it, but things such as "I don't make enough money to be able to save" or "I will never be able to get out of debt." Even if you don't actively think about them, they live in your subconscious. You need to get rid of these limitations, or you will never be able to develop a healthy money mindset. The first thing you have to do is identify when these thoughts come and push them back. This might take a little getting used to because we've been living with these thoughts for a while, and it's hard to break the habit, but when you feel them coming, try to hold them by looking at the evidence. For instance, how is it even possible that you will never be out of debt? It doesn't make sense, especially if you have a plan to pay off that debt. Looking at the real evidence in these cases, you'll find that many limitations are quite absurd. The most important aspect of developing a healthy money mindset is to have control. If you feel overwhelmed or out of control, then you feel more stressed.

In the following section, I will talk about many different techniques, such as setting financial goals and others that will make you more open to the development of your healthy mindset. One that I tend to recommend is to make a plan and create a budget. There are many different tools that can help you do that, and you can even find free templates online. But tools like apps will do most of the work for you and help you take control of your finances. Sometimes simply talking to someone can help you manage your financial stress too. Most of us try to keep everything for ourselves, which is often not a great solution. Communicating with someone that you trust can have a calming effect on you and put things into better perspective. Taking inventory of your finances might be a boring job to do, but it can really help you understand where your money is going and get control over your finances. Again, there are many different tools and apps that can help you track your expenses automatically, such as Mint, Personal Capital, or PocketGuard.

Steps to Develop a Healthy Money Mindset

One of the hardest things someone has to overcome when developing a healthy mindset is forgiving their past financial mistakes. It's way too easy to get hung up on the mistakes we've made and constantly think about what we should have done instead. But the past is the past, and there's nothing we can do to change it. We need to stop wasting our mental focus on things that we can no longer control and focus on the things we can, such as future financial decisions. Focus your money decisions on things that you can control and not on things of the past. Your success is ahead of you.

It's also important to be able to identify the emotions you usually have when it comes to money. This way, you can try to change that emotional state as well as the thoughts that might trigger those negative emotions. A good exercise to identify these thoughts and emotions is to write down what you're feeling after each transaction for a week. At the end of the week, take a look over, and you'll find the necessary purchases and those that aren't. For instance, if you buy a pair of shoes and at the moment of purchase you believe this will bring you joy, at the end of the week, you might feel differently and know that the purchase might have been an impulse purchase. This is also a great way to understand your spending habits and how emotionally connected you are to your purchases. Don't let your purchases be guided by your emotions; think rationally when it comes to financial decisions.

We often compare ourselves to others, and it's not only in financial terms. Either way is a losing game, and it's something that we should try to steer away from. These types of comparisons are never accurate, especially because we often compare ourselves with someone who is apparently much better off than we are and that we know nothing about. This is even more abundant in our social media-filled lives, where often people just post their highlights or only the things they want you to see. Looking at social media posts, for instance, you might see someone enjoying a beach day in the Caribbean, but you don't know how much debt they might have incurred to be there or if they owe money to family or friends. Chances are you will never find out the truth because they won't post it on their social media. Now, when you do these comparisons, you know everything about you, the good and the bad, and that makes it an unfair comparison to make. Even when you compare yourself with people that you know, it's still an unfair comparison because the circumstances aren't similar, even though you might know them a little. After all, even if you realize that they are better off than you are, what do you have to gain from that? You will likely become quite discouraged with yourself, which doesn't help anyone. You should be developing a healthy mindset, which you can't do if you focus on all the negative sides of it. In order to build a healthy money mindset, you have to solely focus on yourself and on achieving your goals. What others do or don't shouldn't be on your mind.

Forming good habits, in general, is not something that will happen overnight, so you have to work on them continuously. This is exactly the same when trying to form good financial habits. You should take some time to do your budget every week, or at least every month, and go over the bills and your spending habits too. This is the only way you will be able to find out what can be improved. Avoiding doing this is probably the worst thing you can do because if there are any problems, they won't go away anyway. Make sure you create good financial habits and work on them, such as making a budget. These habits are the foundation of your personal finances today and in the future.

However, when creating a budget, don't restrain yourself too much, at least not at the beginning. You have to create one that brings you happiness and that you're comfortable with. This often means not restricting yourself from enjoying life. Although you might have to limit this. For instance, instead of dining out every day, you might have to cut it back to twice a week. However, all budgets are different, and we are going through the different budget strategies in the chapter dedicated to budgeting later in the book.

Setting Financial Goals

While the way you set financial goals will differ as you grow, there's always a structure that you might want to follow. For instance, if you're just starting out, your main concern should be focusing on quick wins so you get the feel for it and understand that financial goals are indeed attainable. Starting slowly is important to keep your motivation levels high and pursue other, more ambitious goals. When starting anything, sometimes we have the fear of failing, which often prevents us from reaching certain goals. However, if you're not going to try, you will certainly not accomplish anything at all. For instance, while saving $1000 might seem like a daunting goal, it's much easier to save $200 or $300, and this is where you should start. This will also help you steer away from procrastination and continue to set more goals as the current ones get accomplished.

Having the freedom to set your own goals is great, but you also need to understand the costs and benefits of the goals you want to set. For instance, if you want to take a summer course that will cost you money, how will taking that course benefit you in the long run? Are you going to be able to improve your financial situation because of that course? If so, it's certainly a good investment. Also, it's important to remember that not all costs are monetary; some of them take up some of your time. You have to consider all of the pros and cons associated with those.

Financial goals come in three distinct lengths: short, medium, and long. To determine the length of your goals, you have to look at the cost of the goal, or how much you will have to save, the resources you have to use, and your motivations, since the higher the motivation, the more likely you are to accomplish your goals. But, as a rule of thumb, a short-term financial goal is anything that takes a maximum of a month to accomplish, a medium-term goal is anything between one and three months, and a long-term goal is anything over three months. When setting your goals, it's important that you have a mix of these three so you always have something to look forward to and keep you motivated, but I will develop this in the chapter about budgeting.

Understanding money is the first step to acquiring the necessary skills that will help you as you go from your teenage years into your young adult years, and you will have to rely more on how you manage your money. As we've seen, money is an integral part of everybody's lives, and so making the right decisions is absolutely essential for you to continue to prosper financially. For that, starting with developing a healthy money mindset and understanding how to set attainable financial goals is essential.

In the following chapter, I'll go through the different ways you can start making money and how you can develop skills that will be useful to you later on in your career.

CHAPTER 2

MAKING MONEY

> *Opportunity is missed by most people because it is dressed in overalls and looks like work.*
>
> *–Thomas Edison*

N ow we get to the good part: how can you make money as a teenager? Well, I can tell you right away that there are many different options you can take, and I'm certain you will find some that you will be happy with.

The Different Ways You Can Make Money

Usually, there are three types of work you can do to earn money as a teenager: part-time jobs, freelancing, or entrepreneurship. You might wonder what exactly the difference is between freelancing and entrepreneurship, and while there are definitely some similarities, there are some crucial differences. I believe the main difference between these two is that a freelancer is hired to work or do some tasks by other companies, while entrepreneurs create companies and manage them. While entrepreneurs come up with an idea and develop it into a business model, freelancers give more value to their skills and try to hone them as best they can. While entrepreneurs can sell products and services behind a business to customers, freelancers sell their services and skills to other businesses. Let's delve into it a little more.

Part-Time Jobs

While you're under the age of 18, you can't apply for every single job, but there's quite a lot to choose from, especially if you're looking for a part-time job. Whether you want to work after school, during the weekends, or throughout the summer, I'm going to give you some of the most common part-time jobs you are allowed to do.

For example, babysitting is a very common job for teenagers. I understand it's not for everyone since you might not have the patience to take care of younger kids, but either way, this is a very well-paid job. I'm sure you're familiar with what the job requires you to do, such as looking after young children while their parents are away. To apply for these jobs, while it is not strictly necessary, I always recommend having first aid training because little accidents happen, especially with kids, and you want to make sure you have that covered. If you have a younger sibling, then I'm sure you have some experience taking care of kids; if not, you don't have any previous references to give. I suggest you go around the neighborhoods to find families that you know and talk to them to understand if they would be interested in getting a babysitter.

A sales assistant, sometimes called a sales associate or a shop assistant, is also a job that many teenagers can do, and the advantage of these types of jobs is that you can choose to work in many different industries. Maybe you're interested in fashion, and so working in a clothes shop might be an interesting experience for you, or maybe a video game shop or a pet shop. The options are many, and that's the beauty of being a shop assistant. There's usually some manual work alongside customer service, but it gives you a lot of great experience interacting with people, and it's usually a lot of fun. Many businesses in the retail industry staff teenagers, so you might also find interesting people your age. If you like to interact with customers, then becoming a shop assistant can be something that you will really enjoy.

Barista is another great first job if you want to earn some money. If you already know how to make any type of coffee, that's great, but in most coffee shops, that's not a requirement, and it's a skill you might be able to learn within a week or two. However, the most important skill to have as a barista is your customer service skills. If you are a natural at talking to people and are cheerful, you will love working as a barista. Most of those places also give you some training if you're not proficient at talking to people but want to learn how to interact and be skilled at customer service.

If you enjoy working outdoors, then perhaps you might want to find a part-time job as a gardener. Now, there are many different things to learn when you become a gardener, but as a teenager starting your first job, you won't need to know everything professional gardeners do, plus, you are likely to work with a more experienced gardener, so you can learn. There are also easy gardening jobs that you can do, such as trimming edges, mowing lawns, clipping bushes, watering, or planting. Again, perhaps the easiest way to start making money as a gardener is to go around your neighborhood and ask if they need a gardener for small jobs. While your parents might already have some of the most basic tools, as you progress and continue to do the job, you might want to add a few more tools or upgrade the ones you use to make your job easier.

Being a fast food worker is a very cliche job for a teenager, but it's an easy one to find, and you can make great money even working part-time. Now, most employees in these types of jobs have to be on their feet all day, and that's perhaps the hardest part of the job. But if you can do it, fast food restaurants tend to have very flexible hours that you can accommodate with the other things that you do throughout your day.

If you love animals, dog walking might be the right job for you. In fact, it may not even feel like a job at all. It's quite a popular job for teenagers who like the outdoors and feel confident around dogs. Many dog owners simply don't have the time to walk their pets, but they deeply care about them and have no problem spending money to give their furry friends the best treatment. For you, it all comes down to establishing some good clients, and you can even walk more than one dog, which will increase your income exponentially. This is also a job that is quite flexible, so you can manage your time better.

In recent years, the food delivery industry changed its way of delivering, which allowed teenagers who didn't yet have a full driver's license to do the job by riding bicycles or mopeds. This type of transportation is more evident in large cities with a lot of traffic, where bike couriers have become the norm. While earning money, you might also get a chance to exercise if you ride a bicycle. The amount of money you can make in these jobs is dependent on the number of hours, of course, but also on how efficient you are in quickly getting the food to the customers, where you are then rated. If you do a great job, you are more likely to get tips, which increase your income.

Nowadays, there are many car drivers who use an automatic car wash to clean their cars, but there's still money to be made as a car washer if you do it by hand. This is especially true in smaller cities, where many don't have access to automatic car washers. Alternatively, you can work in these places as a car wash attendant, where you don't have to wash the cars but are there to collect the money and do other smaller tasks when needed.

A quick search online will show you many other options when it comes to looking for part-time jobs; these are far from being the only ones out there. Try to search for things that interest you and that you know you will enjoy doing. Try job search platforms such as Indeed, Glassdoor, FlexJobs, LinkedIn, or Getwork to see who's looking.

Freelancing Jobs

There are a lot of different jobs you can do when it comes to freelancing, but before we get into them, freelancing requires you to take care of how you're going to get paid and to set your own prices. Besides that, because you are your own employer, you need to be far more organized in how you do things. For instance, you need to keep track of the things you need to do, such as tasks and responsibilities, that will help you become more successful at what you do. Freelancing jobs are the most flexible type of work you can find because you can literally work whenever you want or can. However, many of us, especially throughout our teenage years, are far from organized, but you don't have to worry because this is a skill that can be learned and will be very useful for you in the future. There are many tools that you can use, such as online calendars, other tracking apps, and to-do lists. For example, Google Calendar, TimeFree, and Timepage are excellent calendar apps. When it comes to tracking and to-do list applications, some of the best ones out there are Google Tasks, Things 3, or Todolist. Whatever you choose to use, what is important is that you keep everything in order so you know what tasks you should be doing.

Creating an online portfolio is crucial to bringing in clients, and this is not only for visual artists. These are important for any type of freelancing job, from writers to voice actors or transcriptionists. Your potential clients want to know what your level of skill is before hiring you, and this is the only way for them to know. You will also need to know how you're getting paid, and this is something that should be done before you accept your first job. While some jobs might pay directly to your bank account, this method of payment is not very common in freelancing. Usually, online services such as PayPal or Payoneer are far more common and secure to use. You also need to discuss this with the client beforehand to understand the best way for them to pay you. When it comes to actually getting paid, don't deliver any work until at least some of the payment has been transferred to you. The best way to do this and to ensure that no one gets scammed is by getting paid in two tranches: one before the start of the work and one at the end.

Becoming great at marketing is also important because you will find that there's quite some competition, so it's crucial that you understand your target market and spend some time creating your marketing plan. However, nowadays, it has become a lot easier to do this through social media platforms and your dedicated website.

Now, onto the most common freelancing jobs for you. Online tutoring is a great job if you're interested in pursuing any academic field and like to teach. Obviously, you need to teach grades below yours, or if you know a foreign language, you might find yourself getting a great income. Some of the most sought-after subjects are mathematics and science, such as physics or chemistry. When doing this type of work, you need to be extremely organized and have excellent communication skills. Of course, you don't have to be a master at it, but you need to want to learn and become better at it.

Digital artistry is also a job where you can earn a great income, but you need to have a particular skill and be interested in the genre. If you like to create anything through the digital medium, you can sell your art online. Alternatively, you can also work as a digital artist through an agency, but here, you're more likely to have to create art that clients require instead of creating your own and selling it. The requirements for this job differ depending on the type of digital art you want to create, but being good at drawing and understanding at least the basics of animation software can go a long way in this field.

Freelance writing is a job for those who are quite creative with written content, and it's perhaps one of the freelancing jobs where you have the most subgenres to choose from. You can become a ghostwriter, a social media writer, write commercial slogans, etc. There are many different types of writing to choose from. It requires you to have a great knowledge of the written word as well as grammar, and if you want to increase your income, you might want to specialize in a certain industry, such as finance or business.

A virtual assistant, often simply called VA, is a job where you work directly with clients and help them with their daily routine, such as answering emails, doing online research, or keeping track of their meetings and deadlines. Like freelance writing, you can work in many different industries and pick the one that interests you more. You have to be extremely organized since it's a big part of your job, but you also have to be proficient at working with a computer and have great communication skills.

Voice acting is not for everyone, but it's certainly a great job to do if you like it and can. Often, these jobs require you to record readings, such as from a book or other texts, or be a voice actor. However, you might need to purchase some equipment beforehand, such as a microphone or recording software, so you can record your material at home.

If you love video games, you can become a game tester, and it won't even feel like work! Basically, the job is to test new video games to find bugs, typos, or any other type of error before the game comes out to the public. Depending on the platform the games are on, you might have to have that specific platform to test the game, but the majority of these might be done on a computer. A great ability to write reports and good attention to detail are essential for these types of jobs.

Transcriptionists are a common job in the freelancing world, and it often consists of listening to a recording and writing it down. You might also have to proofread your written text or simplify the transcribed text. Much like freelance writing, you need to have a good grasp of the written language.

Regardless of what you want to do as a freelancer, creating accounts on some freelancing platforms is always a great idea, especially if you want to start building your portfolio. For instance, Upwork, 99Designs, ZipRecruiter, or Toptal are great places to start. Again, quick online searches will point you to many other reputable websites and sources on how you can get started.

Entrepreneurship Jobs

Perhaps you want to not only have control over your hours but also start your own business, grow it, and eventually do it full-time (or not). Coming up with your own business allows you to develop different types of skills that freelancing or working part-time doesn't, but you also have quite a few more responsibilities. Obviously, the first thing you have to do is choose what you want to do, such as the industry and the company you want to create.

One of the things many teenagers have, even when they might not have a lot of experience, is knowledge of technology and the online world. And this is certainly something that you can take advantage of since you probably understand the current trends and what people will be willing to use or buy. So, becoming an online marketer might be where your knowledge of the online world and entrepreneurship align. Couple your internet and online knowledge with your social media knowledge, and you can establish your own online marketing company.

Your creativity doesn't have to be bound to digital art; in fact, you can make it big through custom crafts if that's what you like to do. It's quite frequent to see teenagers and others selling things on Etsy; however, you don't have to only sell that, and you shouldn't if you want your business to grow. These crafts can be anything, really, from jewelry to decorations or anything in between, depending on what you want to do. The start is the hardest part, but you can do it by selling your crafts to family and friends and advertising them online.

If you want to run a business in a physical place (as opposed to being at home), something like being a snow cone shop owner might be interesting for you. This is actually one of the easiest ways to start your entrepreneurial career. There are a lot of things that you need to think about, such as what kind of storefront you'd like or what you want it to look like.

If you've washed cars before and want to continue in the same industry, perhaps automotive detailers are exactly what you are looking for. If you think that you don't have the necessary experience, you can start working in the detailing business in another company, but many, after getting the necessary experience, prefer to start their own mobile detailing company.

If you're really great with computers and you believe you have an excellent idea and know how to program, then starting your own tech business might be the single best thing you'll do. Many tech giants started this way, and you can even start working for other tech companies that accept teenagers, such as Vivint.

Obviously, these are just some ideas, and there are many other different things you could be doing. But one thing that I've learned is to first understand what you're good at and what you like to do, and then start from there to try and find what you are going to do.

How to Develop the Necessary Skills for Your Career Ahead?

There are many different skills you will have to learn that will have to do with your career and others that won't, but some of these that will help you progress in your career later in life are general and necessary.

For example, money and budgeting skills are essential, regardless of what career you might follow. Understanding how to make a budget and remain focused on it, how you can open a bank account, transfer money online, apply for a credit card, or write a check. Or how to maintain financial records, understand and assess basic market values, or how to save, purchase, or invest. We will go through this particular subject more in-depth later in the book.

Social skills and manners are also things that will probably help you in your career. This is how you are going to portray yourself in different social settings and will determine the impression you will have on others. Some of the things that might help you with that are learning how to make friendships and maintain them, exploring hobbies and interests, and meeting people with similar interests. Understand the value of the people in your life, and respect their views regardless of how against them you might be. Lastly, learning party etiquette, how to be a good guest, and how to host can help you meet new people and maintain those with whom you've formed a good relationship.

As I've mentioned, organizational skills will come in handy in any career you pursue, so learning as much as you can will make your life much easier. There's a great rule that I always like to mention called the rule of Kaizen, which essentially says "a place for everything and everything in its place." Besides that, there are other little things that you can do, such as declutter your space and reorganize so you know where everything is at any given time.

Communication skills are essential in any job where you have to communicate with others, which is practically all of them, at least to a certain extent. You have to get the message you want people to hear across as cleanly as you possibly can. There are many ways you can practice this, such as being aware every time you have to relay some information to someone on a daily basis. However, there are other things that you need to pay attention to, such as understanding who you are talking to. Everybody is different, and people have the most diverse temperaments, so you might have to communicate in a different manner. Being empathic and trying to understand the other person's perspective can also help you formulate the way you are speaking to them.

Behavioral skills are a way to show your character. Obviously, you build a strong personality, but you have to work on it, not simply wish for it. For instance, admitting your mistakes or taking responsibility for actions you've taken instead of hiding or blaming someone else. Apologizing when you're wrong is also important, and I understand that sometimes it is not an easy thing to do. Always being polite to anyone, regardless of who they are, or understanding the concept of morality so you can rightfully stand up for the things you believe in. Asking for help when you're in need can be a great thing to do. Many of us are too proud to ask for help, but often, that simply makes things worse.

You might also want to develop skills for coping with your emotions. We live in a stressful place where emotions often run high. Camping with these emotions can help you make better decisions or even strengthen ties with other people. For instance, chances are that when you go to college, you might experience loneliness if you leave your parents behind and go study in another city. Self-management allows you to be in control of what is going on in your head. This can be done in many different ways, but meditating or taking time for yourself to let those emotions run through you can help you get through those difficult times. It will also allow you to avoid making impulsive decisions that can have negative consequences.

You will face problems in your career that you will need to solve, and here, problem-solving skills will really come in handy. While your parents might have helped you solve some of your issues, you can't expect them to continue to do that once you grow up and start taking on more responsibilities. While you will get more experience the more problems you solve, this is really a self-learning skill. The first thing you have to do is start facing your problems and stop running away from them. Then, you have to identify the problem correctly so you can start looking for solutions. It's crucial that you analyze the different solutions you've come up with and understand the different outcomes. When you've gone through all of that, you can apply the solution with the best outcome.

Goal setting is essentially understanding how to prioritize the things you have to do. Understand where you want to go and come up with a plan to do it. Here, it's also important that you identify the resources that can help you achieve the goals you've set, and at times, you might even have to change or adjust your goals to suit your needs. The main thing here is to focus on the ultimate goal and devise a plan with smaller goals to get there.

Do you perhaps think that you don't have time to do everything you'd like to? While you might be very busy, there's a chance that your time management is not developed enough to carry out all the tasks you have. There are only 24 hours in which you can try and fit everything you have to do in, and having great time management skills can really help you do that. Using a calendar, a timetable, or even a planner where you can write down all the things you need to do throughout the day is a simple way to keep tabs on everything you have to do. You also have to become good at scheduling and sticking to the things you plan because if you take a little longer on certain things, your time might not be enough to go through everything. Here, it's also relevant that you learn how to prioritize certain tasks over others since some of the things that you might have scheduled might be more urgent or time-pressing. The most important thing, however, is to develop routines so it becomes easier for you to manage your time.

Lastly, another set of skills that will help you in your career are employability skills. These encompass some of the sets of skills I've already mentioned, such as communication, decision-making, and critical thinking. But others, such as work ethic, adaptability, leadership, or teamwork, will make you more likely to be employed in better positions.

As you can see, there are a myriad of jobs that you can take on, depending on what interests you. I've taken on my share of different jobs throughout my teenage years so I could have a solid base of different skills to work with in the future. Obviously, you don't have to work in every industry, but trying out different types of work, such as freelancing, part-time work, or entrepreneurship, might be helpful to learn skills that will stay with you for life. Besides that, you will also have to develop some other skills that you might learn by working and getting experience, but also by practicing them. These are crucial not only to increase your employment rate but also if you want to choose an entrepreneurial path to becoming a great boss.

A Few Words About Taxes

Taxes are mandatory payments to the government and are paid not only by individuals like you and me but also by businesses and corporations. These are used to fund government activities such as services or public works like schools or roads, but also to fund governmental organizations and other programs such as Social Security. Essentially, the taxes that we all pay serve as income for the government to pay for the most varied things. Income taxes are what most individuals pay, and they are automatically taken out of your monthly income, which you can see in your pay stub. But another common tax we pay is capital gains, which are taken out of any interest received from our investments, such as dividends. It's a crime to try and avoid taxes, and it's called tax evasion. However, there are certain things that an individual can do to alleviate the tax burden within the laws, and that's called tax avoidance. Governments use an agency to collect these taxes. For example, in the US, this is called the Internal Revenue Service, or IRS. What you pay in taxes is usually proportional to what you earn, so the more you earn, the more you pay.

While if you work for a company, you don't have to do anything to pay taxes since the company's account does everything for you, and the taxes are taken directly from your pay stub if you are self-employed, then you have to do your own taxes. There are many ways to do this, and many different third-party companies that can help you do this easily, such as TurboTax. However, if you think you can file it yourself, you can go to the IRS website and do it for free. This is for the US; of course, other countries have other entities that collect taxes. For instance, in the UK, it's HMRC. The process is the same; you can do it yourself, which takes some time, or you can find a company that simplifies the process for you. Every other country works more or less the same way; you just need to look for the entity that collects taxes in that specific country. If you need help on how to actually file the forms in the US, you can use the USA.gov website, where they tell you exactly what forms you have to file and how to do it. Every tax collector's website should also have a step-by-step guide on how to file the tax and fill out the form for that specific country.

In the next chapter, I will go through the financial part of things, such as how to open a bank account, what the different bank accounts are and their main functionalities, and many other things that will be useful for you to make the right decisions.

CHAPTER 3

BANKING AND FINANCIAL SERVICES

> *A big part of financial freedom is having your heart and mind free from worry about the what-ifs of life.*
>
> *–Suze Orman*

nderstanding how the banking system works is fundamental to your money skills. There's no other way around it than to open a bank account and be able to manage it. It's actually quite easy, and many teenagers already have some sort of bank account opened by their parents. If you don't, it's alright; simply follow the steps I'll list below.

Opening Your First Bank Account

To open a bank account, first, you need to choose a bank to open with and give them some of your information. If you're under the age of 18, you might need your parents to open it for you, but you will still have access to it. However, there are also teen bank accounts, which are similar to other accounts with only a few features missing. For example, you can't have an overdraft or a credit card, and if you're over 16, you won't need a guardian or a parent to open it for you. Besides that, you can do everything you want with the account, such as setting up direct debits, making bank transfers, etc. However, to register a debit card yourself, you also need to be over 16 years old; otherwise, a parent or guardian will have to authorize it first.

Whether or not you need a parent or guardian to open an account, there's information that needs to be passed on to the bank, such as proof of address, contact information, and proof of identity, which can be a birth certificate, passport, or a driver's license if you already have one. If you have opened a teen bank account, once you turn 18 years old, it usually turns into an adult account right away so you can have all the features that were currently missing, but sometimes the bank provider might request that you authorize this change.

While I'll be talking about the different accounts you can apply for later in this chapter, when you're opening your first bank account, there are a few things that you need to take into account. For example, some bank providers have a minimum opening amount, which means that you need to add some money right away to the account when you open it. The amount differs, and it could be as little as $1, but you need to make sure what the minimum opening amount is before you apply for one. Another thing that you have to take into consideration is the monthly fee. While these often don't happen on teens' accounts, they might once you turn 18. Interest is also something worth checking because the money you have in your account grows depending on the interest rate; however, in regular checking accounts, there's usually no interest rate (we will talk more about this later on in the chapter). Some accounts (especially teen accounts) have limits such as withdrawals or spending limits, so you can't use more money if you reach a certain amount. While it might be a little annoying, it's a great way for you to learn how to handle and manage your money properly. Lastly, when thinking of opening a bank account, make sure it has a robust online banking app where you can track everything from your phone as well as make bank transfers. This makes things a lot easier.

The Different Types of Bank Accounts

There are a few different types of accounts that you can open; however, as a teenager, you can only open a checking account. Besides that, other bank accounts include savings, money market accounts (MMAs), and certificate of deposit accounts (CDs). Understanding the differences is crucial so you can make better decisions.

Checking Accounts

These types of accounts are the most basic ones and are essentially deposit accounts that you can first open. You can hold funds, transfer them, withdraw money at ATMs, or use paper checks. These can also be linked to other accounts (usually through the same bank institutions), such as savings accounts. Banking institutions have many different types of checking accounts, such as teen checking, student, senior, rewards, or interest (since the basic checking account doesn't have interest associated with it). But to start with, a basic checking account is fine as long as you understand the minimum deposit requirements (if any), the minimum balance requirements (if any), if there are monthly maintenance fees, if there are ATM fees, and the ATM network size (this allows you to know how many ATMs you can withdraw money from).

Setting up an account is easy. As a teen, you might need a parent or guardian to do it, but usually, you can do it online or by visiting a branch, and the process is usually immediate. Obviously, you will have to provide some important and personal information, such as an ID and Social Security number. Depositing cash can usually be done through a check or cash, and you will get a debit card linked to that account that you can use to pay for things or withdraw money. Like in many other accounts, your funds are protected up to $250,000 by the Federal Deposit Insurance Corporation or FDIC. This means that if there's any error by your bank or something happens to your money while it's in your bank account, you are covered as long as it's below the threshold. You can usually opt to have an overdraft or not in your account. I personally don't recommend it since this allows for debts where the fees are quite high. Besides allowing you to use an ATM and debit cards, other services used with a checking account include wire transfer, which is essentially moving money from one account to another electronically, or direct deposit, where, say, your employer pays your income directly into your account, which becomes immediately available to you.

Savings Account

The main difference between savings and checking accounts is that with savings, you have an interest rate, which means that for as long as you hold money in the account, the amount is increasing. In other words, the savings account pays you interest on the amount of the deposit you have in the account. All the things that you have to check when opening a checking account, such as the minimum balance, etc., are also relevant when you open a savings account. But while checking accounts usually allow you limitless withdrawals, savings accounts don't because they are not designed for everyday use. They also usually don't have a debit card, which is usually linked to your checking account, so any transfers are usually conducted from there.

These accounts are created to hold your money there and withdraw from it as little as possible because, as I've mentioned, the interest you earn is based on the money you have deposited there. The more money you have there, the more you earn in interest. But the most important thing to look for when opening a savings account is the annual percentage yield (APY), which is essentially the percentage you earn on the money deposited. The higher the APY, the more you earn. Every bank offers different percentages, and while you might think the higher, the better, these high-yield savings often have more conditions that you need to abide by, for instance, fewer withdrawals, withdrawals that take longer, or higher maintenance fees. If you want to have a savings account but don't want to have limited withdrawals, you can choose an easy-access savings account that allows you to withdraw money whenever you want, but these usually have a lower APY. It really all comes down to your needs. If you think you won't need the money, it's best to place it in a high-interest savings account; if not, it might be best to deposit it in a lower-interest account where you have easier access to your money.

There are other accounts that I will just briefly mention, such as a money market account (MMA) or a certificate of deposit account (CDs). MMAs can be seen as a mix of checking and savings accounts where you can deposit money in them, earn interest, have a debit card, and even have paper checks. However, with these accounts, you still have a withdrawal limit, but you can set up direct debits. Some of the main differences with these accounts include, for instance, a higher minimum balance requirement if you want to keep the account open. These are great when you want to earn interest but still want all the convenient features a checking account has to offer, such as the use of a debit card. CDs are time deposit accounts, which means that these mostly work as savings accounts where you leave your money there for a certain amount of time, which in the financial world is called "maturity term." During the maturity term, your money is increasing, or you're earning interest on the balance you have there.

When looking to open a bank account, it's also important that you not only look at the different brick-and-mortar bank providers but also at credit unions and online banks. Credit unions are customer-owned institutions that have many of the same services a big bank has and may even offer you better interest rates (although not always), mainly because they are non-profit organizations. Online banks often offer fewer fees because they don't have branches that they have to pay for, which means they might offer you better rates as well. However, because they don't have physical branches, all contact with the bank is done online through a computer or mobile phone.

To sum up the steps of opening a bank account, first, you need to choose how to apply (whether in branch, online, or through the phone), gather all the necessary information, such as your Social Security Number, ID, and proof of address, provide contact details, select the type of account you want, read and accept the terms and conditions, submit the application, and fund your account.

Managing Your Account

Usually, when you open any type of bank account, you will have to sign a document (usually the terms and conditions, which you have to read thoroughly). While sometimes you might have to sign and mail the documents, more often, you can sign the documents online before you can start using the account.

Checking and savings accounts need to be funded before you can start using them, which can be done in different ways, such as by depositing cash, depositing a check (which usually takes a couple of business days to reach your account), setting up a direct debit from your employer, which is nowadays the most common way to get your income, or transferring funds electronically from another bank account that you might already have.

After that, if you're expecting a debit card, this should arrive at your address in a couple of days. From then on, you can pay bills online, make remote check deposits, and even sign up for alerts on your phone or email when your balance is low or when you withdraw money. Apart from that, the only thing that you should keep an eye on is your balance to see if there are fees incurred or if you need a minimum balance on the account.

Using Online Baking

Online banking, also known as internet banking, allows you to do pretty much everything banking-related online as opposed to going to a banking branch, which might include deposits, payment of online bills, or transfers. Nowadays, every banking institution has online banking in one way or another, where you can access your account through the banking app or through your computer. This makes things a lot easier, especially if you're quite proficient with new technology, and it saves you plenty of time. It's also a lot more convenient because it allows you to make transactions or pay bills anywhere you are, simply from your phone or computer, and all you need is one of those devices connected to the internet. Some financial institutions even allow you to open savings accounts and other accounts linked to your main account online, as well as set up direct debits or report changes in your account.

This advance in technology allowed us to have online-exclusive banks, which offer much lower costs or free banking features and better gains in terms of interest. And even though they don't have branches or ATMs of their own, you are still able to withdraw money from your online bank accounts from any other bank ATMs, so there's little change for you here if you decide to go for an online-only bank.

Advantages and Disadvantages of Online Banking

As I've mentioned above, convenience is certainly the best advantage of online banking, and you can perform the most common things from the comfort of your home on your phone or laptop. Transactions are extremely efficient, can be done almost instantly, and can open and close accounts just as easily. Besides that, you also have a lot of options when it comes to the different types of accounts to open, from high- or low-interest savings accounts to fixed deposits, etc.

Monitoring your finances also became a lot easier since you don't have to go to the nearest ATM or branch to check your funds and can simply do it anywhere on any device. Because of this, you have access to your account 24/7, which wasn't always the case when you had to wait for bank branches to open in the morning.

While I believe online banking makes banking accessible for everyone, including people who are just starting out in the financial world, it also comes with some disadvantages that you need to be aware of. In this case, the disadvantages I'll be listing target online-only banking institutions. For instance, if you are a new banking customer, not having someone to talk to face-to-face might be a little daunting at first, and customer service is only available over the phone or through chat. Online banking depends entirely on access to the internet, and if for any reason you don't have it, you become quite limited. Lastly, while online banking security is constantly improving, accounts are still subjected to hacking, but this refers to any type of online banking, even those belonging to brick-and-mortar banks.

Staying Safe With Online Banking

As I've said, online banking security is constantly improving, and it's quite secure, but it's still susceptible to hacking and other scams if you don't pay attention. There are a few things that you can do to make your accounts more secure and prevent your information from falling into a hacker's hands. One of the easiest things you can do is choose a strong password, as you'd normally do with any other online account. You can also enable two-factor authentication or, if you're on your phone, face identification, which allows you to only access the banking app after your face is scanned.

Alternatively, you can also sign up for banking alerts, so if there are any strange movements in your account, you will be notified right away, and you can then contact your bank to know more or to freeze your account. Steering away from public Wi-Fi connections is also a good way to prevent your information from spreading to other people. Use only private or well-secured Wi-Fi connections. Hackers can get your information through malicious hotspots, through malware and spyware on the Wi-Fi, or through data transmissions over unencrypted networks.

Other than that, simply pay attention to any phishing scams so you don't give your personal information away. There are many different ways these scams operate, but they all have the same finality: you giving your information away. This can be in the form of SMS texts or emails that usually look like they come from your bank. However, they often urge you to insert personal information on the website or to change your information and then redirect you to a website that often looks like your bank. Paying attention to the sender's email address is important, and you can check if that's actually your bank's email address. Alternatively, you can call your bank and ask them if they've sent an email from that email address. Hovering over the links on an email sent to you often allows you to see the webpage it is addressing you to. And lastly, your bank almost never asks you to share your personal information. When in doubt, contact your bank to make sure before you share any personal information.

Understanding Bank Cards, ATMs, and Fees

There's quite a lot more to know when it comes to all these financial services and products than you might think. Things like debit and credit cards might sound and look like the same thing, but they can be very different. The same goes for all the different fees these services and products might charge. So, let's go through all the most important things you need to know to use them with confidence.

Credit Cards vs. Debit Cards

When you look at both a debit and a credit card, there's not much difference, right? They have 16-digit numbers on them, as well as expiration dates, magnetic strips, etc. You can use both in the same way and use them to purchase things, but this is where things get a little different. When making purchases, a debit card draws money that you have in your bank account, while credit cards draw borrowed money from your bank and have a limit. So, in other words, a debit card uses your money, and a credit card uses the bank's money that you will need to pay back eventually. This is not to say that credit cards are bad; they are not. The way you use it might have negative implications for your finances. A credit card offers you security, but you need to know how to use it. Let's get down to it.

Credit Cards

As I've mentioned, a credit card is usually issued by a financial institution where you already have an account. The institution allows you to borrow money from them with the condition that you pay them back with interest, so you will always pay them back more than what you've spent. However, there are many different types of credit cards that might offer you different perks.

Regular credit cards are easy to understand, allow you to pay with borrowed money, make balance transfers, and are usually free (meaning no annual fees). Premium credit cards often have perks for their customers, such as access to special events, airport lounge access, and other things, but they incur an annual fee. Then, there are the specific rewards credit cards that give you travel points, which give you discounted airline tickets, cash back, and other rewards. Balance transfer credit cards usually have extremely low-interest rates as well as low fees from another credit card's balance transfer. Secured credit cards are for those people who can't get standard or any other type of credit card, and they have to pay an initial deposit as collateral to be able to use a credit card. Lastly, there are charge credit cards that do not have a limit, but usually, you'd have to pay the balance within a month before you could use them again.

There are quite a few benefits to using a credit card besides the security and rewards it gives you. For example, they help you build your credit history, which appears on your credit reports. Credit reports are important documents that allow banks and other financial institutions to check if you're financially trustworthy when you're asking for loans or a mortgage for your property. Credit cards help you build a stronger credit report because they show if you have been paying your credit card back on time, for instance. If you use your credit card properly, you can raise your credit score, get higher chances of getting accepted for loans, and get lower interest rates on those loans.

Most credit cards also allow purchase protections and warranties on items that you purchase, besides whatever retail warranty the company producing the item gives you. For instance, if you buy a TV with your credit card, you usually have a warranty that lasts a year or two, but if the TV stops working after the retail company's warranty, you can check if your credit card offers an extended warranty and has you covered. Some credit cards might also offer price protection, which allows you to replace any item that might have been lost or stolen or even get a refund.

Credit cards also have fraud protection in case of theft or loss, and if you report it in a timely manner, this is not exclusive to credit cards and debit cards. The Electronic Fund Transfer Act can give you the same protection, but again, you have to report it within 48 hours of finding out you've lost your card. But with a credit card, you are far more protected. For example, you can dispute an unauthorized purchase if the goods are lost during shipping or are delivered damaged under the Fair Credit Billing Act. If you have bought goods that have been lost or damaged during shipping with a debit card, you can only get a refund if the merchant wants it. Another example of credit cards being more secure is if you were to rent a car. Many credit card providers (but not all) allow a waiver for any collisions you might have.

But of course, there are cons when it comes to using credit cards, and you've probably heard some of them. For instance, the unhealthy use of credit cards can lead to large debts. As I've mentioned, when you're using a credit card, you're not using your money but the bank's money, which you will have to pay back with interest at some point. You have to at least pay the minimum payment every single month, but the more you spend, the harder it becomes to pay at least those minimum payments. Plus, you should only pay the absolute minimum if you can't pay more because if you keep on paying the minimum, you will never finish paying your debt because of the rise in interest rates.

If you fail to make the minimum payments, that will have a negative impact on your credit score, but keeping the balance on your credit card at a low level will help your credit score. But if you do the opposite and fail to make credit card payments, max out your credit cards, or apply for too many credit cards, you will see your credit score decrease.

You can think of a credit card as a short-term loan, and these can get really high-interest rates, which are calculated using your annual percentage rate (APR). The higher the interest and APR, the more you pay in interest when you're paying back the money you've spent with your credit card. Also, keep in mind that the higher the interest, the harder it is for you to pay and the more it will cost you to pay what you owe. Besides the interest on your credit card, there are other fees that might also be applied and that you have to be aware of, such as a late payment fee, a cash advance fee, an annual fee (but not always), a balance transfer fee, or a foreign transaction fee. We will go deeper into credit later in its own dedicated chapter.

Debit Cards

As I've mentioned above, when you're paying with a debit card, you are not using anyone else's money but your own, which comes straight from your checking or savings account. With a debit card, you can only use as much money as you have deposited in the account. Like credit cards, debit cards can also offer some consumer protections, but credit cards usually offer more when it comes to fraud. While most debit cards are linked to a bank account, this is not strictly necessary. In fact, there are two types of debit cards that don't require you to have a savings or checking account: Prepaid debit cards and electronic benefits transfer (EBT) cards. The first is used by people who don't have a bank account but want to make electronic purchases and be able to use all the features a debit card allows. However, as the name indicates, you'd have to preload your card with the amount of money you'd like to have on it. So, for instance, if you wanted to have $300 in the prepaid debit card, you'd have to transfer that money first, and you cannot use more than what you've deposited. EBTs are issued by federal and state agencies, but only qualifying people can use them and have the benefits that come with them. Such benefits can include, for instance, food stamps or cash. Because these are essentially debit cards with a PIN number and a magnetic strip, they can be used in

ATM machines and other point-of-sale terminals. The way it works is that once the recipient gets accepted or approved for benefits, the state they are in creates an account, and the Supplemental Nutrition Assistance Program (SNAP) benefits are placed in the account for them to use every month. By federal law, there are no processing fees or sales taxes on these purchases. These systems exist in the US, but other countries have their own that often work similarly.

When you use a debit card, you don't have the issue of incurring debt since all the money you spend with it is yours, and you don't have to pay it back to anyone. And it is known that people tend to spend more money when using a card (debit or credit) than when using cash, so if you use a debit card, you don't have the issue of racking up large debts. While credit cards still offer better fraud protection, debit cards are becoming better and better when it comes to this subject, and so they have become quite safe. As I've said, the quicker you report the missing card or any unusual activity, the better chances you have of getting the money back. There's also no annual fee on debit cards, unlike many credit cards. You also don't have a withdrawal fee with a debit card, which you do with a credit card.

Now, when it comes to the disadvantages of debit cards, they are not free from some. For instance, there are no rewards, with the exception of rewards checking accounts, but these are not as good as the perks from credit cards. Debit cards don't help you build credit like credit cards do. Essentially, when you pay back your credit card, you are telling lenders that you are financially trustworthy and that you will pay your money back. With a debit card, you don't have to pay it back, so you're not proving that you can be financially trustworthy. Lastly, even though debit cards don't have annual fees like credit cards do, you might have to pay other fees such as maintenance fees, overdraft fees, or even foreign ATM fees.

So, while credit and debit cards might look similar, their advantages and disadvantages are quite different. You need to understand your priorities when thinking about using one or the other. While it's recommended that you have both before you make a purchase, you need to understand if you want to start building your credit or getting rewards or if you prefer to have your finances totally under control. Obviously, using a bit of both might be the wisest thing you'd do, but when using your credit card, make sure you have enough money to pay your debt.

How Do You Use an ATM?

You probably know what an ATM is, and even if you've never used one before, you know it's a machine that allows you to withdraw money from your bank account. Out of curiosity, do you know what ATM stands for? I didn't for a long time after I started using it, but it stands for Automated Teller Machine, and it has many more different uses than simply withdrawing money from your bank account. It also allows you to make basic transactions without having to go to a bank and talk to a teller (hence the automatic teller). While most people use a debit card when withdrawing money, you can also use a credit card, although these usually come with a higher fee. ATMs are spread across the country and other countries and make it easier for you to use financial systems anywhere, which makes them quite convenient even nowadays, where financial services are dominated by the internet and mobile banking.

When it comes to fees, these are usually charged by the ATM operator, your bank, or both; however, if you use an ATM that is operated by your bank, these fees can be avoided. If you use an ATM in a foreign country, you are always likely to pay fees, even if they are only exchange rates.

There are two main types of ATM machines, with the most basic of the models only allowing you to check your account's balance and withdraw money. These are the most common ones seen anywhere. But there is another type that is often inside bank branches, and you hardly see them on a high street, for instance. These allow you to perform more services such as transfers, access account information, accept deposits (often cash), and aid you with a line of credit payments. Obviously, you have to have an account at that same bank to be able to use these more complex ATM machines.

Apart from that, the common design of ATM machines is pretty straightforward. There's a card reader where you insert your card, so the ATM knows your bank details. The keypad allows you to enter your PIN or the amount you want to withdraw or send; there's also a cash dispenser from where the ATM "gives" you the money. ATMs also have a printer in case you want to have a copy of the receipt of whatever service you've just performed, and of course, a screen where you can see what is happening and allow you to guide yourself through the process.

When it comes to using it, it's also quite simple. You will have to insert your bank card, and it will prompt you to type your PIN. From there, you will see on the screen some options, such as withdrawing money or checking your balance. As I've mentioned, if you don't want to be charged for any transactions, you should use the ATM operated by your bank since ATMs operated by other banks or other ATM operators will incur a fee upon transaction. This is especially important if you withdraw money quite often, which might add up at the end of the week or month. There's usually a certain amount that you can withdraw per day, week, or month, but these differ depending on your bank and bank account. While some might limit your daily withdrawal to $300, others might allow a $1500 daily withdrawal. However, if you need to withdraw more than the limit, you can usually get around this by calling your bank and asking for permission, or you can go directly to a branch and talk to a teller.

Opening your first bank account is quite exciting since it will allow you to have a little more financial freedom. It's important that you shop around and check out the best banks for your first account. This should align with the purpose of your bank account—what are you using it for, etc.? Then, you have to choose your account type, and the first one is almost always a regular checking account. In fact, you can't open a savings account without opening a checking account first. Then you have MMAs and CDs, but these can come later. Because you might be tech-savvy, you will have a much easier time managing your account through your phone via mobile or internet banking. The advance of this technology allows us to simplify how people manage their accounts, which has become fairly easy. Lastly, understanding the differences between credit and debit cards is crucial so you don't end up accumulating a lot of debt. To start with, chances are you won't need a credit card, and if you're working part-time, as a freelancer, or even as an entrepreneur but still living with your parents, I don't think you will need a credit card. However, if you do take one, make sure you understand the terms and conditions, the APR, and everything else that is involved when it comes to spending money with a credit card.

In the next chapter, I will talk about budgeting, which is oftentimes linked to your capacity to spend only the money that you have (as opposed to using credit cards). Here, I'll introduce the concept of budgeting, why it's so important, how you can create your own personal budget by tracking your income and expenses, how you can allocate funds to the different categories, how you can manage irregular income (if you're a freelancer or an entrepreneur), and talk about some of the most common strategies when it comes to budgeting.

CHAPTER 4

BUDGETING

> *A budget is more than just a series of numbers on a page; it is an embodiment of our values.*
>
> *- Barack Obama*

B udgeting is the only way we can understand if we are on the right path in terms of finances. Sure, you've heard of a budget and budgeting before, and you might even have a faint idea of what it is exactly. But having a budget is one of the most fundamental things we can do to understand how our finances work and how to be successful when it comes to money. Essentially, with a budget, you can tell where the money is coming from and where it's going, and that's the only way to get absolute control of your money. Now, if we want to get a little more technical, a budget allows you to track your income and expenses and establish a balance of what you can and can't spend throughout a month (or more).

There are several ways to create a budget with more or fewer variants, but a budget always has to have three fundamental things: it has to have an identity, which in this case is you (although there are also budgets for companies, governments, households, etc.). There has to be a defined time period, for instance, a month (businesses tend to do longer budgets). And it has to have detailed information on where the money is coming in (such as from your employer or freelancing work) and where the money is going (where you spend the money, etc.).

Let me give you an example of what the personal budget of a teenager might look like. Say you started working part-time on the weekends, and you're earning $500 a month. Because you are still living with your parents, you are not paying rent, bills, etc. But instead, you're saving a part of it, and the rest is for expenses such as a night out every week and traveling to work on the weekends. Everything else goes to savings.

	Income		Expenditures
Salary	$500	Night outs	$200
		Traveling	$20
Total (savings):	$280		

This is a pretty easy budget since you don't have to pay for groceries, bills, etc., but once you start doing that, things get a little more complex, and you will need to allocate certain amounts to certain places and not exceed them. For instance, if you wanted to save $380 instead of $280, you'd have to cut your nights out in half.

Why Should You Care About Budgeting?

Well, if I haven't convinced you yet about starting to budget, I can come up with a few more reasons as to why you should be budgeting, especially if you want to save as much as possible. First of all, starting to budget at a young age will teach you the basics of money habits and mindset that we've discussed in the previous chapter. This alone should be reason enough to convince you, but there's more.

Budgeting allows you to set and reach your long-term goals, regardless of what they are. For instance, there's this trip that your friends are planning to do, and, obviously, you want to go with them, but while you have money for the flight, you don't have enough for the accommodation. Because the trip is a year away, you might still have time to save some money to go, but I know that when you're a teenager, one year is very far away. Either way, the logic is the same. The accommodation is $1000 for five days, and using the example from above, you are saving $280 a month. This means that in about four months, you'll be able to pay for the accommodation. However, your friends are only willing to wait three months for you to book the accommodation because they say that particular place gets full rather quickly. So, you have to go back to your budget and relocate some of the money so you can save more. Looking at it, the only thing that you can really change is the nights out because you need to pay for travel if you want to continue to have an income. So, if you cut the money you spend on your night outs in half, you'd have $380 saved a month. This means that in three months, you'd have enough time to book the accommodation. Without a budget, you wouldn't know exactly where you'd have to cut and how much you could spend on certain things. It essentially forces you to plan your goals and to know exactly how much you can spend and how much you need to allocate to the different expenses and savings. You have a great overview of money coming in and money coming out, which allows you to know how much you have progressed and how far your goal is.

Budgeting can keep you from overspending, especially on money that you don't necessarily have. Assuming you have a credit card, overspending can become a really bad situation because you are spending money that is not yours, you have to pay it back, and you don't have that money. With a budget, you know exactly how much you can spend and when you should stop. As a teenager, this is easier to understand because you have fewer expenses and, most likely, don't have a credit card yet. However, this will change in the future, and you have to be prepared to plan a budget and stick to it. Before, when people used cash instead of cards, things were also simpler because the fact that you visualized money coming out of your wallet made you think about it. Nowadays, you don't see that money, and so it's easy to simply type a PIN or even touch your card (with contactless payments), and that's it; you don't think about it anymore. This is also one of the reasons budgeting is important: it can keep you in line and make sure you don't spend without thinking.

Budgeting can make your retirement savings a lot easier. I know that retirement is a long way from where you are now, and we will talk about it later in the book. But once you get there and have been budgeting all those years, you will be thankful you've done it. Budgeting doesn't only make retirement savings easier, but all savings in general. It's crucial that you build regular savings and make contributions to your retirement accounts so you don't have to worry about not having enough once you retire.

I've briefly mentioned emergency funds, which are quite necessary if, well, an emergency appears. Budgeting allows you to save, which means that it also allows you to build a financial cushion in case of an emergency. Obviously, as a teen, you might have your back covered by your parents, but as soon as you start your young adult life, you might be on your own, so you will want to save as much as you can to start your adult life and have no issues navigating it.

Budgeting can also reveal your spending habits. For instance, if we use the example above, you know you'd be spending $200 a month on nights out. That's a big chunk of your income. However, when you start your young adult life, you will have far more expenses. Things like TV or streaming subscriptions might add up and take a big chunk of your income. Without a budget, you might not even notice any of that. Only once you list all your expenses do you start to understand how much you usually spend on things that you probably shouldn't. Not only that, but it might also reveal bad spending habits such as purchasing too many clothes, unnecessary food, etc., that you might be able to stop.

How Should You Create a Personal Budget?

While budgets can be created in different ways and also depend on each person's lifestyle, there are a few steps that you can follow to make this right. The small changes you will be able to figure out as you gain more experience creating budgets.

The first step is to create your net income. This might be a new word for you, but it simply means your take-home income. So, if you're only working part-time, you probably are not paying any taxes yet. But once you move to a full-time job, some expenses, such as taxes and retirement programs, will be deducted from your pay. Usually, you don't have to worry about it, and the accountant of your employer does that. The important aspect here is finding out how much you're actually making or how much is entering your account each month. Calculating your income gets a little harder if you have an irregular income, for instance, if you are a freelancer or an entrepreneur; however, you can write down and find out how much you're making.

The next step is tracking your spending, and this is where you might find some revelations about your spending habits. First, you should list your regular spending, such as bills, mortgage, rent, etc. In the example I've used, your regular spending would be your traveling (and not your night outs!). Other things, such as utilities or car payments, are also part of your regular payments. Then, you have to list your variable expenses, and these are a little harder to find out because, well, they are irregular. Your night outs would fall into this category because even though you might spend more or less the same every time you go out, there might be times when you spend a little less or a little more. Other variable expenses would be groceries or gas. This is also the best area where you can reduce your overall expenses because most of them might not be necessary (yes, night outs are not as necessary as paying your rent). But obviously, fixed expenses can also be cut; for example, you could change your phone provider if you think you're paying too much or your energy provider. To help you find all of this information, credit and debit card statements are your best resources because you will have a detailed list of where your money came from and where it went.

When doing your budget, you need to set goals, but it's important that these goals are realistic. Before you even analyze all the information you've tracked, you should write down a list of your goals: short-, medium-, and long-term goals. In the short-term goals, things like setting up an emergency fund should be listed, as well as any other short-term goal you want to achieve, such as going on a trip with your friends. Long-term goals should be things that will take some time to achieve, such as saving for a down payment on a property or retirement. Of course, these goals can change over time, which will change the way you set up your budget, but what's important is that you have them so you can keep yourself motivated.

When that's done, it's time to make a plan. This is where you take all the information you've gathered and bring everything together. The first thing is to look at what you're actually spending and compare it with what you actually want to spend. When you have those side by side, then you have to start looking for ways to cut down on some of the expenses. It's easier to cut down on variable costs such as going out, TV or streaming subscriptions, etc.

Again, you have to do your budgeting at least every month because it will need constant adjustments. But you also have to adjust your spending so it stays within your budget. Once you've followed all the steps until now, you'll have a much clearer idea of the things you need to adjust and where you can't overspend. Here, I like to make two columns of my expenses, one with my wants and another with my needs. The first thing that you can cut is anything in the "wants" column. For instance, do you really need to go to the movies once a week? Or can you have movie nights at home? Either way, movie night is not a need; it's a want. Food, rent, mortgage, transport, etc. Those are needs, and even for those, you might find a solution on how to decrease spending. The main thing to take from here is that even small decreases and changes can add up at the end of the month.

The last step is to regularly check on your budget, ideally every month because expenses and even income might change. The hard part is starting, but once you have a budget, you can simply adjust it every month. This is a habit that you should try to incorporate into your routine, and you will see the difference that will make.

Budget Allocation

While right now you might not have as many sections in your budget as you will once you have your independence, it's important that you understand what budget allocation is. There are many different categories that you can make when setting up your allocation, which might be a little daunting, but there are a few that should always be incorporated. It all comes down to how much more control you want over your money, your spending habits, and your goals. All of this will allow you to organize your money and reach your financial goals faster.

When you're just starting to budget, I find it easier to first catalog the different sections as "essential" and "non-essential." As we've discussed, essential spending has to do with the things that you have to spend money on regardless, such as rent or mortgage, groceries, travel, etc. Non-essential is everything else that doesn't fall into the first category.

There's a very popular budget rule called the 50/30/20 rule, where you allocate 50% of your income to your needs (essential), 30% to your wants (non-essential), and 20% to savings. Of course, this is just a guide, and you might have to adjust it. Also, there are many other budgeting strategies that I will talk about later in this chapter. Now, once you get independence, there will be many other categories in your budget, and I like to divide it into five different categories: Housing that encompasses rent or mortgage; transportation that involves public transportation tickets, gas, car maintenance, car loan payment, etc.; utilities such as electricity, water, mobile, internet, and cable; food and supplies, such as groceries, household items, cleaning supplies, and savings. These categories might expand if or when you have a child or a pet, or both, in which case you'd add another category, childcare, where you'd insert babysitting, nursery, and daycare, and a pets category, where you'd add pet food, vet bills, flea treatments, toys, etc.

This is quite a basic budget category, but obviously, there are other things that you will need to add as you get better at budgeting, such as healthcare, insurance, personal care, or clothing. You can add more categories as you see fit for your lifestyle, as these are just simple ideas.

Now, you might be asking, "How much money should I be allocating to the different categories?" Well, that depends on your needs. I've already given you an example with the 50/30/20 method, but it really depends. One thing is certain: your needs have to be met, and that's a great way to start your budget. But the different categories you add simply have to work for you. After all, it is a personal budget and a personal process. Everybody has a different income, different expenses, needs, and goals, and it's hard to give the right number.

What If I Have an Irregular Income?

If you have an irregular income, then things get a little more complicated, but nothing that you can't overcome. Here, you need a different approach. You might not know your income for sure, but you know your expenses, at least the fixed ones. This is where I would start when budgeting on an irregular income. For instance, you'd still have rent or a mortgage, bills, groceries, and maybe travel costs. While these can also vary, they are easier to predict. When you've written down the fixed expenses, you need to make sure that you can at least cover them every month.

Another thing that you can do is budget for the lowest monthly income you can have. It might be tempting to budget for a good month when your income is irregular, but you should budget for your lowest income so you know for sure you can make it. Here, it's also important that you think ahead since different months and seasons could mean more or less income. This is especially true if you're self-employed. There are certain industries where certain seasons, such as Summer or Christmas, might bring in more money while others might bring in less. You should try to save more during the higher income periods so you can then pay for those months when business is less stable.

Different Budgeting Strategies

As I've said before, there are many different budgets, but they simply serve as a template from which you have to make your own adjustments so they fit your lifestyle. In any case, I'll show you some of the most popular budgeting strategies used in personal finance so you can have a better idea of where to start.

Again, I like to emphasize that when you start budgeting, it might be hard to stay on track, and that's one of the reasons you should start now when you have fewer expenses so you can create the habit. But let's get to the strategies.

I've already mentioned the 50/30/20 formula, sometimes known as the balanced money formula, but I want to explain some of its benefits. This is an easy budget to start with because it only has three simple categories, which means less calculation and fewer worries. However, overspending can happen when using this strategy because there's more leeway, and it's not as strict. This comes from the fact that you are not budgeting for every category, like food or gas, which might mean that if you don't pay attention, you might overspend. If you follow this budget, I recommend that you overestimate a little so you have some room for overspending.

Cash-Only Budget

This strategy is exactly as the name indicates: You only use cash (if you still remember what cash is, of course). This strategy is also called envelope budgeting because you place the cash in different envelopes, and on each one of those envelopes is written the purpose of that money. This means you wouldn't be using your bank cards. Nowadays, using this method is not as easy as it once was because most things we pay are standing orders, but there are certain categories where you can only use cash. For example, you can add $200 to an envelope named "groceries." So, you would withdraw $200, write "groceries" on an envelope, and place that cash on that envelope. That's all you can spend on groceries. Once that money is gone, you can't purchase more. You can also do this for gas, clothing, etc.

This is a great strategy if you overspend often. It's quite simple: once there's no more cash in that specific envelope, you can't spend more. To make this method more efficient, make sure you leave your bank cards at home. One thing that you should pay attention to when using this budgeting method is to be extra careful since you're using cash and can lose it. Make sure all the money you carry is in a safe place.

Zero-Based Budget

The zero-based budget, which many refer to as the budget where you "give every dollar a job," is exactly that. Every income money has a purpose, meaning that your income matches every money outgoing from your account. Obviously, this doesn't mean you spend all your money, but instead, at the end of the month, you shouldn't have any money in your checking account because you've also transferred some to an external savings account. Essentially, all your money has a purpose, and you shouldn't have money in your regular checking account because it's not bringing you any benefits.

Some of your income has the job of paying the bills, paying rent or mortgage, while another portion goes for savings, groceries, etc. You should use this budget technique if you want absolute control of your money, where you essentially micromanage everything. In other words, you wouldn't spend any money unless it had been planned before. However, this is quite a time-consuming budget because it involves a lot of planning, and you'd be recording every single transaction. So, while it gives you total control over your income, you need to have time to actually make it work.

The 60% Solution Budget

This budget strategy is in many ways similar to the zero-budget one in the sense that you use every single dollar of your income somewhere. Essentially, 60% of your income goes to committed expenses, and this includes both fixed and non-fixed expenses, so you can have a mortgage or rent, but also gas, cable, streaming services, etc. In other words, every expense that comes every month falls into this 60%. The rest (40%) is then divided into four 10% groups, such as long-term savings, short-term savings, retirement, and wants. Long-term savings include emergency funds and any investments you might want to make. Short-term savings is any goal that you want to save up for that is coming soon, such as vacations. The retirement allocation is the money that goes to retirement accounts such as 401(k)s (which I will discuss later in the "Retirement" chapter). If these are done through your employer, then you don't have to do them. Then, the want is anything that you want to do with the remaining 10%, such as going out for dinner, going to the cinema, etc.

This is a less intensive budget to follow while still using every dollar of your income for something. The issue with this method is that you might lean on percentages quite a lot and forget to track your expenses. You should still track everything so that you know that you're on the right path. Another thing to take into consideration is whether you're in a good financial position to actually follow this budget since not everybody is.

Value-Based Budget

This budget strategy works best if your income is high, so if you don't think you're in the higher-income bracket, this budget strategy is not for you. Also, this budget requires you to actively think about yourself and the things you want to do. In sum, this budget allows you to spend money on things that you give value to (which you still have to track) instead of making sure a certain percentage of your income goes towards a certain allocation. Here, you have to write down the things that you value most. So, for instance, if you value going out for dinner or traveling, that's what you should be writing down. Anything else that is not on your list, you shouldn't be spending money on.

This budget is also better suited for those who have some level of discipline and already have some savings. It also saves you more time since you're not trying to track every single dollar of your income.

If you don't have the discipline, this strategy is not for you because chances are that you will get off track easily. If you tend to spend money on things that are not really of any value to you, then this is also not for you. But this soul-searching when writing about the things that you value can be a way to really understand the things you like. For instance, you might think that you like to go watch an NBA game every month or so, but after some thinking about it, there might be many other things that you value more, so you don't add NBA games to your list.

Again, these are just guidelines that will help you come up with your own budget that will suit your needs. The most important thing is feeling comfortable with the budget you are creating every month. And don't forget that your income changes, as do your priorities, so make sure you adjust your budget accordingly.

Budgeting is a crucial thing to do when we are handling money. Without a good budget, you simply can't save enough money for the things you want to do and for your future. For this, you need to analyze how you spend your money and what your income is. Once you know exactly how these things work, you need to be able to properly allocate your income to things that matter to you, and that will help you reach your goals. However, budgeting is not an easy thing to do, and that is why it is so important to start now so you can create healthy habits that you will bring with you into adulthood. It is also not something that you do once; it needs to be constantly changing and adapting to fit your needs and your lifestyle, but it needs to be done.

The next chapter is like a continuation of this, where I will be talking about your spending and paying the bills. I'll dive into how you can make informed purchasing decisions, how you can differentiate between needs and wants, how to practice smart shopping, such as comparing prices, and other tips on saving money on bills.

CHAPTER 5

SPENDING AND PAYING BILLS

> *Do not save what is left after spending, but spend what is left after saving.*
>
> *–Warren Buffet*

Once you reach adulthood and independence, you will find that you have more freedom when it comes to the things you want to purchase. However, if you have not developed control over your finances as a teenager, in the form of budgeting, for instance, you will have a much harder time making the right financial decisions. This will then have consequences for your overall spending and needs, such as paying bills, etc.

There are other things that during your teenage years you can develop and become better at, such as differentiating between your needs and your wants, how to practice smart shopping and using other techniques such as comparing prices, and many other things I'll talk about in this chapter.

How Can You Make Informed Purchasing Decisions?

As the name indicates, to make better buying decisions, you need to be informed. So, the key here is to understand what you're buying so you can choose the best product or service over others.

The first thing you should do is ask yourself some questions. For instance, "If I buy this, how will it improve my life?" or "Do I really need this?" If whatever you're buying does improve your life significantly and you do need it, then you can ask, "Is a purchase the right thing to do? Couldn't I borrow it instead?" This often happens when what you are buying might be important and essential, but it's something that will only be essential once. And so, it begs the question, "How often will I use it?"

If it will make your life better, you cannot borrow it, and you might use it more than once; the questions don't end here. You should ask yourself, "Is now the best time to buy it?" These are the types of questions you should ask yourself before any purchase you make so you can determine if you should make one or not.

You also need to consider your current savings, especially if it's an expensive thing. Imagine that you need that, but it's quite expensive, and you don't have the savings for it. Is it worth it to take out a loan for it? Is this a planned purchase? If this is planned and you have savings, then by all means; however, if it was planned and you don't have the savings, perhaps you might consider holding off on the purchase until you can afford it. Taking out a loan to purchase something should be your last resort, especially if what you're purchasing won't bring you any income.

What I like to do when facing some purchases is look at the cost-per-use. Here, you will be calculating the value of the good or service you are thinking of purchasing, and with that, you will have more information about the potential purchase. It is also quite simple to calculate; all you have to do is divide the total cost of the item or service by the estimated number of times you will use it. You also have to think about the benefits of what you're buying. Here, you have to consider all its advantages and disadvantages. Will it bring in more money? Will it boost your productivity? If you purchase a new computer and work from home, perhaps in the long run, it will bring you some advantages, such as performing jobs quicker. If you invest in solar panels, in the long run, they will save you more money. On the other hand, purchasing a car is almost always a necessity if you live in an area where there's no public transport or it takes too long to get you where you want to be. This is because a car decreases in value from the moment you purchase it, plus you have to pay for maintenance, gas, insurance, etc. So, unless a car is the only way you can get to work and make some income, it is usually a bad investment.

Needs vs. Wants

I think one of the hardest things to do when you get financial independence is to distinguish between needs and wants, which is the basis for creating a good budget and making the right financial decisions. This is something that you have to do yourself. Of course, there are basic needs that we all have to prioritize, and I've mentioned most of them, such as rent or mortgage, groceries, or utility bills. Essentially, there are basic requirements that you must fulfill to live properly. They are things that you must have; they tend to remain constant over time, and their non-fulfillment can have serious consequences. Wants, especially in this context, can be described as services and goods that you might like to have, but they don't represent a necessity like needs do and are often a desire that is non-essential for you to live. They tend to change over time, unlike needs, and the non-fulfillment of these does not result in any tragedy, but it might result in disappointment for some time.

If you want to get a little more technical about needs and wants, I will give you another definition. Needs are requirements that are necessary for you to live and survive. If we go back to ancient times, humans had three needs: food, shelter, and clothing. But as time went on, our needs increased to encompass healthcare and education, not so much to survive as to improve our lives.

Wants, from an economic point of view, are things that you might wish to possess, often now but also at some point in the future. Most goods and services stem from wants and not needs, and that's one of the reasons many businesses are extremely wealthy because people really crave their wants. For instance, why would you want to buy the iPhone 14 when you bought the iPhone 13 last year? Your current iPhone 13 still works perfectly fine, but your desire to have that, for various reasons, will make you buy the new iPhone. This lack of control over our wants can really have a negative impact on our finances, and that's why it is so important to understand the difference between these two definitions and develop control over our wants.

How Can You Shop Smart?

While fixed expenses are hard to modify, you can save some money by reducing the price you pay for variable expenses, and this often comes in the form of smart shopping. There are many different ways you can reduce the cost of things, and I'm going to give you some ideas on how you can do that. While you might use many of these throughout your adulthood, it is important that you practice these methods and strategies so that when the transition to adulthood comes, you will be more prepared.

I think we can all agree that consumerism is a long-lasting trend nowadays, and people just want to buy and buy without even thinking if they actually need what they are purchasing. This is also a fast way to increase debt, especially if you don't have a budget. Just to give some actual research, the average person spends about $161 on clothes monthly, and the average child in the U.S. has about $6,000 worth of toys by the time they reach their teenage years (Bowling, 2019). That's a lot of wasted money, in my humble opinion, and this also reveals the lack of budgeting skills most people have. Many of these come from impulse purchases and bad spending habits. But let's look at some ways you can shop smarter.

Let's first look at online shopping, which is something that has been growing over the last few decades with the advent of technology and some companies such as Amazon. However, online shopping made it far easier to compare prices with other online retailers. And this is exactly the first thing you should do. You can quickly go to other websites, search for the same or similar items, and check their prices. This is a great way to get a bargain on certain items. Reading the reviews is also important, which is also something that online shopping makes easier. When reading the reviews of a certain item, if they are simply bad, you tend to give up on the product and move on. If you don't usually read reviews and you like what you see, chances are that you are going to purchase it and possibly be disappointed. Reading reviews stops many people from making purchasing mistakes. Sometimes the reviews don't need to be all that bad, but they might point out the capabilities of that item, which you might find to be of no use to you.

The world of coupons is gigantic, and more people should use it. Coupons allow us to get cheaper prices on certain things. But you have to be careful and only use coupons on things that you were looking for before because many people tend to buy things with coupons that they wouldn't even think about buying if they hadn't seen the coupon. For that, make sure you know what you want, and don't let yourself be persuaded by these marketing tricks. Waiting for a sale, especially an internet sale, might be quite convenient since you can simply sign in and order the items once the sales start, which is far easier than offline shopping. If this is something that you can purchase later, then by all means, you should wait for a sale if you know one is coming.

Always double-check the return policy when you shop online because, especially with clothes, we often purchase the wrong size. However, if you don't know how the return policy works, you might find yourself unable to replace the item. Some return policies last only two weeks, while others might last a month, two, or even three. Either way, you need to make sure you check it and know when you have to send it back. Imagine that you buy a jacket, and the policy states that you have 15 days to return it. The jacket takes eight or nine days to arrive, so chances are that you're not going to be able to return it in time.

Let's move on to purchasing clothes since this is where many people spend a lot of money. The first thing you should do is refer back to your budget and understand how much you can spend on clothes. Without this, chances are that you are going to overspend. Knowing exactly what you need is also important because it stops you from purchasing things that you might like but don't need. If you go to the mall with no clear idea of what you need to buy, you are probably coming back home with too many things and sometimes without the things you need. When shopping for clothes, you need to take your time, especially if you are in a shopping center or mall, and go around other shops to check on prices. If you're looking for a shirt, don't buy the first one you like because it might happen that later on you will find another one that you like more at a cheaper price. So, shop around and come back to the one that you liked more.

Buying clothes off-season tends to be a little cheaper. This can be better done after the season ends because merchants tend to lower their prices so they can sell the remnants of the previous collection and have more space to place the new collection. Alternatively, you can go to thrift stores. I do understand that not everybody likes to purchase clothes at the thrift store, but if you don't mind, it's a great place to find good brands at lower prices. Lastly, you should always go for quality over quantity. It's better to buy one pair of high-quality jeans than four pairs of lower-quality jeans because chances are that those cheap jeans will all wear out faster than the single high-quality one, and you will be back to shopping faster.

Groceries are a necessity but are not a fixed expense, so you could apply strategies and methods that will reduce their cost. The first thing that I would recommend is to always have a grocery list with you when grocery shopping. Planning ahead is fundamental so you don't get caught up in purchasing things that you weren't meant to purchase. It's also important so you don't forget to purchase important goods. It's important that you buy fruits and vegetables locally, not because they are necessarily cheaper (although they might be), but because they are certainly fresher than those you can find in a supermarket. Before you head out to go grocery shopping, have a look at your fridge and cupboards so you don't buy goods that you wouldn't need, and that would eventually be thrown away. Here, you should always plan to avoid wasting food. To do that, everything you buy should have a planned purpose. For instance, don't buy tomatoes if you're not planning on using them next week since chances are they will expire, and you will have to throw them away.

It's always better to buy groceries for the whole household since it's cheaper to buy in bulk instead of going grocery shopping every few days. Bigger packs are usually cheaper than smaller ones. However, you should always check expiration dates as well as prices so things don't go to waste or you buy alternative products that will cost you more.

Once in a while, we need to make big purchases, and these require more thorough planning. I'm talking about cars, fridges, tables, TVs, etc., things that you buy once every few years. And exactly because of that, you need to think more about them. Here, you should be researching as many options as you possibly can and even asking for professional advice if possible. When you are divided about what to purchase, you should know everything you can, from the model to the consumption, reviews, etc. It is even worth talking to friends or family members who have made similar purchases before to help you make a decision and talk to you about the item. But I'll leave the different strategies about big purchases for a dedicated chapter later in the book.

I've mentioned this before briefly, but when making big purchases, you should go for functionalities over big-name brands. The first thing that comes to mind is mobile phones. There might not be any point in purchasing the latest version of an iPhone if you can find another phone that has the same or even more functionalities but whose brand is not as recognizable. Here, it's also important that you look at reviews before purchasing, of course. Usually, with big brands, you rarely pay for how good the item is and pay more for its name. If you can, you should consider purchasing in installments; this is especially true if there's no interest on the items you are purchasing. If the interest is minimal, you can still consider it since you might not be able to purchase the whole amount in one sitting or if this would disrupt your budget and take from your savings.

While you might not really think about having kids, it's important to understand that they will be a sizable part of your budget. This also has to be thought out thoroughly. When shopping for kids, one thing that you should often keep in mind is that, in most cases, you probably don't need to buy anything. I'm mostly talking about toys and other things to spoil your kid. They will probably throw a tantrum, but that's fine; they are kids, after all, and they will get over it. You have to be reasonable and explain to them that they can't have everything they want. However, it's also important that you consider their opinion on certain things. If you want to buy something for them, you should probably take them with you, as it is more likely that they will use it or play with it for longer periods, and you won't need to purchase something else in a short period of time.

How Can You Compare Prices?

As I've noted above, purchasing online or in-store items is a little different, and as such, you should use slightly different ways of comparing prices. Let's start with comparing prices online.

The easiest way to compare prices online is to use a comparison tool. These are usually websites where you can compare online products side by side. There are many different ones that you can use, and amidst so many to choose from, you have to actually use some of them to see which ones you prefer. I tend to use more than one so I can have more information and make a better choice. Some of the most popular ones are Google Shopping, Shopzilla, and

Shopping.com. Bear in mind that these are popular ones in the US, there might be different ones in different countries.

A quick Google search will allow you to check out many different comparison websites. Some are better at comparing prices in specific stores, while others are really good at checking certain types of items, so do your research and decide which ones you want to use. Alternatively, you can also use mobile apps if you find them more convenient. Then, once you've decided on what websites or app comparison tools to use, you can go on and type the product in the search bar. Here, you will find that different tools display items and prices differently. You can also look for the type of item or for specific brand products. Usually, the tool will give you some other options to look at. If you don't have any specific brand in mind, you can also search for different categories or departments and browse through the different items.

Then, all you have to do is browse through the different results that appear. Some of these tools allow you to see the number of stores selling a certain product, but you can filter it to look for other results or list them in different orders. Then, you can click on the item that interests you, and a list of different merchants selling the same item will appear. Here, you can filter for the best or lowest price. Keep in mind that the lowest price might not be the best deal you will find. Sometimes the merchant might be more reliable, and you will know you won't have any issues with the product or the delivery. If there's not much of a discrepancy, or if there's a discrepancy between a reputable seller and one that doesn't have a good reputation, I always go for the one with the best reputation. Researching the seller is something that you should always aim to do, especially if you don't know them, regardless of how reputable they are. Usually, you can purchase right from the price comparison page; other times, you might have to go to the merchant's website.

Of course, some people still prefer to compare prices manually, even though they use computers. Here's what you can do: First, you need to make a list of stores that you know are reliable. Before this, you should have a product in mind, and depending on the product you want to purchase, the type of stores you will be listing will be different. Then, you should visit each store's website. Even if you don't know the website, this can easily be found by Googling the name of the store. Every merchant's website has a search bar where you can simply type the name or the kind of product you want, and it will appear. You then proceed to write down the price and the brand. It's always wise to check shipping policies since a product might be cheaper at one merchant than at another, but the shipping price might be a lot higher, which makes the whole item more expensive. Ideally, if you can find a merchant that ships the product for free or you pick it up in-store, that would definitely be the cheapest option. Then, as you do your research and write everything down, you can compare it at the end and check out the best options for you.

Now, when it comes to comparing and calculating prices at the store, it might take a little longer than when done online. This is especially true when you're looking at bigger packages and trying to figure out if the overall price is really that much better than smaller packages. Usually, checking the unit price of the item can give you a better idea of how much you are actually saving. When we talk about unit price, we are usually referring to its cost per quantity. However, here this can mean that the quantity is per item or per unit of measurement, but don't worry, I'll go through all the processes.

In order to calculate the unit price, all you have to do is divide the cost of the product by its quantity (what you are actually receiving by purchasing the package). There are two ways of doing this. The first is, as I've said, calculating the unit price. The first thing to do here is to check the item's total price, which is usually a smaller percentage of the total cost of the packaged product. This can usually be found on the product's label at the store. You might have a coupon, and if you want to calculate the unit price with the coupon, you need to subtract the coupon's value from the overall price before you calculate the unit price. Then, you have to find the quantity that the package has. You can find this on the label of the product. While some goods are sold by item, such as pencils or toilet paper, others will have a unit of measurement, such as liters, ounces, or gallons.

When comparing, it's important to make sure that the two products you are comparing are in the same units of measurement when not compared by item. It is very common that two products you are comparing might be in different units of measurement, which makes it harder to compare. If this is the case, then you will have to convert the units of measurement so they are the same. You can simply use a measurement unit online to figure this out. Let's look at milk, which is sometimes measured in gallons and sometimes in quarts. If a quart of milk is priced at $2 and a gallon is $8, then these two products cost the same because a gallon is four quarts of milk, so $2 x 4 = $8.

You can then divide the total price by the quantity of the item to figure out the unit price. Here, I would say using a calculator would be faster. For instance, if you are looking at a 4-roll pack of toilet paper at $5 and you want to know the unit price, you'd have to divide $5 by 4, so the unit price is $1.25 per roll of toilet paper. Again, most stores have the unit cost on their label, so you don't have to make any calculations, but it is always better to know how it works in case some products don't display that.

The second method is comparing unit prices. Here, to calculate the unit price of the goods you want to purchase, you need to divide the total cost of each good by the quantity in the package they are sold in. So, for example, one package of 4-roll toilet paper is priced at $5, and another package has 6 rolls and is priced at $6.30. Which one do you think has the cheaper unit price? First, you need to calculate $5/4, which is $1.25 a roll. Then you need to divide $6.30 by 6, which is $1.05. The 6-roll package of toilet paper is cheaper. In general, the product with the lowest unit price is the best value, but you also have to look at the quality. If the quality is similar, then you should go for the cheaper one, but if not, you need to try and understand if it's worth it to pay less for worse quality. While these two methods have the same results, the first allows you to calculate unit prices to understand the price of each unit, and the second allows you to take two items with the same function but different prices and figure out which one has the best value.

How to Save Money on Bills and Other Purchases?

The best way to increase your savings is to make a budget, but there are other ways you can retain more of the money you earn and add it to your savings, such as by cutting your energy bills. You might have heard your parents talking around the house about the incredibly high cost of bills at the moment. While this might change by the time you have to pay your own bills, you can always try to save as much as you can. One thing that you might not be aware of is that usually, energy bills such as electricity and gas are paid through direct debit from your card, and this can be changed. What energy companies usually take is an estimate to cover what you have spent. This is because we use more energy in certain months than we do in others; for instance, in the winter, we tend to use more energy so we can warm our houses. However, while some months you might have a debt on your energy account, other times you might have credit. But you need to keep checking that to make sure you are not overpaying your energy bill or falling into a large debt. Sometimes, the energy company increases the direct debit on your card, and this might be for some reason, such as if you've moved on to a more expensive bill or if your contract with them has expired. They usually put you on a higher tariff. You need to contact them to renew your contract or look for a new energy provider. It can also happen that you are in a variable tariff contract, in which case the rates have increased. If you don't want that to happen, you would have to get into a fixed tariff, which might look more expensive but is often better since you know exactly how much you will be paying per unit of energy. If your energy use has increased, this could also be another reason why your direct debit has gone up too. If you're not sure why the direct debit has increased, you should always contact your energy provider to make sure there's no mistake on their behalf.

Now that this is out of the way let's get into the real tips. Heating your home is where most people spend the most energy. So, you might ask, What is the most energy-efficient way to heat a room? Well, central heating is definitely the most efficient way to do this, but not all properties have it. This is especially true if you're renting and you don't have another choice but to use what is provided to you. However, if central heating is not an option and you only need to heat the room you are in, then a portable heater is definitely the second-best choice. However, you need to pick one that is cost-efficient. You can use the price comparison tips I've mentioned above to pick the best one. Ideally, you'd pick a portable heater that has a timer and a good thermostat so it doesn't overheat and you don't spend too much energy and money on it.

Cooking is another thing where a lot of energy is consumed. Here, electric ovens are far more efficient than gas ones. The same is true for electric hobs. However, here, more efficiency doesn't mean cheaper since gas tends to be cheaper than electricity. However, air fryers and microwaves (for small things) tend to save you more money in the long run. Apart from that, there's not much you can do when it comes to cooking besides trying not to have your oven on for too long and preparing everything before so you can cook as fast as you can. However, if and when you have your own property, purchasing energy-efficient appliances can really make a difference in your energy bill. Again, when doing this, make sure you compare all the appliances so you can have the most energy-efficient and not the cheapest appliance since, in the long run, you'd be paying more.

Insulating your home is also a good way to save energy. Once again, if you're renting, there's not a lot you can do. But when you're looking for properties to rent, you should keep in mind that properties that are better insulated tend to waste less energy. So, properties that have the attic insulated, have draft proofing installed, and have double-glazing tend to be more energy efficient.

Not everything is gas and electricity when it comes to bills, and there are other things such as cellphone contracts, broadband, and insurance where you can also reduce costs. When it comes to an internet connection, unless you are out of contract, in my experience, there's no point in changing because you most certainly have to pay an early opt-out fee. However, if your contract runs out, this is an excellent opportunity to get a cheaper and faster internet connection. If you don't have fiber yet, then this is the best time to upgrade. While it usually costs the same as standard broadband, it is a lot faster and more reliable. When it comes to your cell phone, you should keep an eye on your data and check if you are really using all the data you are purchasing every month or if you can reduce that data and the price you're paying for it. While many providers offer high amounts of data and sometimes even unlimited data, most people use between 5 and 10 GB, so there's no need to purchase all that data most of the time.

One thing that I had to learn with time and experience is that when it comes to cell phones and broadband, you can haggle the price. Yes, nothing is really set in stone, and if you've been a customer with them for quite some time, your chances are even higher to get a better price. If you think that negotiating can be overwhelming, you can do it over a text chat or email. But to be prepared, you should compare the services with those of other providers so you can back up your negotiations.

At some point in your adult life, you will have home and car insurance. These are needs because you need your valuables protected. The best way to reduce them is when it's time to renew them. Obviously, when you got them the first time, you should have gone through comparison websites and checked out the best available deal for you. But this insurance industry is always on the move, and when it is time to renew, chances are that you will find a better deal. You do the same thing you've done before and do your research with the help of comparison websites. Even if you're not near renewal, you can always check with other insurance companies, and perhaps an early switch might be able to save you some money. Here, you have to take into account the cost of early cancellation, of course, but if the rival's prices are that much better, you should consider switching. The way you pay is also important. These usually come in monthly or annual payments, and annual payments are almost always cheaper. But this is a calculation that you can do quickly; simply divide the total amount of the annual insurance payment by 12 and check if it's cheaper than paying monthly. It's also important to have a close look at the extras insurance companies often add to the contract; most of the time, you won't need those extra covers, and you can save money that way. A good piece of advice that I would give and that you could probably follow is to put the name of someone with more driving experience if you don't have that much experience because young and inexperienced drivers tend to pay more.

Fuel is a necessity if you, like many people, rely on your own method of transportation. The question that should be on your mind when the time comes is, How can I drive and spend less on fuel? Well, the first thing that comes to mind here is to drive as smoothly as possible, try to preserve momentum, and don't accelerate if there's no need to. This might not be much of a tip, but trust me, in the long run, it will save you a lot of fuel. For instance, if you have a good idea of what's ahead of you when you drive, you will better control your acceleration or know when you should and when you shouldn't. Essentially, anticipating what is ahead and not using braking and acceleration for no reason. By the way, breaking also wastes fuel since you then have to use more fuel to accelerate. While in the U.S., manual gears are not very common, if you do ever drive one, shifting gears as soon as possible will ease the work the engine will have to do and, with that, consume less fuel too. In fact, if you drive a new-ish car, they already indicate when it is best to shift gears. Plus, new cars have other modes where you can switch to Eco, for instance, which will allow you to consume less fuel too.

Perhaps you've seen your parents use the car on cold days, and they run the engine while staying stationary so the engine heats up. This is hardly needed with new cars because the engine is designed to heat up way faster. Only use air conditioning when strictly necessary since these waste quite some energy, but using it once in a while will also prevent it from having issues more often. Heated seats are hardly ever necessary unless you live in a very cold place. These seats also consume a lot of energy, most of the time unnecessarily. Also, checking your tire pressure can often help you save some fuel since the more deflated the tires are, the more energy the engine wastes.

Reducing your overall spending as well as your bills can have a huge impact on your savings. It all starts with making informed decisions when purchasing goods or services. Understanding how to shop smartly and how to compare prices is fundamental to all of this. There are many comparison websites where you can find the most varied goods to do your research. You also have to have a clear idea of your needs and wants, and when shopping, it is best to bring a list with you so you don't forget anything and don't spend unnecessarily. With the tips I talked about on how to save money, while I don't expect you to memorize everything or even apply all of them, it is important that you are aware of them and that when the time comes, you know the things you can do to increase your savings.

CHAPTER 6

CREDIT, CREDIT CARDS, AND DEBT MANAGEMENT

> *Don't let your mouth write no check that your tail can't cash.*
>
> *–Bo Diddley*

C redit, credit cards, and debt might be something that scares you. Perhaps you don't fully understand it, but you've probably heard your parents talking about it, someone in your family, or even on TV. The truth is, while debt and credit cards can have a negative effect on your finances, they also have a positive side. I've briefly talked about it before, but now I'm delving more into the topic.

What Is Credit, and Why Is it Important?

While the word "credit" might have different meanings in the financial sector, it often means an agreement where an individual, also called a borrower, gets money but at the same time states that they will give it back at a later date, usually with interest. But credit can also refer to the credit score or credit history of someone, so you can have good or bad credit. Don't worry; I will get to that.

There are many different forms of credit, but the most common one is a credit card; however, there are also mortgages, car loans, and personal loans. With a credit card, you have a line of credit where you have a certain amount that you can spend on that specific card. There are two main types of credit, and all of the forms of credit I've mentioned above fall within one of them. These are revolving or installment loans. Revolving credit is, for instance, a credit card where you can continuously borrow more and more money as long as you pay the minimum balance at a certain date. An installment credit is, for example, a mortgage where you have fixed amounts to pay every month, and you don't continuously take out money. Usually, this comes as a lump sum. Both of these usually have interest.

When somebody says that credit is important, it usually refers to your credit score or history. This is what banks and other financial institutions refer to when deciding if they should lend you money or not. They often look at your credit report, which often states things like payment history, which tells them how often you make credit payments on time; credit utilization, which means how much of your credit in your credit cards you have used (usually the less, the better); length of credit history, which refers to the amount of time you have had credit, whether it is a credit card or a car loan (where usually the longer, the better); credit mix, which is how diversified your credit is, such as credit cards, mortgages, car loans, etc.; and new credit, which tells them how often you take on a new credit card (opening too many credit accounts throughout a small period of time is usually not good).

The health of your credit is important because it opens the doors for many things, such as applying for a credit card, purchasing a house, renting a house or apartment, applying for a job, buying a car, or even starting a business. This is because, for most of these, you need to borrow money, and the lender is going to look at your credit score and credit history to understand if it is safe for them to actually lend you the money. It's also important to note that even with a bad credit score, financial institutions can still lend you money, but oftentimes this will have a higher interest rate. This is something that you want to avoid because it means you'd be spying on a lot more than what you are borrowing.

So, as you can see, having a credit card is not so bad and allows you to build your credit score and credit history. However, you have to manage it properly.

How Can You Manage Your Credit Properly and Responsibly?

Managing your credit responsibly is the important part. You want to get a high credit score so you can borrow higher amounts and pay less interest. If you miss payment dates, default, or file for bankruptcy, your credit score will decrease. This is also true if you, as I said, use too much of your credit or open too many credit card accounts in a short period of time.

So, in order to manage your credit responsibly, I have a few tips for you. Always make your credit card payments and other credit payments on time. While paying more than the minimum payment is better because it means in the long run, you will be paying less, you have to at least pay the minimum amount. In fact, if you don't make a single payment on time, this can stay on your credit report for years to come. Another thing you should not do is spend more than you can afford to repay. It seems easy enough, but many people fall for this mistake. You should never live off your credit card unless you have absolutely no money for your basic necessities. What I like to do to ensure I never miss a payment is to set up a reminder or a direct debit.

Credit cards should strictly be used to build credit, so you should pay small amounts with them and not big amounts unless you have the money ready to pay them. One last thing: you should keep your old credit card accounts open even if you don't use them because they count toward your length of credit history.

How Can You Build a Good Credit Score?

Some of the things you can do to build or maintain a great credit score have already been mentioned. But there are other things. For instance, getting on your electoral roll is an easy way to get some points on your credit score. This is often used by lenders to check your address as well as your name and to verify if everything is up-to-date.

Getting credit, as I've mentioned, is also a great way to improve your score. But remember to take out a small and manageable amount so you can pay it back on time and fully, and don't get overwhelmed by the amount of debt. Sometimes, you can get a score boost too. The three major credit bureau companies are Experian, Equifax, and TransUnion, and sometimes all you need to do is link your current account to one of the credit bureau companies. This is an easier way for those companies to know how well you manage your credit. When it comes to credit score levels, what you want to achieve is "excellent," but a "very good" or even a "good" level of credit score points can give you quite some rewards. Here's a table of the credit score range for your credit level:

Poor	300–579
Fair	580–669
Good	670–739
Very good	740–799
Excellent	800–850

Here's a summarized list of things you can do to increase your credit score, besides some of the things I've already mentioned before:

- ✦ Setting up automatic bill payments
- ✦ Paying down credit balances
- ✦ Getting a credit-builder loan
- ✦ Disputing credit report inaccuracies

✧ Keeping old credit card accounts open

✧ Limiting the number of lines of credit you get

✧ Paying off credit card balances every single month

✧ Keeping track of your credit score

✧ Adding to your credit mix

✧ Adding rent payments to your credit score report

✧ Asking for an increase on your credit card limit

How Can You Manage Your Credit Card Debt?

Although most people understand the risks of taking on large amounts of debt, there are times when they fall into these debts and struggle to pay them. It's important that you don't shy away from or try to ignore this problem. In fact, you have to face it and look for solutions. While it might look bad, and it is, it's not the end of the world, and there are things you can do. But first, let me explain to you the process if you fall into overwhelming amounts of debt and can't pay them.

Every credit card is covered by the Consumer Credit Protection Act, which means that lending companies such as banks and other financial institutions have to follow some rules if the debtor (you) is struggling to pay. So, it all starts by not paying the minimum amount in a month, after which your bank will contact you and demand that you pay that month's amount. If you don't, then they will put your account in default. If you still don't pay, then they might bring in a debt collection agent to recover the money you owe. It sounds a little scary, but at this point, you've had enough time to do something about it, as I'll explain below.

Banks and other financial institutions, to help their customers that are struggling, can do a few things: they can give you a credit card payment "holiday," which means you are "off the hook" for three months (obviously, you still have to pay it). They often make sure that your credit score is not affected during this three-month period. And they can also increase your credit card limit; however, you should be careful about this because it means that later on, you can incur more debt.

Now, onto things that you can do to pay off your credit card. The first thing you have to do is really try to understand your finances. This means fully understanding what you can afford every month. You have to budget! If you have been forgetting to budget, you will have to do it because this is the only way you can understand how much you can spend. When doing your budget, make sure you set aside a part of your income so you can pay your debt. You have to absolutely stop using your credit card. You can't afford to incur more debt than you already have.

You can also negotiate your credit card debt by contacting your bank and explaining everything to them. Here, you can also tell them how much you can pay each month, and believe it or not, many banks agree to some of the terms you might bring up and even agree to an affordable repayment plan.

How Can You Deal With Debt Collectors?

Hopefully, this will never happen to you, and if you ever have an overwhelming amount of debt, you will follow the steps I've written above to avoid it. But if you are ever in a situation where you have to deal with debt collectors, there are also a few things that you can do. Usually, debt collectors will contact you about an unpaid debt. Remember, you have to face your problems here, and hiding is never the solution because it can get much worse. While you have to deal with them, it's important that you understand your rights under the Fair Debt Collection Practices Act (FDCPA). For instance, debt collectors cannot threaten you, lie to you, or insult you in any way (they can't even say they will sue you if they don't intend to do so). They can't add interest to your debt unless it is written in the contract on your credit card or other agreement, and they can't threaten to take your property (or even take it) unless the property is served as collateral when you take out a loan.

They have to first notify you in writing (this could be by mail or online) at least within five days of any contact you've had with them. And they have to give you 30 days from their notification to ask for any more information about the debt. Also, there have been some recent rule changes where debt collectors can't call you more than seven times in a single week, and they can't talk to you from any social media platform.

You can also check if your debt is actually valid. This means that you need to check the notification the debt collector gave you and make sure that it is yours. It could be that the amount is wrong, or perhaps you've already paid the debt. Understanding your statute of limitations is also important. This means that debt collectors have a certain amount of time to claim the debt, but this amount of time differs depending on the state you are in. If they come after you after that statute of limitations has expired, you don't have to pay, and in fact, you can sue them.

Of course, you can always consider negotiating with a debt collector. This is after you've checked your statute of limitations and know for sure the debt is yours, but you can't afford to pay everything right away, you can try and negotiate with them. For instance, you can try to get an agreement where you pay back the debt in installments, or you can propose a settlement where they will have to agree not to pay the full amount of debt. However, if the debt is legitimate, you should always try to pay it in full, even if it is in installments, because this will hurt your credit score.

If you believe that a debt collector is harassing you, you can send a cease and desist letter, which basically tells them to stop contacting you. This can be done if the statute of limitations has run out or you don't have any assets, which means you won't be able to pay anything even if they sue you and you lose.

Credit is quite important to understand and to build as soon as we possibly can. Having good credit allows us to borrow money for large expenses such as buying a car or a house. However, credit can also be quite dangerous if we don't pay attention to it. We could become overwhelmed with the amount of debt we accumulate, which would make our financial lives quite complicated. It's important that we always pay back whatever we have borrowed and don't borrow more than we can pay; that's how debts get out of hand. But again, we need to use our credit cards to build a good credit history. If, for some reason, you accumulate more debt than you can pay, you should never try to hide from it, as it will always find you. This is one of those problems that don't go away until we face them. As I've explained in this chapter, there are ways that you can actively work to reduce your debt, such as by fully understanding your finances, creating a budget, or, in extreme cases, contacting your bank.

CHAPTER 7

INVESTING

> *Invest for the long haul. Don't get too greedy, and don't get too scared.*
>
> *–Shelby M.C. Davies*

Investing is another one of those things that people get a little scared of when mentioned. Many believe it's a way to lose all your money. But I assure you that those people have never invested in their lives. Yes, it is true that you can lose money if you don't have the faintest idea of what you're doing, but you can also make a lot of money just by understanding the basics.

The Basics You Need to Know

People have been investing for many years, and it is a tried and true way to put your money to work for you. You should be able to invest at regular intervals as you get your income, and once you know the basics and have the possibilities, it should be a part of your budget to set aside some money to invest. This is also the reason why investing as soon as you possibly can might allow you to make a lot of money. The thing is, you don't need a large amount of money to start; you can simply begin with $10, $25, or even a single dollar. But of course, you need to know what you're doing, and while many people feel daunted about the stock market and investing in general, the basics are not that hard to grasp.

Now, before we get into it, I want to talk about the three most common ways of investing: stocks, mutual funds, and bonds. You've probably heard about these but don't know exactly what they mean.

Let's start with what I believe to be the most popular of them all: stocks. These are often referred to as equity, and essentially, they are a small part of a business or corporation. Every time you purchase a fraction of such an organization in the stock market (where they are sold), you are buying what is called a share. This officially tells you that you are the owner of a portion of a corporation. In case your head is still wrapped up in what you might have heard about stocks, the trading of these is regulated by the government to protect investors like you from fraud. Now, businesses and corporations issue these shares or stocks to raise funds for their businesses so they can operate. Now, to buy stocks, you have to get them through stock exchanges, or more commonly, the stock market, such as the New York Stock Exchange (NYSE) or the Nasdaq. However, you don't have to physically go there, and nowadays, buying and selling stocks is easier than ever. There are many mobile applications that you can download, sign up for, and use from your mobile phone. For instance, a popular one is called Robinhood. You have to be over 18 years old to hold an account and trade stocks, plus you have to give ID proof and proof of address, as well as have a bank account. Although you might be asking, How do I earn income from owning stocks? There are two ways you can do this. The first, and probably simpler, is when the stock increases in value. Say you buy a single share of Microsoft for $100, and after a year, the value has risen to $150. If you sold at that time, you would take $150 or a $50 profit. Another way is through dividends, but this is only specific to some stocks. In fact, Microsoft also offers dividends on its stocks. Dividends are a small percentage of the value of the stock paid to shareholders or investors. This is usually paid every quarter, and you can check how much the corporation pays to the investors by looking at the dividend yield (also, most of this information can be looked up online or through your brokerage app). For instance, using the same example above, if you have a share of Microsoft valued at $100 and the dividend yield is 1%, you'd get paid $1.

Getting Started

Before you get started trading stocks, you need to learn the basics, of course, but there are other things that you need to establish. The first thing you should do is define your tolerance for risk. In basic terms, tolerance for risk is what you can afford to lose when investing. There are many categories within stocks that can tell you more or less about their risk (obviously, investments are never 100% sure); for example, you have large, medium, and small capitalization stocks, meaning the larger the capitalization, the smaller the volatility of the price, but also the fewer chances you have to make big money. Then you have value stocks and aggressive stocks, and all of these have different levels of risk. Once you know your risk tolerance, you can start really looking at the types of stocks to buy.

You also have to understand what your investment goals are. For most people, investments mean the long term. This means that you usually purchase some stock that you believe will go up over a long period of time (say five years, for instance. Other, more professional investors, like to invest in the short- or medium-term. This is something that I wouldn't recommend, especially if you're just starting out. Of course, your goals could also change over time; for instance, you might start by simply trying to increase the amount of money you have, while later on, you could try to get an income from your investments through dividends. Other more concrete investments could be purchasing a car or a house, saving for retirement, or paying for tuition.

Then, you have to determine your investment style, which basically means how you want to manage your portfolio (all your stocks). Many people prefer to purchase something and forget about it, meaning that they are not constantly checking it. You believe that they will continue to slowly go up. Others prefer to be more thorough, check their portfolios more often, and tweak here and there for maximum profitability. There's also something called the robo-advisor, which is an automated tool where you insert your goals, and add money to them (often through a stockbroker's app), and the robo-advisor tweaks your investments to align with your goals. Lastly, you can also pay for a financial advisor to give you some tips. However, these can be quite expensive, and unless you have a lot of money invested, they are probably not worth it.

Then, you will have to choose your investment account. Here, you have retirement plans usually sponsored by your employer, such as a 401(k), where you can choose from stocks, bonds, mutual funds, etc. However, I'll talk about all of this later. You can also choose to open a taxable account or IRA with a brokerage instead of an employer-sponsored one. These can also be retirement accounts, and you can have your own as well as employer-sponsored ones. Robo-advisors also have a specific account.

Lastly, you have to really learn the basics and learn how to diversify so you can reduce the risk. Diversification is perhaps the most important thing when it comes to investment. Let me give you an example of diversification. Say, you have $1000 invested in the stock market, but all the money is on Microsoft stocks. Here, your portfolio has zero diversification because everything is in one single stock. What happens if Microsoft has a bad quarter or some negative news? All your portfolios will suffer. But now, you have put only $250 on Microsoft, $250 on Nvidia, $250 on Apple, and $250 on Facebook. There's some more diversification, without a doubt, because even if Microsoft goes down momentarily, you have the other three stocks to keep your portfolio from free-falling. However, as you might have noticed, all of these stocks are in the technology sector. What if this specific sector is having a rough time for whatever reason? What if you put $250 on Microsoft, $250 on Apple, $250 on Coca-Cola, and $250 on Fiat? Your diversification would be a lot better, and you'd reduce the risk of losing a lot of your investment money.

Mutual funds are managed funds that use money from several investors to invest in stocks. This way, you don't have to manage it yourself. It's also important to understand that in these mutual funds, there can be stocks as well as bonds (which I will mention later in the chapter). These funds are managed by professional money managers, and their goal is to try and maximize gains for the investors, although every mutual fund has a different way of investing, such as being risky or risk averse, and the securities (both stocks and bonds) can be tailored depending on the mutual stock. For instance, you might choose a mutual fund whose premise is to invest in green stocks and bonds. This means that the companies the manager invests in are environmentally friendly. This also means that when you gain or lose money, so do all the other investors in the mutual fund.

However, you must be thinking, How are mutual funds priced? After all, they must have a price since you have to invest a certain amount of money, right? Well, you can look at it as if every time you invest in a mutual fund, a share of it is the average of the prices of all stocks and bonds within the fund. So, for example, if you invest in a mutual fund with two stocks (which is impossible since they usually have more, but bear with me for the sake of explanation) and one stock is currently priced at $200 and the other at $100, a share of the mutual fund would be $150. So, in other words, when you invest in a mutual fund, you are investing in many different stocks and bonds, which is good for diversity. You can also get income from dividends when investing in a mutual fund that holds stocks that distribute dividends.

As I've said, there are many different types of mutual funds, but I'll give some examples of the most common ones. Stock funds, as the name indicates, invest almost exclusively in stocks. Of course, here you will have many more subcategories, at least as many as there are subcategories of stocks and companies. For instance, you might have growth funds that invest in companies that focus on growth, but they usually don't pay dividends. However, you are more likely to gain from the increase in stock price.

Index funds also exclusively invest in stocks but focus on index stocks. These are like mutual funds that you can purchase straight away from the stock market, which can also be called ETFs. One of the largest ones is the S&P 500, which tracks the value of the 500 largest companies in the U.S. ETFs are also an excellent option if you want to diversify your portfolio, and there are many different types.

Balanced funds are a hybrid type of mutual fund that has stocks, bonds, and sometimes even other investment vehicles.

Bonds can be seen as fixed-income investments. They are loans made by a part of a government (for instance, a local government) or a corporation to raise funds. In this particular case, you are the one loaning the money to these entities, and in return (after some time), they will give you back the money plus interest. As you might have guessed, bonds have an end date, which is the date the loan (called the principal) has to be paid back to you. These are called fixed-income because you know for sure they will be paid back, and you know when. Bonds are also much more risk-averse than stocks in mutual funds; however, they are not risk-free, especially bonds from corporations, because they can default. However, this is rare, and even more rare, if you purchase a government bond since these almost never default. Government bonds are issued at literally all levels, so you can have, as I said, local governments, but you also have federal government bonds. Because these are a lot safer, the profit is usually a lot less than in stocks, for instance. Governments usually issue bonds to pay for infrastructure such as schools, hospitals, roads, etc. While corporations might do it to expand their business or raise capital for a new product launch. When you purchase a loan, you have all the necessary information, such as the expiration date, principal per bond, and interest rate (called the coupon rate), so you can clearly understand what the benefits are and how much you can actually receive back. However, after you've purchased a bond, you can resell it at a higher price, or you can also buy bonds from other investors and not directly from the source.

There are other types of bonds. I've already mentioned corporate bonds that are issued by companies. Governmental bonds are solely issued by the U.S. Treasury, and municipal bonds are issued by municipalities and states. Then, you can also have agency bonds, which are issued by government-affiliated organizations.

What Is Compound Interest When Investing?

Compound interest is a very interesting concept that you should be fully aware of because it can allow you to increase your money and wealth. Compound interest can be seen often in savings accounts but also when investing. Many savings accounts only earn interest on the initial deposit. For instance, if you deposit $100 and the interest rate is 5%, after a month, you will have $105. The next month, you will have $110 because the interest is only applied to the initial deposit of $100. However, if that savings account had compound interest, the second month's interest would be applied to the $105, so, you'd have $110.25, and in the third month, you'd have $115.76 instead of $115. While this might not look much, it actually is because if you leave the money for a long time, you're incrementally increasing your money. This, added to the large amount, makes a massive difference in your earnings. Compound interest is often referred to as having interest in the interest. In other words, with compound interest, your money grows faster than if you had applied simple interest.

In investments, you can choose to have a broker's account with a dividend reinvestment plan, also known as DRIP. This automatically reinvests any dividend you receive. This is why, even though you might prefer growth stocks, dividends can really boost your returns.

The "magic" about compound interest is that because it accumulates interest from the previous month (or periods), it grows exponentially, meaning that the accelerating rate is always increasing. These periods, we call compound interest periods, are the intervals of time between when interest is added to the investment or your account. Now, this can come in different ways: annually, semi-annually, quarterly, monthly, or daily. Even if the account you have accrued compound interest daily, often you get paid monthly, and while it's daily, the additional interest is added to when the previous interest gets to the account. So, as you might imagine, the more frequent the compounding interest is, the better for you. But, as you probably figured too, if you are a borrower, compound interest works against you, and when it comes to the frequency of compound interest, you want as sparsely as possible. So, when looking at the benefits of compounding interest, it can help us build wealth in the long term, whether it is through investments or savings, and it mitigates inflation. However, if you are the borrower, compounding interest is not beneficial. It's also important to note that the returns you earn are taxable. Let's look at a table illustrating how much you'd get with compound interest. Here, your initial investment is $5000, and it has a 3% monthly interest for one year (12 months).

Month	Interest	Accrued Interest	Balance
0			$5,000
1	$150	$150.00	$5,150.00
2	$154.50	$304.50	$5,304.50
3	$159.14	$463.64	$5,463.64
4	$163.91	$627.54	$5,627.54
5	$168.83	$796.37	$5,796.37
6	$173.89	$970.26	$5,970.26
7	$179.11	$1,149.37	$6,149.37
8	$184.48	$1,333.85	$6,333.85
9	$190.02	$1,523.87	$6,523.87
10	$195.72	$1,719.58	$6,719.58
11	$201.59	$1,921.17	$6,921.17
12	$207.64	$2,128.80	$7,128.80

As you can see, the accrued interest as well as the interest increase exponentially which by the end of the year has grown quite significantly. If you were to have only simple interest at the exact same rate, your interest would always be fixed at $150 a month. By the end of the twelve months with compound interest, you're earning $207.64 by simply not touching your money.

Long-Term Investment Strategies

There are quite a few strategies to invest in; some are short-term, others long-term, but as you're starting out, I'm going to talk about long-term ones because they require less knowledge of the market and are far safer.

The "ride a winner" strategy means that in your portfolio, you'd have a really good winner," meaning that one of your stocks was really increasing, and you'd only consider selling it after it increased tenfold. However, you have to be quite disciplined and do your due diligence because even if a stock is going to increase ten times, there will be periods where it will go down before going back up, and you need to resist the temptation to sell it. In other words, you have to believe in the stock you've bought and not sell it because it went down a little.

Selling a loser is another long-term strategy where you essentially have to come to terms with the fact that a stock is not going to go back up (at least not any time soon) and cut your losses before it does more damage to your portfolio. I'm talking about drastic or continuous losses, not simply losing a few dollars. Also, you need to understand what is going on in the market to understand the reason behind some stocks losing value before deciding to sell.

Again, don't panic if the stock goes down for a little bit; these are short-term movements, and they are part of the market. You have to zoom out and take a look at what is happening in the big picture of the stock. Also, you should never chase a stock that has increased exponentially within a week. For instance, you see a stock that has increased 50% in the last week, and you have the urge to buy it because it's going up so fast. But chances are that you already lost the ride, and once you buy it, it might come crashing down or won't increase that much anymore. Stick to your strategy and do your due diligence on the stocks you've bought.

Dollar-cost averaging is quite a common strategy in the investment world, and it's often used to manage the price risk of your investments. You apply this strategy every time you're purchasing investments such as stocks or ETFs, and instead of purchasing five shares of a certain stock at one time and at a single price point, you purchase them at different times. So, you're buying that same investment at regular intervals and in smaller parts, independent of the price. Let me give you an example: if you buy two Microsoft shares at $100, your average cost per share is $100, but in the next month, the shares drop 50%, and your share value drops from $200 (since you had two shares) to $100. But what if you bought one share of Microsoft for $100, and the next month you bought it for $50? A month went by, and there was no significant price change; this would be because your average cost per share was $75, and so your investment only dropped 25% instead of 50%. Essentially, you are averaging the cost of your investments by diluting the price point and making them more secure. At the end of the day, you still have the same number of shares, but you bought them, on average, at a cheaper price.

Lastly, you have to focus on the future. You have to study the companies and try to understand where they will be in 5 to 10 years. Understand their business model, read the news, and look at their quarterly and annual reports so you have a better chance of making money.

Investing is a very important part of your finances, and fortunately, people are starting to be more involved in it than other generations were. It is not a place where you lose money; it can happen, but if you know what you are doing, it is often a place where you can make quite a lot of money. As I've mentioned, there are many different options when it comes to investing, such as stocks, bonds, and mutual funds, but a mix of them will make your portfolio more diverse and give you a much better chance at creating returns for you. I would advise you to start with mutual funds because they are more risk-resistant, and you don't have to pick your investments yourself; instead, you have a professional do it for you. Then, I would move on to stocks once you understand the market better and how everything works and have more confidence in your skills. Compound interest is a great way to make returns, and you should use it as often as you can, whether it is in your savings accounts or through your investments, because in the long run, it can make you a lot more money than using simple interest.

In the following chapter, I'm going to talk about insurance, what it is, why it is so important, and the different types of insurance you can have.

CHAPTER 8

INSURANCE

> *Because of the risks, the insurance premium may not be.*
>
> *–Dwayne Brown*

I nsurance is an important aspect of life as well as finances if you're looking to protect your assets, your property, or even your family from financial risks. We tend to have a greater peace of mind when we have insurance that can protect us and maintain us financially secure from many risks that life might bring us.

For instance, without car insurance, we would have to bear the burden of paying for all the expenses of the car in case we had a car accident. The same with health insurance which can really cripple our finances. It's quite simple to understand how insurance works. You pay a fee, whether it is monthly or annually, it depends, and the insurance covers the majority of the things that can happen. Of course, this depends on the insurance you have and the many add-ons you might want to have.

Understanding Insurance

As I said, insurance is quite easy to understand, but its benefits are far greater than you might think. For instance, insurance plans might help you pay medical bills, emergencies, hospitalizations, and any medical care you might need in the future. If you don't have that, and with the lack of free healthcare in the U.S., you and your family can be really drained of savings. There's also life insurance that gives money to the surviving members of the family. This is especially good if the person who passed away was the sole earner of the household. This way, the family can pay any debts, mortgages, or anything else. It might not be something that you think too much about now, but once you have family and kids, you will definitely try to inform yourself about it.

Life insurance can also help you with retirement planning and stay financially independent throughout your retirement. Property insurance allows you to get paid in case of a natural disaster or any other kind that might destroy your property or if someone gets in and steals valuable things. Your insurance has coverage for that. It is a really good thing to have because life is unpredictable, and you don't know when something might happen. It is always best to be prepared.

What are the Types of Insurance Out There?

There are quite a lot, but I'm just going to name a few. While some of them I've already mentioned, I'll just go a little deeper in explaining what they are.

Life insurance, as I've said, is what can safeguard your family in the event of death. In simple words, it can help the family financially, usually with a lump sum of money that is paid to them if something happens. Health insurance covers medical expenses in many different ways. As I've mentioned, treatments, hospitalization, or any other treatments you'd need afterward. Child plans are great because they work as a sort of savings for when the child is ready to go to college or university.

Home insurance covers any damages to your property caused by accidents, natural calamities, mishaps, and pretty much anything else. And auto insurance is for vehicles, and these are mandatory. These cover accidents with other vehicles as well as natural disasters. They also protect damages to third parties during an accident where you might have hurt somebody while driving your car.

Evaluating Your Options Before Purchasing Insurance

Like many other things when it comes to finances, it's important that you properly evaluate insurance before purchasing it. The first thing to do is assess what you need. Having a look at your requirements is key to fully comprehending the policies you need. Usually, the most important thing is to protect yourself and your family financially. For instance, if you want to save money for your kid's education or buy a property, you should perhaps look into a unit-linked insurance plan or ULIP. An insurance pension account, on the other hand, will give you an income once you retire.

However, purchasing your insurance is not something that you should do and forget. You have to review it throughout your life and change it as your needs change. Essentially, you should try to protect yourself and your family from all financial liabilities. For example, if you are purchasing life insurance, you need to make sure it is big enough to cover any debts.

As with many other things, comparing plans will give you a much better idea of the insurance you are purchasing. There are many different solutions out there, and it is important that you take your time to choose the best one, as well as the one where you pay the lowest premiums. However, I believe that the benefits of a plan are more important than its pricing. I know many of us don't read the terms and conditions, but when it comes to insurance, it's crucial that you do. Not only read them but understand them fully.

Buying insurance is not as hard as it seems, but you need to be absolutely sure of what you are buying and that you are making the best possible decision for you and your family.

In the next chapter, I'll be talking about big purchases, whether material or to improve ourselves and others, such as paying for college. I'm going to go through how you can plan for significant purchases, understand the financing options and explore the different strategies you can use.

CHAPTER 9

BIG PURCHASES AND PAYING FOR COLLEGE

> *Education is the most powerful weapon which you can use to change the world.*
>
> *–Nelson Mandela*

Big purchases don't always mean buying properties and cars (however, I will start with those); they also mean investing in our future. For that, you need to plan carefully so you don't end up making mistakes that might affect you in the future.

How Can You Plan For Big Purchases?

When planning for big purchases (yes, I'm talking houses or cars), you know that you will need significant funding. For that, you really need to think about how you are going to actually do it. You need to think about how much money you can put up front and all the consequences that entail.

The first thing to do is assess your needs, goals, and timeline. The latter is especially important because you might have to pay it for quite a few years, such as on a property through a mortgage. Determining the true cost of what you have to pay is also important. For example, if you are thinking about purchasing a property, you need to determine the down payment; if you are purchasing a car, you need to figure out the upfront money. So, for that, you also have to think about how long you have to save (a budget with this in mind is your best tool). For instance, you need to save $20,000 in the next two years so you can pay the down payment for a property. How much do you need to be saving every month? You have to save roughly $850. From there, you have to budget and make changes so you can reach your goal.

One thing that I like to do is set up a separate account. This means staying away from your regular savings, your checking account, and your emergency fund. Ideally, you could put it to work earning interest in a savings account. But the goal is to have it separate so you can clearly see it growing and know that you are getting closer to your goal every month.

However, it's important that you don't ignore your other financial goals, so don't make unrealistic goals for large purchases. It's crucial that you build yourself a good and strong financial foundation before taking on large purchases.

Financing Options When Making Big Purchases

If you're buying a property, the best financing option is definitely a mortgage through a bank. Again, you have to shop around and talk to several banks and financial institutions so you can get the best possible mortgage with lower interest rates.

Now, if you're purchasing another big purchase that is not a property, there are options. For instance, if you want to purchase a car, car financing is possibly the best option. There are different options when it comes to this particular financing option. For instance, you have a car loan where you choose the loan amount that you need and for how long you need it. If approved, this money will be paid into your account, and you will purchase the car. Then, you pay this loan in installments. Having a great credit score will ensure you have the best possible interest rates and that you are approved.

You also have a hire purchase, or HP, where you have to also pay in installments (both the loan and the interest), but unlike a car loan, usually, you have to pay something upfront (usually 10% of the car); however, the larger the upfront money, the lower the interest rates are. Here, you can also choose the length of time that you want to pay it back.

For other purchases, you have other options. For instance, you could use your credit card. Of course, this should be done if you can pay the balance off as quickly as possible or if, by any chance, the interest is at 0%. You can also take out a personal loan. These require a great credit score and usually have fixed interest, but you can use them for many different purchases, such as home renovations. At times, it might also require collateral, which means you have to put something where if you can't pay the loan back, they will take it from you, for example, a car.

Depending on what you are buying, the merchant might offer an installment plan where you pay for the purchase over several months. These are usually quicker to get approved, but you still need to have a good credit score. They obviously come with interest when you pay them back.

The Different Ways You Can Save for College

College is important for your future. Nowadays, while there are alternatives, people who go to college usually earn more throughout their lives. However, it's expensive, and if you haven't been saving, it can become difficult to pay for it. Although there are many different ways that you can pay for your college expenses. The examples I will give below are exclusive to the US, but most countries have similar options available.

The first one that comes to mind is the 529 Education Savings Plan. This is a state-sponsored investment account that helps save for college expenses. Any money in here can be invested in many different investment vehicles, such as mutual funds or ETFs. But it gets better: any earnings from this are not taxed, unlike other investment accounts. However, you can only use these funds for anything related to education, such as the cost of tuition, transportation to college, or educational materials. In fact, there are high penalties if you use it for anything else but education-related things and your portfolio is usually a lot more limited than other investment accounts.

Another savings account you can use for your education is the Coverdell Education Savings Account. Usually, your parents have to open these because they are custodial accounts before you are 18 years old. Like the 529, you don't pay taxes on earnings, but your parents have to have a low annual income to apply for it, and they can only contribute $2,000 per year.

Another option is scholarships, grants, or work-study programs. Before talking more about it, you can visit studentaid. gov to check all the options for grants, scholarships, and other financial aid for your education.

Let's start with grants. These are financial aids that don't need to be paid back unless you withdraw from school. The Department of Education has many different grants that can help students pay for their education. Some of them are the Federal Pell Grants, the Federal Supplemental Education Opportunity Grants, and the Teacher Education Assistance for College and Higher Education. While eligibility changes, grants are only given to students who actually need financial aid to pay for their tuition.

Scholarships are offered by private and nonprofit organizations to help students pay for their education. Eligibility depends on many factors, such as talent or academic merit, but some are also based on financial need. Each scholarship has its own requirements, but a quick online search will give you all the websites you can visit to check on particular scholarships.

Work-study jobs are programs that allow you to earn money that you can then use to pay for your education. Usually, this work is part-time, so you can attend your education. While you can earn more than the minimum wage, this is not guaranteed. What you get from these work-study jobs depends on your level of financial need, the funding level of the organization, and when you apply for them.

Alternatively, you can also apply for a loan to pay for your education, but as you already know, this has to be paid back with interest, so it's important that you plan everything properly before doing it.

Big purchases and paying for college are things that might seem daunting, but they are part of life, and we need to go through them. In fact, with enough planning, they are not so hard to achieve. There are many different things that you can do and many different strategies that you can follow to reach these goals faster.

In the next and last chapter, I will talk about retirement, how to plan for long-term financial goals, explore retirement saving options that you can start right away, and the different strategies available.

CHAPTER 10

RETIREMENT

> *Retirement from work, but not from life.*
>
> *–M.K. Soni*

Yes, I know it's a long way until you retire; after all, you haven't even started to work, right? However, planning for retirement starts right now. In this last chapter, I'll be talking about retirement plans and the many different strategies you have, as well as the benefits of starting to plan this early in life.

How to Start Planning for Retirement?

When it's time to retire, you have worked all your life for yourself and your family. Now, you want to spend some quality time with your family and do what makes you happy—if you've planned properly, of course.

A retirement plan simply means that you have followed the right steps to live a comfortable life when it's time to stop working. There's not a single formula to plan for retirement, but there are guidelines. A retirement plan is important because you will have a regular income after you stop working, but you are also ready for any emergency and prepared to live a long, healthy life.

You have many investment options that will allow you to properly plan for when you retire. But like all kinds of investing, there are some with higher risks and higher rewards and others that help you protect your wealth. Let's take a look at the most common ones.

The Different Retirement Options

Before I get into the different retirement options, the examples I'm going to talk about below are specific to the US, but other countries have similar options available. The two most common retirement investment options are 401(k)s and IRAs. A 401(k) is a retirement savings plan that you often get through your employer, and it has tax advantages for you. When you are working, your employer will offer you a 401(k) that you have to sign up for if you want, and here, you are agreeing to give a percentage of your monthly income to your 401(k) savings plan, which is just like an investment account. Then, your employer usually matches what you have contributed. While you don't have all the options you'd have in your personal investment account, you can still pick from several investment options, but these are usually mutual funds because they are safer. In a traditional 401(k), any contributions you make are pre-taxed, which essentially means that you are not taxed on them now but will be when you eventually withdraw the money in your retirement. A Roth 401(k) works the same way, but it's after-tax, which means that your contributions are taxed right away but not when you withdraw the money in your retirement.

Then, you also have an Individual Retirement Account or IRA. This type of account also has tax benefits like a 401(k), and you can also contribute with pre- or after-tax money. This is a long-term savings account that works similarly to a 401(k), but it's not done through your employer. This is what self-employed workers use more often, and you can open it through your bank or even a brokerage. Here, you have four different types of IRAs: the traditional, Roth, Simplified Employee Pension (SEP), and Savings Incentive Match Plan for Employees (SIMPLE).

The differences between them have to do with the contribution limits. For instance, with a traditional IRA and a Roth IRA, you can contribute a maximum of $6,500 or $7,500 if you are 50 years old or older (however, these limits change every year). With a SEP, you can contribute a maximum of $65,000 or the lesser of 25%, and with a

SIMPLE retirement account, you can contribute a maximum of $15,500 or $19,000 if you are 50 years old or older.

CONCLUSION

That's it! That's all you need to know to start your financial journey on the right foot and prepare for what's coming. I know, at times, it might seem a little overwhelming, but once you know how things are done and you allow yourself to create routines, everything becomes a lot easier.

Starting with the basics and understanding what money is and how to make money is fundamental. A good foundation will allow you to prosper in all the other areas of your personal finances. When it comes to making money, there are many different ways you can do it as a teenager, as you have seen in Chapter 2. Just pick whatever you are most comfortable doing or something that you believe you will be doing in the future. Gaining experience at this stage of your life will make it easier for you in the future. If you can, open a bank account (if you don't already have one) since understanding the basics here and how you can manage your account will make you more comfortable with these services. Understanding the two basic accounts—checking accounts and savings—will allow you to not only get paid but also grow your money effectively. Nowadays, everything is gamified, and bank accounts are no exception. With mobile and internet banking, it is a lot easier to understand what you are doing.

I cannot emphasize this enough: budgeting allows you to reach your financial goals, and you should make it a habit. Regardless of the type of budgeting you follow, it's important to have one so you have your finances under control at all times. The more you know and the more you are in control, the better purchasing decisions you will make. This brings us to the different techniques when it comes to purchasing goods or services: practicing smart shopping and comparing prices can save you a lot of money in the long run and is one of those things that you want to have in your routine. Credit, credit cards, and debt can all sound scary, but as you've seen, credit can actually help you with your finances as long as you keep it under control. It can build your credit score and allow you more opportunities.

While savings are important, so is investing. In fact, investing, when done properly, can increase your wealth exponentially. Having savings goals is important, but having investment goals is also crucial so you can create a good financial foundation and be prepared for any financial emergencies that might come your way. Preparedness is everything. And don't forget compound interest, which can exponentially increase the value of your savings and investments even without adding any more money to them.

You might never have associated insurance with money or savings, but as we've seen in Chapter 8, it can be a great protection for your wealth, yourself, and your family. There are all types of insurance, such as health or auto, and while some are mandatory, others are recommended. This is especially true for health insurance in the US since these are mostly not covered by the government, and any minor medical emergency can become very expensive. It's important that you know how to evaluate insurance policies and coverage so you know you are properly protected, but you can also save money.

There's always a point in our lives where we have to make big purchases or have big expenses, such as purchasing a car, a home, or paying for our education. It's crucial that you plan properly and in advance, know how to evaluate your options, and explore the different strategies on how to save for these big expenses. Lastly, retirement might seem very far away, but we've seen the importance of starting early. This is probably the longest-term financial goal you will have, but even at your age, there are things that you can do to start planning for it.

However, I believe the most important thing you can do is apply the knowledge you have acquired in this book on a daily basis. There are many concepts here that might take a while for you to make a habit of, but with practice, everything is possible. Taking control of your financial future is something that many of us adults didn't have the chance to do, mainly because we didn't have the knowledge, but you do. If you apply everything you've learned in this book, you will not only have total control of your finances, but you will also live a stress-free life.

SOCIAL SKILLS

FOR TEENS

A Simple 7 Day System for Teenagers

to Break Out of Shyness, Build a Bulletproof Self-Confidence, and Start Overcoming Social Anxiety to Excel in Social Interactions

 **EMILY CARTER**

INTRODUCTION

> **❝**
>
> *No one can make you feel inferior without your consent.*

–Eleanor Roosevelt

✦ ✦ ✦ ✦

While it's a good quote—a great one even—I have some notes. First of all, as much as we try to deny it, we are not in control of our thoughts and emotions. Sure, there are a lot of mental exercises and practices that can improve our self-awareness and emotional intelligence, which might lead us to better understand (and control) our *reactions* to the world around us—and to what goes on in our minds when life happens.

However, to say that we can choose not to be offended, hurt, or made to feel inferior to others' words and actions is implying we should deny or ignore our thoughts and emotions altogether. And honestly, I'm offended by that. We can learn how to respond to our emotions in a way that's healthy, but there's no magical switch you can flip to suddenly not care; this isn't *The Vampire Diaries*.

Now, you might be thinking, what do our emotions have to do with building confidence and self-esteem in social interactions? And the answer is: Probably more than you might realize. You see, your emotions shape your perspective on life, and perspective controls your thoughts, and your brain will believe everything it tells itself because it's biased.

Each and every one of us have what are called "automatic thoughts." These are thoughts that are influenced by things like past experiences, perspectives, and emotional triggers. If your automatic thoughts are negative by nature, they can wreak havoc on the way you see yourself, especially if you're still getting to know who you are and where you fit into the world as a teenager.

"I'm just introverted," your brain might say. And that might be true, but there's a difference between preferring to be alone and feeling like you're not socially capable of building meaningful relationships. Introverts are still confident in their ability to interact with the world; they just don't feel the need to.

If the only reason you don't like talking to other people is because it feels hard, you never seem to know what to say, you believe they don't like you based on zero evidence, you feel you're too awkward, you assume they're judging you, or you believe they're better than you, then you might not actually be an introvert after all.

Your inner monologue can make you believe things so strongly that you don't even question them. And it's only when you make a conscious effort to challenge your own beliefs, values, and perspectives that you start the process of rewiring your brain to be kind and more accepting of your flaws and perceived shortcomings. Becoming aware of your self-sabotaging thought processes and tendencies is the first step to a healthier self-image.

Building and practicing social skills in your teen years are important for a few reasons. Mainly because, as an adult, it's necessary to be willing and able to communicate effectively in unfamiliar circumstances. Whether it's for work, friendships, or romantic relationships, social skills are the foundation of any meaningful interaction. It helps avoid miscommunications, resolve conflict, build trust, set boundaries, and so much more.

If you think about it, the absolute best time to work on these skills—and practice using them—is during your teen years. Sure, you might make a fool of yourself once or twice, but everyone is so focused on themselves and their own presence in the world at this age that your mishaps go unnoticed most of the time. When you compare how many cringeworthy moments you've had to what you remember your peers having, it paints a clear picture.

The thing is, you don't remember their awkward moments because they've had less of them; you just don't think it's worse than yours. And that right there is a prime example of how powerful the brain can really be. It would be foolish to assume that they're watching and waiting for you to do or say something embarrassing as much as they're trying not to do or say something embarrassing themselves.

But let's say they do make a big deal of something you did or said. Oftentimes, when others are inflating your misgivings, it comes from a place of low self-esteem and a lack of confidence in themselves. It's a way to redirect attention away from themselves, so they can feel secure and lower their guard—even if just for a moment. It's never fun to be in a situation like that, but how you respond to it (regardless of how you feel) can make a world of difference to how others perceive you and your self-confidence.

The anxiety that comes with low self-esteem and social interaction is not going to go away on its own. Unfortunately, you're going to have to face your fears at some point or another, and it all starts with rebuilding the foundations of a positive self-image and finding your voice.

You might be thinking, "It's impossible to build confidence and overcome social anxiety in only seven days." And, of course, you'd be absolutely right. The idea— or my idea, at least—of the seven-day system is to build a habit. When you know exactly what to do every single day, and you have a clear strategy and plan in place, you're not left wondering what you should be doing.

Week after week, you follow the same steps of doing something small and seemingly insignificant every day until you've built up enough tolerance to face your fears (or hesitation) surrounding social interaction. Only once you're able to go through every exercise comfortably do you move on to more advanced or intimidating situations.

Throughout this book, we'll be doing just that. You'll learn effective and easy ways to work on personal growth, communication skills, and handling difficult or awkward situations using a seven-day system that will kickstart your journey to self-discovery and self-acceptance.

And remember, social skills—just like any other skill— require practice and perseverance (even when it's hard).

By taking one tiny step at a time, you'll build tolerance and maybe even realize that it's not half as bad or difficult as you may have thought.

CHAPTER 1

Day 1　　**SELF-AWARENESS**

> **"**
>
> *We don't see things as they are,*
> *we see them as we are.*

–Anais Nin

✦✦✦✦

The term "self-awareness" gets thrown around a lot, and I believe that a lot of people don't truly understand what it means. Everyone is technically aware of themselves, but an overused profound quote that gets posted alongside a selfie with a grayscale filter on it isn't exactly the epitome of self-awareness.

Don't get me wrong; I hold cheesy philosophical quotes very near and dear to my heart. A lot of them inspire creative thinking, ideas, introspection, and new perspectives. The way that everyone can look at the exact same piece of art, for example, and come up with their own unique interpretations of what's happening based on their own unique set of brainwaves, the emotions they think it's meant to conjure, and the general "vibe" or meaning they personally look for behind it will forever fascinate me.

Levels of Self-Awareness

You are not born self-aware; it's something that develops over time—much like self-image. It's how you make sense of the things you do based on your opinions, emotions, values, and belief systems. There are five key elements (or levels) of self-awareness:

1. **Consciousness.** By the age of five, you'll have the basic understanding that you're a person with your own thoughts, emotions, and experiences. You can recognize your own reflection and identify yourself in a picture or video.

2. **Self-knowledge.** You know your current likes, dislikes, and preferences. It also includes your motivations, beliefs, and opinions.

3. **Emotional intelligence.** This is your ability to understand, manage, and express your emotions in a healthy way.

4. **Self-acceptance.** You're able to recognize your flaws and admit mistakes while still showing kindness and compassion for yourself.

5. **Self-reflection.** You reflect on your emotions and behaviors and whether or not they align with who you believe yourself to be. You use this feedback for self-improvement rather than self-hatred.

Furthermore, there are two distinct types of self-awareness: public and private. Public self-awareness is when there's a lot of attention on you from other people, like when you're delivering a speech or presentation—you have the spotlight. You're, therefore, hyper-aware that you're being watched and evaluated. This pressure usually causes us to behave in ways that are considered to be more socially acceptable. If you have social anxiety (or even something akin to "stage fright"), you're focused and concerned about what everyone might think of you–especially if you were to do something embarrassing or "wrong."

Private self-awareness is when you become aware of certain aspects, features, or traits about yourself privately. The way you feel or what you think when you look in the mirror, when you realize you forgot to study for a test and your stomach drops, when your crush walks into the classroom and your heart starts beating faster. These are all examples of private self-awareness. You can feel and recognize what's going on in your mind and body.

Being self-aware is a good thing; it allows us to put the things we do and feel into perspective. It allows us to become better people. However, it's possible to be overly self-aware— it's called being self-conscious.

Most—if not all—people experience bouts of self-consciousness every now and again. Honestly, it's impossible not to in the era of social media, unachievable societal expectations, and impossible beauty standards. But it's not normal to be experiencing excessive amounts of self-consciousness. If it's to the point where it's affecting your quality of life on a daily basis, it might be worth speaking to a mental health professional about.

Limiting Beliefs and Self-Sabotage

As part of your self-discovery journey, you'll have to come face-to-face with the fact that it was you holding yourself back all this time. Now, you might not be ready to hear that just yet, and that's okay.

The brain is biased, and it will convince itself that something is true even when it isn't based on facts. These are called limiting beliefs, and while some limiting beliefs are necessary to keep us safe and to form a productive and healthy society (like believing you can't fly so you don't try to jump out the window of a ten-story building or believing that stealing is wrong so you stop yourself from hotwiring a car).

However, some of these limiting beliefs keep us from achieving goals, experiencing new and exciting things, or taking advantage of great opportunities. For example, you might think you don't have what it takes to be a doctor, so you settle for being a teacher. You might think you won't get into the college of your dreams, so you don't even apply.

You believe no one finds you interesting, so you sit alone at lunchtime.

There are unhelpful limiting beliefs, and they keep you stagnant, unable or unwilling to move forward, take on new opportunities, and grow as a person. Whether you have limiting beliefs about yourself, the world, or life in general, the first step is to identify them. And you do that by thinking about a goal you have had stored in the deepest pits of your medulla oblongata that never seemed to leave despite how many times you've shot it down.

This could be anything from learning a new skill to making new friends. Now, ask yourself why you aren't actively working on it. I can guarantee you there's a limiting belief somewhere surrounding it. For example, let's say you're into DIY and you've flipped furniture pieces for your own room. The idea of turning it into a side hustle has popped up in your head a couple of times, and even though it gets you excited every time, you haven't taken it further.

The limiting beliefs here can be that you don't think you have enough skill, knowledge, or creativity, or that no one would buy second-hand furniture from a teenager. See how none of these beliefs are rooted in reality? How none of them are based on evidence or facts?

If you're still having trouble identifying your limiting beliefs, here are a few alternative ways (besides thinking of a goal you're not working toward and why) that might bring more clarity:

✧ **Get rid of mind clutter.** Your mind, just like your desk or your bedroom floor, can get cluttered if you don't make an effort to get rid of all the unnecessary thoughts. Unnecessary thoughts are things that stick around in your mind and can be hard to get rid of: Fears and worries, wants and desires, the upcoming test you haven't studied for, your to-do list, negative experiences, lingering emotions, things you can't control, and so on. Either way, having too much going on upstairs makes it harder to think clearly or focus on anything. The easiest and most effective way to reduce and prevent mind clutter from accumulating to an overwhelming level is to write it out. The act of putting your thoughts onto paper (or even typing it out in your notes app) helps you let go of these unnecessary and negative thoughts. You could also try meditating, taking a nap (and making sure you're getting enough sleep in general), decluttering your physical environment (i.e., cleaning your room), spending some time in the sun, limiting external distractions and stimuli for a bit, or adding ten minutes of physical activity to your daily schedule. Keep what works; leave what doesn't.

✧ **Be curious.** Limiting beliefs are often associated with being closed-minded, and closed-mindedness is synonymous with having a fixed mindset (the idea that we can't change who we are or improve ourselves to any degree). You can start working on moving toward a growth mindset by adopting an "everything is figure-outable" mentality and being curious about yourself, your past experiences, and your current sense of reality (and whether it's possible that it might be warped). So be curious, doubt your mind's intentions for you, ask questions, and challenge yourself.

✧ **Work on self-improvement.** Self-improvement is kind of the entire goal of this book. And by admitting change is needed, being willing to change, and being open to the words written on these pages, you have already taken the first step! But self-improvement isn't a one-and-done type of deal; it's a life-long journey—one that is continuously changing who you are for the better. As part of the first step in self-improvement, you'll need to dig deep and identify your personal values. This is a list of what's most important to you in life. To identify your core values, start by answering the following questions:

- Think of a time (or times) when you felt most at peace, happy, or fulfilled. Who were you with, and what were you doing?

- Think of a time (or times) when you felt hurt, angry, or unhappy. What happened?

- What inspires you the most?

- What are you most proud of?

- If you could change anything about the world, what would it be?

Based on these answers, you should be able to see certain themes pop up. Maybe a majority of the moments when you were most happy were with family—you value family. Your worst moments were when someone betrayed or lied to you—you might value honesty, trust, and loyalty. If music inspires you, you could value creativity. And so on. By the end of this exercise, you should have a good idea of what your core values are. You can then do some soul-searching and define them better, add new ones, and remove ones you don't strongly identify with—until you're left with just a handful. This doesn't mean they can't change over time as you grow and gain new perspectives, but it's a pretty good starting point. You might also discover you have some unhelpful or negative core values, such as valuing money a bit too much, being dishonest at times, the need for attention or being liked all the time, being rude, superiority, entitlement, and so on. If you do find you have a couple of negative core values, these are the ones you focus on correcting while on your journey to self-improvement.

✧ **Counseling.** There comes a point where all the self-help books in the world won't help you break free from the shackles of your own mind. If you think you might already be too far down the rabbit hole, rest assured there's still hope. I can only give you so much advice and cheesy philosophical quotes from here. Sometimes you need someone right there with you on your self-discovery journey that can give you personalized support and course correct you when you veer too far from the path. Therapists and counselors can help, and there's nothing wrong with needing support until you can take the reins and continue on your journey alone.

Self-Acceptance 101

Self-acceptance doesn't mean making excuses for your bad habits or bad behaviors; it simply means acknowledging them, being aware of them, and admitting you need to work on them without creating resentment toward yourself. It also means being proud of your accomplishments, your progress, your contributions, and your skills.

Someone who is self-aware is able to view themselves realistically. They know what their strengths are and don't feel insecure about their weaknesses. For example, they don't look at a video of Tony Hawk skateboarding online and think they're useless because they can't perform at that same level.

Someone who accepts themselves will see themselves as a whole person with flaws, quirks, emotions, traits, and past experiences instead of defining themselves based on a certain or singular incident, ability, characteristic, or weakness. They believe they are worthy of respect and love because their sense of value comes from within—they respect, value, and love themselves unconditionally.

The good news is, you can become this person too!

Once you've identified your core values, you can adjust your actions accordingly. This strengthens your sense of identity so you feel more grounded and able to challenge negative self-talk and distorted thoughts.

Practice self-compassion and standing up to yourself, for yourself. Negative self-talk and distorted thoughts are a result of those pesky cognitive biases we talked about earlier. The more you entertain negative self-talk and allow them to go unchallenged, the stronger they get. Then, just like Mario when he eats a mushroom, they grow into distorted thoughts. When this happens, the constant negative self-talk has done its job and the distorted thoughts and beliefs take on a life of their own.

Distorted thoughts and beliefs can make spotting negative self-talk more challenging, but with a bit of practice and conscious effort, you'll be able to deconstruct your entire self-image and build it back up stronger and more accurately.

Self-Assessment

You can't accept yourself if you don't know who you are. Not only is knowing who you are necessary for self-acceptance and self-improvement, but it also plays a huge role when it comes to setting goals for yourself in every aspect of life. If something isn't important to you, if you're not good at it, or if it goes against who you are, you're not going to make progress in a way that's meaningful to *you*. And that defeats the whole purpose of life.

Let's start with something simple: What do you like to do? Keep it as broad and general or as detailed as you want. Look at your day-to-day life; what do you look forward to every day? Maybe you enjoy the bike ride home from school, the earthy smell when it just starts to rain, reading, listening to indie music, cosplaying, playing video games, rearranging your room, roller skating, watching movies, ASMR. Maybe you actually like pineapple on pizza!

Nothing is insignificant; even the small things—that many other people might also like to do—are what make up who you are.

Now ask yourself the opposite: What do you not like or not like doing? Start with the biggest, most obvious things like maybe school, homework, chores, and vegetables, if applicable. Once these are out of the way, go deeper. Maybe you don't like the color red, going into direct sun, taking a bath (because in your mind it's like making human soup), exercising, wearing jeans, the taste of artificial grape flavor, and so on.

The next question you're going to ask yourself is: What are you good at? You may find that the things you're good at are closely related or overlap with the things you enjoy doing. You like playing chess because you rarely lose. You like baking because it always turns out great. Maybe you actually enjoy school because you love learning new things, and you get good grades. You get the point. Evaluate the things you're good at to find the soft life skills that often lurk beneath the surface: Creativity, patience, kindness, curiosity, determination, and many more.

You probably saw this coming, but the next question is obviously: What are you bad at? The answers to these might also be in relation to the things you don't like doing, or it might be because you simply have no interest in them. For example, you might tell yourself that you're bad at socializing because you have no interest in it when in reality, you're just bad at socializing. So be honest with yourself here. Because being bad at something can be fixed, having no interest in it is a different story.

You can write down your answers to all of these questions separately and keep it as a reminder that you are a whole person—which includes the good and the bad. Try to approach your answers from an analytical standpoint (no judgment, just curiosity). Come back to it every now and then to add to the lists, take things away that no longer apply, or just read through it for fun.

If it helps, you can also find self-assessment tests online, which include personality tests. Though, I would advise using personality tests as rough or inspirational guidelines only since they tend to be anecdotal (not to mention your own bias can influence the results greatly). Don't take them at face value, is all I'm trying to say.

Once you know your true strengths, weaknesses, interests, values, and beliefs, you have a pretty good idea of who you are—in theory. Now, you might not be ecstatic about what you discovered about yourself in the process. No one is 100% happy with who they are. But again, self-acceptance isn't about whether you like who you are; it's about acknowledgment.

"Am I flawed?" Yes. "Do I still deserve love, compassion, empathy, and respect?" Yes, just like everyone else.

Self-acceptance means to treat yourself the way you would a close friend or loved one. You'd never tell someone you love that they're not good enough, not pretty enough, not talented enough, or not smart enough. And if you would say something like this to someone you care about, you need to acknowledge that your values and behavior toward others are bad and toxic, and take accountability for it.

But either way, the call is coming from inside the house. Whether you treat yourself badly or treat others badly, it's your responsibility to see the light, see that it doesn't serve you, and willingly choose to do the work in order to change for the better.

Self-Actualization

There's a lot of debate around what the term "self-actualization" really means. Some say it's the act of becoming who you were meant to be as a person; others say it's about reaching your fullest potential. But for the sake of our purposes, I'm going to define it as becoming the best possible version of yourself.

However, while self-actualization can be interpreted in a lot of different ways, none of the definitions involve being perfect. Unrealistic expectations, perfectionism, or anxiety about making the "right" choice can actually hinder your progress when trying to live authentically.

Becoming the best version of yourself is about living your life in a way that takes full advantage of your strengths while also taking your limits (or weaknesses) into consideration.

People who are actively being who they were meant to be (or self-actualized individuals) don't let what other people think of them get in the way of their reality and truth; they don't depend on external approval or validation. They let their creativity, intuition, and spontaneity guide them, they don't pretend to know things to impress others, and they are comfortable with uncertainty and constructive criticism. They don't take themselves too seriously, and they can admit when they've made a mistake and take responsibility for their actions and behaviors. They dedicate themselves to doing things that bring purpose, happiness, and fulfillment to their own lives while not harming others in the process. They consider the bigger picture while also being able to appreciate the smaller things in life.

Self-actualization goes hand-in-hand with self-awareness and self-improvement. In fact, working toward being more self-aware and wanting to improve yourself will most likely put you on the path to self-actualization, whether you like it or not. There's no endgame here; all of it is a lifelong journey without a destination.

Daily Task

Becoming self-aware takes practice and time. It's not going to happen after just one self-assessment session. It's not a possession; it's a skill. It's the ability to analyze your thoughts, habits, actions, and emotions—without judgment—and determine whether they are true to who you really are or who you want to become. And then gradually and consciously working toward positive change until the changes become subconscious or automatic.

This is why your first daily practice or task will be to start journaling. Regardless of whether you think it's silly, intimidating, or embarrassing—just try it. Challenge yourself: Journal every day for a week, and then stop for a week. Pay close attention to how you felt during the week you were journaling versus the week when you weren't.

Document the results by giving your mental clarity or general state of mind a rating (out of 5 stars, or 0–10, for example) every day during the two weeks of the challenge so you can compare your findings accurately.

If there's a visible improvement in your ratings during the week you were journaling and then a steady decline during the week you weren't journaling, you should continue the habit (and you owe me $5). If there's no improvement, or your rating gets worse when journaling, then journaling probably isn't for you, and you should maybe look into different ways to improve self-awareness—there are plenty to choose from, so don't panic.

And to prevent you from backing out because you don't know where to start or what to write about, I'm going to walk you through a few ideas and prompts to inspire your one-week daily writing challenge:

- **Day 1: What are three things that challenged me today, and how did I handle it?**

  This could include physical, mental, or emotional challenges of any degree of difficulty or significance. You couldn't find your socks this morning, you missed the bus, you messed up your verbal assignment, your dad was in a bad mood when he got home, the batteries in your controller dead, you have to work in a group for a project with someone you don't like, PE class, the girl you liked rolled her eyes at you. Anything goes!

  Then write down how you handled it, what you did before, during, and after, how it made you feel, and any further information that's relevant (or not relevant, it's *your* journal). Now, write how you think you should've handled it based on your ideal values and beliefs—only if how you handled it in reality doesn't align with who you want to be. And what you can do to realize these changes if you were to ever be in that situation again.

  You can also write about life challenges you face in general, not just for the day.

○ **Day 2: What are my three most recent limiting beliefs, and why are they not true?**

It might help to think about recent situations where you found yourself holding back or avoided doing something. For example, you avoided showing your art to someone, you held back when doing a presentation, or you avoided having a discussion with your parents about something that's bothering you.

Now dig deeper. Try to remember the thought that came to mind or the reasoning behind why you didn't do something. The personal reasons you have for not doing something are, more often than not, due to a limiting belief. Sure, there are instances when holding yourself back from doing something is valid, for instance, when it involves hurting other people unnecessarily in any way.

But when it involves you doubting your experience, abilities, or value, it's a limiting belief that doesn't serve you. Once you have your three recent limiting beliefs, challenge them. It might help to not think about them as your own limiting belief but rather something someone you care about said to you about themselves. What reasons or assurances would you give them in order to convince them it's not true?

○ **Day 3: What is something nobody knows about me?**

Again, it could be something small and superficial or deep and profound. It could be the first thing that comes to mind, maybe you already know the answer, or maybe you need to sit on it for a couple of minutes.

It could be anything that you haven't told anyone yet for whatever reason: a skill you taught yourself, a unique experience, a quirk or trait, a preference, a hobby, a hidden talent, or liking something controversial (like butter pecan-flavored ice cream). It could be as many things as you can think of or only one example. Take a second to let whatever it is resonate. You can expand on what you wrote down—the why's, what's, when's, and where's—or not.

The goal of this prompt isn't to justify, debunk, or prove anything but rather to appreciate yourself and acknowledge that you are a whole person regardless of what other people might think or say about you.

O   Day 4: What things have I avoided doing because of fear?

It might help, once again, to think of a recent example since you might not remember specifics or details about something that happened years ago—but feel free to still write about a distant past experience.

This prompt in itself might help you uncover deeper or stronger self-limiting beliefs. Don't be scared to dive into it and give all your thoughts, emotions, and theories on the fear itself, what caused it, how it has impacted you now, and how it can potentially hinder your growth in the future.

○ **Day 5: What do I need to let go of?**

Let me be clear: Letting go of something and forgiveness is not the same thing. You can let go of something and move on while still holding someone accountable for their hurtful actions against you. Letting go of negative, debilitating thoughts, emotions, and experiences is about and for *you*. Forgiveness is for those who deserve it, but it's not necessary for healing.

With that in mind, think of a negative feeling or thought you've been holding onto for a long time. Write as much detail as you can remember about the incident. Don't hold back; let your emotions take over and spill out over the pages. Write until there's nothing more to write about, until every last drop of resentment, frustration, regret, or devastation has been captured in ink.

Feel the weight of having to hold on to this burden for so long slip off your shoulders, feel the negative emotions seeping out of your pores and vaporizing, feel the hold it has had on your heart loosening. Take the deepest breath you've taken the entire day, breathe as if it's the first time your lungs are filling with oxygen, and let go—whatever that means to you.

○ **Day 6: What would my ideal life look like?**

What would your ideal life look like right now with regard to yourself, your habits, your accomplishments, and your skills? Yes, it would be nice to live in a mansion, be driven (or drive) to school in the newest Mercedes, and have more money than you know what to do with. But that's not what I'm referring to with this question.

The more specific you are, the better. For example: "I would exercise and make my bed every day, I wouldn't freeze or stumble over my words when having a conversation, I wouldn't care what other people say or think about me, I wouldn't doubt my place in the world, I would get into that program," and so on.

This prompt is about self-discovery. But instead of saying everything you think you aren't or can't do and getting down about it, you're reframing it a bit. It might reveal things about you that you might've not considered, and it might make you aware of things you didn't know you wanted to do or become. And at the very least, it gives you an idea of future goals relating to self-improvement that you can start working on.

O **Day 7: If I had to choose a mantra or quote to live by, what would it be and why?**

Feel free to search for inspirational or meaningful quotes from philosophers, inventors, or whoever else tickles your fancy for ideas. Choose one that has a lot of meaning to you and explore why.

For example, my favorite quote that I live by is from Joshua J Marine: "Challenges are what make life interesting and overcoming them is what makes life meaningful" (2022).

The way I interpret this quote—and the reason why it's so meaningful to me—is that there will always be challenges in life, some bigger than others. Some mildly derail your plans or ruin your mood for the day, and others bring your entire world to the brink of collapse. There are a lot of things in life you can't change, but you can change your perspective. You can choose to overcome and learn from it. You can look back one day and see that everything turned out okay in the end anyway. You can admit that while it sucked at the time, it put into motion a butterfly effect that has gotten you to where you are today; it opened new doors and shut ones that you were too afraid to shut yourself.

The fact that I'm still here means that, so far, I have a 100% success rate at overcoming the biggest obstacles and challenges that I have faced. And that counts for something!

The seven prompts I provided above are for if you are the type of person who needs a guideline to follow or you don't know where to start. You can absolutely rearrange the order, make adjustments, or discard all of it and just write whatever comes up when the pen hits the paper—or your thumbs hit the screen. You can look up different prompts or ideas on what to write about, and you can create your own. There are no rules!

One suggestion I do have is that you stop here, do the first journaling prompt, and only continue on to the next chapter tomorrow. But keep journaling every day as you proceed with the daily tasks of the upcoming chapters. Doing this will prevent information overload.

Day 2   SELF-CONFIDENCE

> *You're never as good as everyone tells you when you win, and you're never as bad as they say when you lose.*

–Lou Holtz

✦ ✦ ✦ ✦

As with many things in life, everyone has their own thoughts, feelings, and ideologies on what self-confidence actually means and what it looks like. Some people think it's good to be confident since it's connected to self-esteem, success, and good mental health; others think it's bad because they confuse it with vanity or narcissism.

According to the Merriam-Webster dictionary, the word "self-confidence" is defined as "Confidence in oneself and in one's power and abilities." Thanks, that's... revolutionary information.

Let's clear things up. Self-confidence means believing you have inherent value regardless of your mistakes; feeling worthy despite your flaws; respecting and loving yourself; having the courage to stand up to others and defend yourself; living in a way that feels true to who you are; and loving yourself as a whole.

As you can see, it can mean a lot of things—and all of them are accurate descriptions. But what being self-confident *doesn't* mean is that you're perfect or you need to be perfect; that you're better than others; that you should have and achieve high standards, goals, and expectations; that you won't have problems or struggles in life; that you can't be humble; or that you should be selfish.

Developing A Growth Mindset

"You can't teach an old dog new tricks." A common saying implies that once a dog has reached a certain age, they are set in their ways and can't improve their behavior, skills, or abilities. Except, it's not true. One study that was published in 2016 shows that while older dogs might take longer to learn new tricks, it's still possible to teach them (Wallis et al., 2016). And this is only one of many.

But this phrase is also used amongst people, usually the older generations. In my opinion, using this term is a way to justify being stuck or stagnant. It's a way to get out of having to put in the work or effort to improve yourself. It's a way to absolve yourself of any responsibility regarding a need for change. It's lazy and outdated.

But this kind of mindset can happen to anyone at any age. It's called a fixed mindset and it will hold you back for your entire life. You have a fixed mindset if you believe that people are born with talent instead of having worked hard for years to develop it. You have a fixed mindset if you think there's a cap on what you're destined to become. You have a fixed mindset if you believe that not being good at or not knowing something is a permanent state of being.

People with a fixed mindset will avoid challenges because it could lead to failure, and since they believe that their attributes and skills can't be improved upon, failing at something means they are automatically a failure. It becomes so much more intense. They will also avoid or ignore constructive feedback from others (because they view it as a personal attack), feel threatened by others who achieve success, hide their flaws or mistakes, and give up easily.

When you believe that trying is futile, you become hopeless, and this only feeds into the narrative of someone with a fixed mindset. "I can't be better or do better, so why even try?" This black-and-white perspective of "you either *are* something or you're not" has a snowball effect on your self-confidence, self-esteem, self-image, and self-talk.

Getting out of a fixed mindset can be tricky because in order to do so, you first have to believe that change or improvement is possible—which literally goes against everything that someone with a fixed mindset believes. However, this is an instant where, once you've taken the first step, the most difficult part is already over.

What It Is

Now that you know what a fixed mindset is—and whether or not you have one—let's talk about the alternative. A growth mindset is basically the complete opposite of a fixed mindset. Even if you don't have a fixed mindset (or you're not really sure and haven't given it much thought), you can still benefit from strengthening and developing a growth mindset.

So, what even is a "growth mindset?"

Well, a growth mindset means you view setbacks and failures as valuable—a necessary part of the learning process. Someone with a growth mindset recognizes that learning and the ability to learn has no expiration date. They are open to constructive criticism because it might bring forth ideas and perspectives that they might not have considered. They get inspired by the success of others and see challenges as opportunities to grow, learn, and improve.

Having a growth mindset has a huge positive impact on your motivation and academic performance and achievements. And that's a fact! (Yeager et al., 2019).

Here's another fact: You can change your mind. Even if you're stuck in the negative feedback loop and thinking patterns of a fixed mindset, you can rewire your brain to be more open to growth and learning.

How To Change Your Mind

Don't get me wrong, changing your entire outlook on life will take time and practice, as most things do. But in my humble opinion, it's worth doing. What you need to understand is that if you believe anything, your brain will interpret and warp any information to prove itself to be right. There's that internal bias again.

And while there are certain things that will help you overcome a fixed mindset (like challenging your limiting beliefs and thoughts), I want to be even more specific about how you can go about changing your perspective—and, as a result, your mind.

✧ **Know that, scientifically speaking, it's possible.** Your brain might not believe you if you simply tell it that developing, learning, and growing is possible. Luckily, there are studies that prove—without a doubt—that it is possible to change your mindset from negative (fixed) to positive (growth).

Neuroplasticity refers to the brain's ability to change, modify itself, and adapt its physical structure, as well as how it functions throughout your lifespan in response to various internal, external, and environmental factors (Voss et al., 2017). What this means is that your experiences and environment during childhood plays a huge role in how your brain's neural pathways form. These neural pathways are how your brain makes sense of the world around you and your pathways are different and unique to everyone else's—but they can also be changed or "rewired."

We see this with people who have lost one or more of their senses all the time. In someone who has undergone sensory loss, their remaining senses compensate for it. This is a prime example of neuroplasticity in the works. In order for their other senses to strengthen, their brain structure physically changes (Merabet & Pascual-Leone, 2009).

It's also proven that your thoughts have an effect on your emotions, and the stronger the emotional reaction to a thought, the more your brain believes it to be true. And since beliefs have the ability to change your brain structure (your neural pathways), it stands to reason that the only thing you need to do is change your beliefs. Sounds simple enough, right? However, it's exactly the "changing" part that many people struggle with. But again, just because it's going to take time and effort doesn't mean it won't happen or it's not worth it. So, in essence, the first and most important step in this journey is to convince yourself (through research and facts) that it is possible to change your mind.

✧ **Reward your efforts, not your results.** Remember, growing is a journey without a destination, which means that, oftentimes, you never get to see the end result. Stepping away from only feeling good about what you manage to accomplish and giving yourself a pat on the back for simply trying and making progress can be extremely validating and motivating.

For example, reward yourself when you manage to spot a limiting belief or negative thought, not just when you manage to successfully challenge or reframe it; reward yourself for recognizing that your body language might be telling people you're unapproachable, not just after you've fixed it.

Rewarding yourself could come in the form of anything you enjoy doing or what makes you feel good such as spending time in the sun, playing with a pet, having a movie night, taking a bubble bath, spending time on your favorite hobby, fixing yourself your favorite snack, and so on.

✧ **Relabel, reattribute, refocus, revalue.** Relabel negative thoughts as soon as you recognize them. If you did poorly on a test, for example, and your first thought is, *I'm so stupid*, pause and relabel it as anything other than true. Because it isn't. You can call it a brain glitch, a false message, an impulsive thought, a mental invasion, or anything else that questions the validity of the thought.

Reattribute the reason for having the thought in the first place to something that's out of your control. Because it is. Remind yourself that your mind is still stuck in a negative feedback loop based on old beliefs, experiences, and emotions. And that it's going to take a while to reprogram and get used to the new features and commands.

Refocus your attention to actively and consciously change your recurring negative thought patterns. This is when you replace the negative thought with one that's more realistic and accurate based on the evidence you have. Think of it as a manual override—since the automatic system is not doing what you need it to do. Using the example of automatically thinking you're stupid when you get a bad grade, you can counter it by following it up with, "Now hold on a second, since when does failing one singular test mean that a person is stupid in general? That doesn't seem like a fair analysis of overall intelligence." Go over the evidence and reality of the situation; maybe the truth is that you failed because you simply didn't study, studied the wrong material, or misunderstood a lot of the questions on the test. But again, none of the reasons for failing a test means you're not capable of passing the class in the end.

If you consistently follow the first three steps when negative thought patterns emerge, eventually, your brain will revalue them as mere distractions and untruths. Your mind catches up and drifts away from negative automatic responses because they don't hold as much weight anymore. Through practice and persistence, your relabeling, reattributing, and refocusing of negative thoughts will become easier and more automatic. You will have trained your brain to react with more positive and reality-based thoughts, which will also change your limiting beliefs.

- ✧ **Pay attention to what you're being exposed to.** This is especially true in the era of social media. The algorithms dictate what's on your feeds and "for you" pages. But the thing is, negativity is more popular than positivity—because it generates a stronger emotional reaction. You're more likely to react to, comment on, and stay tuned (or read) to the end of a post that talks about all the bad stuff that makes us lose faith in humanity.

  But when you do this, you'll only be fed more of the same stories! I'm not going to go into how social media is all marketing and engagement, but just know that your mind will grow off of whatever you feed it. So be wise about the content that you consume.

  But this also counts in real life. You can't control what other people do, say, or think, but you can remove yourself from certain situations or take steps to protect yourself and your mental health.

- ✧ **Tap into the power of "yet."** The word "yet" is a great subtle reminder that improvement and growth are possible. "I'm not able to identify and challenge all my limiting beliefs and thoughts—yet." "I'm not as confident in myself—yet." "My skill isn't on the level that I want it to be—yet," "I'm not very good at social interactions and situations—yet." It changes the narrative from hopeless to hopeful. It opens up a small window of possibility, and that's all you need to cram a crowbar in there and break it right open.

✧ **Build mental resilience.** Mental resilience refers to one's ability to adapt or recover from things like stress, emotional dysregulation, or other mentally exhausting challenges. And one thing you'll need on your journey to self-improvement through self-awareness is mental "toughness."

Mental resilience doesn't mean you should suppress or ignore your emotions or that you shouldn't have emotional reactions at all. It simply allows you to be courageous despite your doubts and fears, to stay in control of your thoughts and actions despite involuntary emotional responses, and to get where you want to be in life regardless of your past or current hardships.

How do you build mental resilience? By living life. By practicing and giving it time. By taking care of yourself, finding a purpose, establishing realistic goals and working toward achieving them, being mindful of how you talk to yourself, keeping things in perspective, and building meaningful connections. By accepting the things you can't change and finding a way to push through them anyway, you're proving to yourself (and strengthening the idea) that you're capable enough.

Believing in yourself—as corny as it might sound—really has a big role to play in self-confidence. In order to raise your confidence, you have to change the way you think of yourself and your true abilities. You do this by getting used to correcting your knee-jerk assumptions and automatic thoughts and slowly turning them around until they cave in on themselves.

Building Self-Confidence

There's a reason why the majority of this chapter is filled with developing a growth mindset and setting goals. It's because believing that you are capable of improvement and achieving the goals you have been wanting to achieve (but might not have thought were possible) improves your self-esteem, and healthy self-esteem warrants self-confidence.

Self-esteem and self-confidence are a packaged deal; you can't authentically have one without the other—but they're separate concepts. Self-esteem is how you treat and value yourself in private and isn't always obvious from an outsider's perspective. Self-confidence is how you present yourself to the outside world and other people (and is typically based on self-esteem).

However, people with low self-esteem might present themselves as having a lot of self-confidence in order to make up for the former. In essence, "fake it 'till you make it." And while that sentiment might be helpful in many different, unrelated aspects of life, pretending to be confident in yourself only leads to a deeper identity crisis because you're living in two different realities where what you think and what you do doesn't line up—which may cause imposter syndrome (feeling like you're a fraud or you don't belong). It could also fuel anxiety and create mental exhaustion from always having to put on an act or a show—leading to eventual and complete social withdrawal and isolation.

Here's a fun fact: Opinions are not facts at all—not even when they're your own.

Your self-image is influenced by things such as your appearance, personality, the opinions of others, or past experiences. In a nutshell, your self-image is your opinion of yourself. It affects your behavior and how you interact with the world and other people. And most importantly, it affects your happiness, relationships, and overall well-being.

A negative self-image will impact the quality of your relationships. Whether that's because you doubt their intentions, aren't communicating your needs effectively, take constructive criticism personally, or feel like you can't be yourself around them, it all comes down to what goes on in your own head.

Expanding on that, people with low self-esteem might tolerate unhealthy or even abusive relationships because they will do mental gymnastics to excuse or defend the other person's behavior. They might even go as far as blaming it on themselves.

The inability to fully trust someone and open up to them will make it hard to connect on a deeper level, which will eventually lead them to believe that you're the one who's unwilling to build a relationship. As a result, they will withdraw, leaving you feeling confused and hurt once again, watering that now flourishing tree of doubt even more.

It's a vicious cycle, one that keeps you from living up to your potential, having people around you who care for you, and enjoying all the wonderful experiences that life has to offer.

Since self-esteem is the building block upon which self-confidence is built, it's easier to start there. So what can you do to work on improving your self-esteem?

First of all, stop comparing yourself to others. And yes, it's one of those things that's easier said than done. When the negative thoughts and emotional reactions start to creep in when looking at other people's lives, achievements, or success, do that thing where you challenge it. "I started my YouTube channel at the same time as [insert classmate's name here]. How come they have way more subscribers than me? That must mean I'm [insert limiting belief or cognitive distortion here]."

Now you follow up with the facts, but be careful not to assume things that you can't possibly know or verify. Sure, you may have started your respective channels at around the same time, but your niches and content are different; they post much more frequently than you and on a consistent schedule; they have better equipment and software, so their sound, lighting, and editing results in an overall better viewing experience. Maybe I could actually talk to them and find out what they're doing differently to me in terms of tags, titles, and all the other technical stuff.

See how the narrative changes? How it doesn't have to be so self-sabotaging and self-imposed?

It's normal to want to be extraordinary, and seeing others in a position that we want to be in right now can be demotivating. It rips our time and attention away from ourselves and our own goals and leaves us feeling defeated. Instead, compare yourself *with* yourself. But not in a mean, resentful type of way. Think of what you do differently today than you did yesterday. Did it improve your life? If not, think of what you can do today that your future self will thank you for.

Be your own hype man or woman. You can't always count on validation or acknowledgment from others, so tell yourself what you want to hear, be on your own side, comfort yourself, and reassure yourself—even if you don't believe it yet. Some additional small things you can do that will accumulate interest over time and build up your self-esteem—and inadvertently, your self-confidence—are:

- ✧ Make a list of things you're good at (big and small) and be proud of yourself for it.

- ✧ Stop focusing your attention on people who make you feel bad about yourself and gravitate toward people who are actually nice to you.

- ✧ Stop trying to convince people that you are cool, smart, chill, or whatever you think they want you to be or don't want you to be.

- ✧ Stop trying to please everyone with your words or actions; say "no" more often.

- ✧ Challenge yourself to step out of your comfort zone every day with small things and build up to bigger things.

- ✧ Stand up for yourself.

Daily Task

Positive self-talk is advised to patients by licensed therapists as a way to combat negative or distorted thoughts, limiting beliefs, anxiety, stress, and even depression. It's a form of dialectical behavioral therapy (DBT) and it can have a huge impact on your overall mental and physical well-being and performance.

There are many ways to implement positive self-talk into your daily life, and the more you practice it, the easier and more natural it becomes. Negative thinking usually comes in four forms and can even overlap each other or occur simultaneously. The four forms of negative self-talk are:

- ✧ **Personalizing:** Blaming yourself for everything.

  Example thought: *It would be so disappointing and inconsiderate of me if I change my mind.*

  Corrected thought: *I have the right and power to change my mind, even if others might not understand.*

- ✧ **Magnifying:** Focusing so much on the negative— or even blowing them out of proportion—that you ignore any and all the positive aspects.

  Example thought: *I completely embarrassed myself by doing that; I failed.*

  Corrected thought: *It was hard to put myself out there like that, and I'm proud of myself for even trying, even if it didn't turn out the way I expected it to.*

- ✧ **Catastrophizing:** Always expecting the worst despite logic or reason.

  Example thought: *There's no way I'm going to be able to accomplish that, so why even try?*

Corrected thought: *I will try my best; this is a great opportunity to learn something new.*

- ✧ **Polarizing:** You categorize everything as either all good or all bad with no middle ground.

  Example thought: *I didn't clean my room; I am the laziest person in the world.*

  Corrected thought: *I needed that hour of rest today; I'll get to it tomorrow.*

Something you can do every day that ties in with positive self-talk is words of affirmation. I've mentioned this earlier on, but positive affirmations are a set of affirming statements that you tell yourself every day. They could be the same or different every time, and it can form part of your self-care routine.

With that being said, taking care of yourself is very important for your self-esteem and will contribute to building unshakable self-confidence. In order to feel good about yourself, you need to take care of yourself. It reinforces the idea or belief that you are important—which you are—and that your well-being is important to you—as it should be.

And that is why today's task will be to say some positive things *about* yourself *to* yourself. It's going to feel awkward, but push through the cringe and try to really take them in. You can craft your own positive affirmations or choose the ones you like the most from the following list:

- ✧ I'm strong enough and capable of reaching my goals.

~~~~~~

- ✧ I will grow and learn from my mistakes.
- ✧ I don't need to be perfect.
- ✧ I am worthy.
- ✧ I am enough.
- ✧ There is no shame in being wrong or making mistakes.
- ✧ I'm patiently changing into the person I want to become.
- ✧ Getting to know myself is exciting.
- ✧ What others think of me is not my responsibility.
- ✧ I get to decide what's best for me.
- ✧ It's okay that I don't have all the answers.
- ✧ I'm proud of myself.
- ✧ I give myself permission to be myself.
- ✧ I am allowed to feel my emotions.
- ✧ I am open to opportunities and challenges.

Please don't dismiss the power of positive affirmations until you've tried it. You can combine it with the journaling challenge or do it on its own. Choose different ones every day or recite the same ones. There's no wrong way to approach it; whatever works for you. But don't resist doing it because you're afraid of how it *might* make you look or feel—for starters, no one has to know that you're doing it; it's for you, not them. But also, stop assuming things and just give it a go for a couple of days. See how you feel then. Keep doing the things that help you, leave the things that don't—but at least do them first.

Remember, the journey isn't linear; you don't know what the future holds. It's okay to reassess your goals or methods for achieving them if things aren't working out or if you come to find that you want something completely different. You have the right to change your mind.

CHAPTER 3

Day 3   SOCIAL SKILLS

Be courteous to all, but intimate with few, and let those few be well tried before you give them your confidence.

–*George Washington*

✦ ✦ ✦ ✦

Y ou might find you know most (or all) of the "rules" regarding socializing already based on common sense and experience alone, but it can't hurt to go over the principles and theoretical aspects of how to build rapport with others.

However, the last thing I want is for you to find yourself in a situation that's upsetting or severely uncomfortable before you're ready, which is why this chapter is going to go over the basics of socializing, social skills, and social cues. The goal of this chapter is to arm yourself with knowledge, that's all.

Knowing what to say, when to say it, and how to say something; knowing whether a conversation or interaction is going good or bad; and reading non-verbal cues and body language are all important factors to consider. But before you get overwhelmed, our subconsciousness picks up on most of this stuff already. The issue is that your subconscious mind might not always interpret things correctly. By being aware of social cues and how to respond to or interpret them, you ditch the guessing game altogether.

And by improving your social skills, you'll not only experience less social anxiety and be able to build stronger, more meaningful relationships, but it also raises your self-esteem and self-confidence as well as improves overall mental and physical well-being.

The Basics

I find it ironic that social skills are so important, and yet we don't know exactly what they consist of. It's not like we're born grasping a pamphlet explaining this stuff, and it's also not something that's actively taught to us. I mean, the info is there; it's just not really presented to us in the same way as math or biology is. Okay, sure, the mitochondria are the powerhouse of the cell, but how much eye contact do I give before it's considered creepy?

Social skills and etiquette are necessary and important, especially once you enter the realm of young adulthood and beyond (which will come a lot sooner than you realize). One minute you're calling your mom "bro," and the next, you're getting excited in the home appliances aisle for 45 minutes.

My point is that humans are social creatures, and a lack of social skills can hold you back both from a personal and professional standpoint. Poor social skills might, for instance, ruin platonic and romantic relationships and be the cause for you not landing your dream job.

Social skills are how we express our feelings, communicate our thoughts, and relate to those around us. But being aware of how we do this is also important. It's not the easiest concept to wrap your head around. It's a lot to be aware of and pay attention to, and it's not like you've had much experience or time to polish these skills. So try not to feel bad about not having mastered the art of social interaction yet.

Before I go into detail on what individual skills make up "social skills," there are a few things I think are worth keeping in mind. First is that you don't need to get everything *just right* in order to build good and lasting relationships. You don't have to focus intently on just one factor or skill; they all work in unison. And you will mess up from time to time—even the most charismatic people can sometimes come across as rude or uninterested.

There are two main forms of communication, namely verbal and non-verbal. Verbal communication happens when you verbalize your thoughts, feelings, opinions, and ideas, either through talking or writing them down. Non-verbal communication happens through things like eye contact, gestures, facial expressions (including micro-expressions), and body language. Let's break that down.

Verbal Communication

Many argue that your tone and volume of voice don't (or shouldn't) fall under verbal communication. For one, you can't really discern tone or volume through written text—unless they're typing in all caps, then it's safe to assume they are, in fact, shouting. Nonetheless, I do feel like the way you say something does affect how it's received.

A simple example of this is when you look at what happens to the underlying implication of the sentence when you place emphasis on certain words:

"**I** didn't say you should do it." Someone else said it.

"I **didn't** say you should do it." I explicitly told you not to do it.

"I didn't say **you** should do it." I said someone else should.

It's the exact same sentence, but it means something different depending on where you place the stress. Here are the most important individual elements that form part of effective (or ineffective) verbal communication:

- ✧ **Form of language.** Knowing when and how to use either informal or formal language. This doesn't necessarily mean having a large vocabulary with big fancy words. A simple example of this is not cursing or swearing when talking to an elderly lady or your principal.

✧ **Clarity.** Pronouncing words correctly and articulating sentences so you're coherent and easy to understand. Stating your thoughts or ideas with confidence.

✧ **Tone.** Where you place emphasis changes the meaning or intention behind a sentence. This influences how your words are received by others.

✧ **Pitch.** Raising or lowering the pitch in your voice for effect. An example of this is when you're being sarcastic or trying to imitate someone else.

✧ **Pace.** Talking slowly might indicate that you're bored or uninterested, while talking fast can mean you're excited or angry. It speaks to the energy you're exerting while in conversation.

✧ **Volume.** Talking loudly or softly. Again, talking loudly might mean you're fired up, excited, passionate, or angry. Talking softly can mean the conversation is more intimate or even private—or that you're just shy.

The way you combine all these elements will depend on the situation you're in, your mood, the environment, the people you're talking to, and so on. The way you talk to your sibling is different from the way you talk to your parents or a teacher, for example.

Verbal communication, simply put, is the physical act of conscious communication—you turn your internal dialogue into an external one. The type of language you use, along with clarity, tone, pitch, pace, and volume, are just tools you can use to effectively drive forth the intended meaning behind your words. The way you use these tools can also differ depending on who you're talking to and the circumstances surrounding the interaction.

Misunderstandings happen when the message you're trying to convey gets lost in translation somehow. This most often happens when there's a discrepancy between what you're saying and how you're saying it—or how you're using the different elements.

There are a lot of other things that affect how you present yourself to the world verbally, but this is the basics of verbal communication.

Non-Verbal Communication

Non-verbal communication is how we send messages or convey information—either about ourselves or in reaction to others—through things like eye contact, body language, facial expressions, gestures, and even our appearance.

Did you know that 80% of communication happens non-verbally (Hull, 2016)? This means that the actual words that come out of your mouth only account for 20% of overall interaction. You could effectively have full-blown conversations with others without saying a single word.

Before we break down the elements of non-verbal communication, I want to talk a bit about first impressions. There's a famous quote from both Oscar Wilde and Will Rogers that you've likely heard by this point already: "You never get a second chance to make a first impression." (1966)

I mean... yes and no. From a literal standpoint, sure, you only get one shot at a first impression—unless the person forgot they met you in the first place. However, I think first impressions are overrated. You're going to tell me that you've never met someone, immediately didn't like them, but after spending some time with them, thought, *They're actually pretty cool?*

First impressions are a thing, but they don't hold nearly as much weight in casual everyday settings as people imply they do. Humans have a natural tendency to judge, and first impressions are a prime example of this. You can't possibly pretend to know me based on the first two minutes of meeting me (the average time "experts" say a first impression lasts). You can make judgments, assumptions, and form opinions, but once again, none of these are based on facts and all of it is subject to change over time.

I only bring this up to shed light on the fact that even if you mess up a first impression due to social anxiety, low confidence, or any other reason, you're not irredeemable; you're not doomed.

Here are the most important elements of non-verbal communication:

✧ **Facial expressions.** You can tell a lot about what or how someone is feeling simply by looking at their face. Facial expressions for emotions can differ between cultures around the world, but the main ones (happiness, sadness, anger, and fear) are pretty universal and usually hard to hide.

✧ **Gestures.** These are any deliberate movements you use to add emotion or more influence behind your words, such as pointing, waving your hands around, rubbing your eyes, pinching the bridge of your nose, and so on. But it can also include things like giving someone a thumbs up, high-fiving, and so on.

✧ **Body language.** Your posture and subconscious body movements also signify your reaction or emotions. For example, crossing your arms is said to be a defensive gesture, fidgeting with something could indicate nervousness, and so on.

✧ **Eye contact.** Facial expression and emotion rely heavily on our eyes—they are the windows to the soul, after all. But they also play a big role in non-verbal communication through eye contact. Eye contact is important for establishing a connection.

✧ **Physical appearance.** It's not something we as a society should be proud of, but the way you look does have an impact on how people view and judge you. Your style is an extension of your personality, and by no means should you alter the way you dress or how you style your hair based on what other people may or may not think of you. The implication here is more on neatness and cleanliness. However, everyone has a different idea of what a neat and tidy appearance looks like—or should look like.

You don't need to be an expert on the theory of communication to communicate effectively. However, knowing the basics of verbal versus non-verbal communication can open up a whole new world where you're able to tell whether someone is authentic (their words match up with their behaviors) or being deceptive with malicious intent.

Conversation Skills

My mom always said, "There's a difference between hearing and listening." And while I used to roll my eyes at the time, as an adult, I get it. What she really meant was there's a difference between simply listening to respond and listening to connect.

A conversation can be superficial. You don't have to form a deep and meaningful connection with the person who happens to be seated next to you on the bus or the guy who asks you if you know where the nearest bathroom is at the doctor's office. But if you are looking to start any type of long-lasting relationship with anyone, communication will be a big part of that.

There are four types of conversation:

⬥ **Discourse.** A one-way cooperative conversation where the purpose is to deliver information. A teacher presenting a lesson or presentation is a good example of this.

⬥ **Diatribe.** A one-way competitive conversation where the purpose is to inspire or express emotions (usually negative ones). An example of this is when your parents express concern over your latest test results.

⬥ **Dialogue.** A cooperative two-way conversation where the purpose is to exchange information and build a relationship. For example, two friends discussing what they did over summer break, there's a back-and-forth exchange of questions and answers that spawn from genuine curiosity and interest.

✧ **Debate.** A competitive two-way conversation where the purpose is to win an argument or convince someone. You and your sibling disagree over which fast food restaurant has the best fries. You're arguing each other's reasonings and opinions in a way that's non-aggressive.

There's a time and place for each of these types of conversations; in fact, all of them are necessary depending on what you're trying to accomplish. They allow you to express your emotions, connect, and even disagree with people respectfully. That's the key word here: Respectfully.

I tend to agree with the phrase, "Respect is earned," but you can still lead with it and react accordingly. A rule I follow is that if I'm the one initiating contact or starting a conversation, I'm always respectful. Most of the time, people return the same energy, but I'm not going to continue being respectful if my respect is met with disrespect. And if someone comes up to me and doesn't lead with respect, I'm not wasting time or energy on the conversation because they clearly don't value me as a person.

There are some soft skills that come into play when engaging in conversation, most of which fall under verbal and non-verbal communication skills, such as eye contact, tone of voice, body language, yada, yada. But there are also things like active listening, reciprocity, social cues, and a host of other things that are important for engaging in a conversation and keeping others engaged as well.

We went over what verbal and non-verbal communication is—most of it is pretty straightforward and you probably understand and do most of it without trying already—but now we're going to break down the less obvious aspects of having a conversation and establishing a relationship.

Social Strategies

Maybe your problem isn't actually with reading social cues but with initiating conversation and actually getting to a point where the interaction means something. You grasp the mechanics behind social interactions and have a good idea of how to participate, but it never seems to get past the small talk phase.

A good conversation is one that's pleasantly memorable; you wish you could've stayed longer, talked more, and can't wait to talk to them again. And yes, it's possible to feel all these feelings in regard to someone you don't necessarily want to pursue romantically.

You'd obviously feel more connected to someone who shares the same values, morals, and interests with you than you would with someone who doesn't. But that doesn't mean you can't form deep connections with someone who thinks differently than you. In fact, it's usually the people who bring up a different perspective that we might not have thought of that intrigues us.

Granted, if someone says something that you wholeheartedly disagree with, you might not want to be friends with them—and if they have extremely negative beliefs and values that are objectively immoral, you definitely shouldn't be. However, sometimes a good debate with someone who sees things in a different light is exhilarating and refreshing. If you only surround yourself with people who agree with you and never engage with people who don't, you risk being trapped in an echo chamber where you'll never be challenged to question yourself at all.

With that being said, there are some things that might be the cause for you not being able to hold a conversation or make it evolve into something deeper over time. Now, you might not even be aware that you're falling into these potholes, or it might not be something that's in your control, but keep in mind that you can work on improving them, which is the entire premise of this book:

- ✧ **Social anxiety.** Yes, yes, this isn't exactly new information. You've known about your social anxiety for a long time. But this *is* the most prominent reason for not being able to build or advance meaningful relationships.

  Building a relationship with someone relies on your willingness to open up and be vulnerable. And with the probability of saying or doing something embarrassing being so high, you avoid it at all cost, which means avoiding social interaction altogether. The issue isn't in the act of doing or saying something embarrassing; it's in the fear surrounding it. You think you won't be able to redeem yourself after.

- ✧ **Fear of rejection.** Awkward moments and silences are a natural part of communication between one topic and the next—it's a turning point. No one likes awkward silences, but in your mind, it's a sign of rejection. And rejection is humiliating to most people.

Whether your cognitive distortions make you believe that someone is going to scoff in your face or flat-out ignore you when you try to talk to them, the fear of rejection is very real and can lead to social anxiety and, by extension, social withdrawal.

✧ **Lack of social skills.** Whether it's you not pulling your weight or them, a lack of social skills is a conversation extinguisher. It's hard to participate in a conversation when it seems like one of the participants is totally disengaged or uninterested.

Because that's what it looks like from the outside. Someone who lacks social skills may come across as rude when in reality, they just don't know what to say or how to reciprocate. Either way, it will lead to an abrupt end of any dialogue.

In order to have productive conversations that gradually evolve from generalized small talk to heart-to-heart personal deep dives, there are a few things to keep in mind. You're aiming for dialogue (from the four types of conversation), meaning that it's a two-way street, give and take. But how much is too much to give? How much is not enough?

Here are a few strategies and general guidelines to keep in mind and follow when talking to someone you really want to establish a continued relationship with:

✧ **Actively listening.** I don't mean just processing what someone is saying; I mean taking their facial expressions and body language into consideration as well as paying attention to what they're *not* saying. This prevents you from judging, jumping to conclusions, and assuming what other people are thinking or feeling.

For example, if someone says, "Your hair looks different today," unless there's something in their tone of voice or body language that suggests they're trying to mock you, don't just assume they are. They simply made a statement.

Actively paying attention to what someone is saying also includes not getting distracted by your phone or anything else and not interrupting them. This will help you remember what they're saying for future reference. You can also ensure you really understood what they were saying by rephrasing their words and asking clarifying questions if you're not sure that you're understanding correctly.

✧ **Ask open-ended questions.** Questions that can only be answered by a simple yes or no answer aren't the plague, and you don't have to recast or avoid asking a question entirely just because the answer is closed-ended. But you can follow it up with a question that requires a more elaborate answer. If someone says they've never heard of the band you like, ask them what type of music they're into and recommend a few songs from the band that fit that vibe.

And when someone asks you a yes or no type of question, try to add some additional yet relevant information. For example, if someone asks you if you like a certain band, instead of saying just yes or no, add on why you do or don't like them.

- ✧ **Be genuinely curious.** This kind of ties in with the previous bullet point, just on a much deeper level. Asking questions is a great way to get to know people, but showing genuine curiosity about other people's lives is more than that.

  What I mean by being genuinely curious is, when they reveal something about themselves that you find interesting, don't just nod and say, "Oh, that's cool." Be curious! For example, let's say someone mentions that they dabble in music production; ask them if you can listen to some of their stuff, ask them how they got into it, what software they're using, how long they've been doing it, or if it's just a hobby or something they're serious about. Be excited for them, hype them up, and tell them if you're impressed.

  However, don't force it. People can tell when you're being insincere. So this should only be done if and when you come across someone whose hobbies or skills you're truly fascinated by. Just make your curiosity apparent.

✧ **Relate.** Being able to relate to others is the most powerful way to form a connection. And this can happen in many aspects, but most commonly, it's similar or shared interests, hobbies, opinions, experiences, beliefs, and values. However, relating to someone doesn't guarantee a healthy, strong, or long-lasting relationship.

But it is a good way to open up a dialogue or initial conversation in order to figure out whether or not you are compatible. You might see someone drawing a character from your favorite anime series and you compliment them on their artistic talents. Maybe you become best friends, or maybe you realize after a while that besides having something in common, you don't really enjoy their company. But the only way to find out is to take that initial leap of faith.

✧ **Keep it light.** Don't reveal your deepest secrets or your entire life story in the first five minutes of introducing yourself. Small talk, although tedious and sometimes dull, is necessary. It can actually reveal a lot about you and the person you're talking to.

For instance, it can reveal whether someone has a good sense of humor, their communication style, or personality traits, and oftentimes provides us with useful information. So while small talk is usually about trivial, unimportant, or light-hearted topics, it lays the groundwork for future interactions.

You don't know them well enough to decide whether it's worth investing more time into the relationship. Small talk is limbo, in this case, a period of uncertainty as well as discovery.

And while you certainly can comment on the weather, there are also plenty of other menial topics to discuss: Movies, TV shows or series, music, and books; sporting events and championships, your favorite sports teams, exercise routines; favorite food, restaurants; culture; travel; celebrity gossip; hobbies and interests; family, where you grew up, the list goes one.

✧ **Go with it.** You don't—and shouldn't—do all the heavy lifting. Give the other person a chance to speak, ask questions, and reciprocate. Don't force abrupt subject changes and don't come on too strong with rapid-fire interrogational questions about their lives, hobbies, interests, and so on.

Let the conversation unfold naturally, and if a pause or awkward silence does inevitably happen, allow it to. Nothing is going to happen other than your brain making you hyper-aware that things are awkward right now. Building your tolerance to a point where you're able to endure the occasional awkward moment is a superpower!

Additionally, if you do get the vibe that someone might not be open to a conversation, don't take it personally, and don't force them into one. Don't keep on talking to someone if they aren't actively contributing for whatever reason.

✧ **Reflect.** Reflecting on the type and "quality" of the conversations you're currently having will help you improve your conversational skills and strategy. Think back on the conversations you've had over the past couple of days. How did you feel directly afterward? How did it start, and where did it end up? At which moments did it seem to be going well? What happened? Were there any moments where it seemed like it wasn't going well, and why do you think so?

The information from these questions might be able to give you an idea of what you're doing right, as well as areas that need improving. Be careful not to answer them with assumptions or negative beliefs, and be rational and realistic—look for evidence to confirm or deny your answers.

Daily Task

There are many resources available that will help you improve your social skills, including books (like the one you're reading right now), podcasts, blogs, and worksheets. Your task for today is going to be broken up into a few simple steps that you might have to do over a period of time.

First, you're going to do some observing. Without changing anything about what you're doing during conversations today (or tomorrow if you're reading this late in the afternoon or right before bed), you're going to simply pay attention. Make notes after every social interaction if you're afraid you might forget things, such as others' reactions to something you did or said, your own reactions and body language, and so on.

At the end of the day, write down each area of social interaction that you believe you struggle with based on what sticks out to you (or your notes). Maybe it's reading and interpreting body language, active listening (or constantly interrupting people), taking part in group conversations, conflict resolution, and so on. It might help to ask for honest feedback from people who know you well, but try not to get discouraged or defensive when they list things you didn't even think or realize you do (or don't do). Though, you can also phrase the question as if you're asking for advice since some people might be afraid to offend you with a list of things you're doing "wrong."

Next, you're going to remind yourself that socializing is a skill and that you will improve with time and practice. Isolate one thing from your list of social skills that you can benefit from improving, and think of ways to do so. For example, if you find that you generally don't pay attention to people's facial expressions, challenge yourself to scan their faces every now and then and take in their expression at that specific moment (their eyebrows are raised, they're smiling, etc.). Even if you don't consciously know what it means, just noting or becoming aware of their facial expressions will give you a certain vibe.

Once you've improved that one area, then move on to the next one. Set small milestones and give yourself a pat on the back when you reach them.

You might have to do some additional research on social skills, cues, norms, and etiquette since I can't possibly cover everything there is to it in a single book, let alone a chapter, but you'll at least be able to get somewhere with what's covered here. And remember, perfection is overrated, not to mention subjective—aim for progress and you'll never fail.

CHAPTER 4

Day 4 SOCIAL ANXIETY

> **"**
>
> *Courage is resistance to fear, mastery of fear, not absence of fear.*

–Mark Twain

✦ ✦ ✦ ✦

H umans are social creatures; we need connection and interaction to live a fulfilling life. Being afraid of rejection or embarrassment can definitely form part of social anxiety, but in its most severe form, it's a debilitating phobia that can present itself as physical symptoms like dizziness or full-blown panic attacks even during low-risk, casual, or fleeting interactions.

Common Triggers

Social anxiety doesn't just randomly happen one Tuesday morning. There are lots of catalytic reasons for someone experiencing severe social anxiety, such as meeting new people, having to perform in front of a crowd, or fear of being embarrassed or humiliated. However, there's a difference between just experiencing nervousness and having social anxiety.

Social anxiety goes beyond being shy or feeling nervous in group settings or around people you don't know. Someone with a more severe form of social anxiety might go so far as to skip school, avoid grocery shopping, or cross the street when someone is about to walk past them on the sidewalk— they fear social situations *so* much that the mere thought of someone potentially greeting them is too much to bear.

Unsurprisingly, the root cause of severe or debilitating social anxiety is trauma (either domestic or social) related to negative past experiences such as having been bullied, teased, rejected, ridiculed, abandoned, and abused. Typically, the symptoms of social anxiety start in early childhood, but it's also possible to develop it later in life as a teenager or even as an adult.

Having social anxiety usually interferes with every aspect of a person's daily life and their ability to function normally. They don't simply get jittery right before they give a speech; they have sleepless nights about it for weeks or even months in advance. They worry about potentially being in a situation where they have to communicate with others—and they will go out of their way to avoid it at all costs.

It is possible to overcome social anxiety, but know that it will require you to face your fears (in small, manageable increments) and build up a tolerance to your triggers and reactions. And that is exactly what we'll be going over in this chapter. And even if you don't have social anxiety, these techniques could still be useful for putting yourself out there if you struggle with nervousness or shyness.

Managing Symptoms

The whole reason why social anxiety makes it so hard to function is because of the symptoms. A trigger sets off your fight or flight response, which makes your body pump out adrenaline like it's going out of style. This leads to physical symptoms such as shortness of breath, upset stomach (nausea or an intense feeling of "butterflies" that doesn't go away within seconds), shaky voice or hands, tight chest, fast heart rate, sweating or hot flashes, and feeling dizzy or faint. All of these symptoms, stacked on top of the mental aspects of social anxiety, could cause a full nervous system meltdown, resulting in a panic attack.

It's automatic and unavoidable; every fiber in your being is screaming at you to run because the situation is dangerous— even if you consciously know that's not true most of the time. By re-regulating your nervous system when the involuntary fight or flight response kicks in, you reduce the symptoms. And by reducing the symptoms, you're better able to face the fear and eventually even overcome it.

A few ways you can re-regulate your nervous system and manage the physical manifestations of social anxiety in the moment are as follows:

✧ **Breathing and relaxation exercises.** This is arguably the most effective way to relieve the uncomfortable and alarming symptoms of social anxiety quickly. All there is to it is taking a big breath in (the deepest you can manage) and slowly breathing out. Try to elongate the time it takes to breathe in and out with each breath, so start with two seconds per breath and work your way up to ten seconds or longer. While you do this, try to become aware of some areas or muscle groups where the tension might be residing (the jaw, shoulders, hips, etc.), and focus on releasing it. Picture the tension leaving your body as you exhale.

You might have to excuse yourself if you're feeling really overwhelmed and do this in a bathroom or somewhere else that's private, but you can also do it on the spot if you feel comfortable enough to do so.

✧ **Grounding.** A common tactic usually used in people who are on the verge of an anxiety or panic attack, but it works for social anxiety as well. It's called the 5-4-3-2-1 coping technique and it requires you to (when you feel dysregulated or overwhelmed) name five things you can see, four things you can touch, three things you can hear, two things you can smell, and one thing you can taste.

The goal of this exercise is to bring you back to the present moment instead of letting the panic or fear take over and progressively worsen.

✧ **Challenge your thoughts.** Break down your thoughts and fears and, using logic and objectivity, debunk them or challenge them. In the case of social anxiety, negative thoughts and fears are usually rooted in doing or saying something that you believe others might judge or ridicule you for. More on this later.

✧ **Acknowledge your symptoms.** Admitting to yourself what you're feeling and how these emotions are physically showing up in your body can bring comfort and relief in and of itself—to some degree. This could look like thinking something as simple as, "I am feeling really anxious right now because I'm about to talk to someone I don't know," or "There's a pit in my stomach and I feel dizzy because of my social anxiety."

You could also pair this with some form of reassurance phrase or affirmation like "I'm not in danger" or "This feeling will pass; just breathe."

Relieving symptoms of social anxiety in stressful situations is very helpful, but there are also some lifestyle changes you can make that will reduce your social anxiety in general and in the long term:

✧ **Diet and exercise.** Dietary changes don't have to be drastic or restrictive. Even small changes like limiting caffeine while making sure you're adding protein, fiber, and fruits or vegetables to most daily meals can make a difference.

Exercise includes any form of movement, bonus points if it's actually something you enjoy doing, like hiking (or just taking a walk), totem tennis (swingball), or jumping on a trampoline. It doesn't have to include repetitive movements, weight lifting, or excessive sweating. Increased activity not only takes your mind off of the things making you anxiously overthink, but it also decreases long-term muscle tension and encourages the production of stress-relieving hormones. It even helps you manage future nervous system reactions to perceived threats, meaning that it literally helps you deal with triggers relating to social anxiety (Ratey, 2019).

✧ **Sleep.** It's hard to get a good night's sleep if you have social anxiety, and ironically, a lack of sleep (or sleep deprivation) actually worsens your symptoms of social anxiety—it also takes a toll on your general mental and physical health.

Sleep deprivation or difficulties with sleep that persist and don't improve when you're taking measures to reduce overall anxiety should always be taken seriously and checked out by a medical professional.

✧ **Meditation.** There's a lot of debate about what meditation really is and how it should be done. I'm here to tell you that, once again, there are no rules. If the way you approach it works, it's worth doing.

Now, there are many ways to meditate, some more serious than others. But you don't have to be sitting cross-legged, eyes closed, with your thumb and middle finger touching on your knees for hours to benefit from it. Meditation is simply the act of focused concentration and staying in the present moment. You pick something neutral to focus on (like your breathing, a phrase or mantra, the texture on the wall, or your movements) and you stay there for a bit—as long as you need to.

Your mind will get bored and wander; when this happens, you gently nudge it back to whatever your neutral focal point is. You can also adapt this so you're focusing intently on whatever mundane tasks you're doing, like walking, brushing your teeth, packing the dishwasher, and so on. Feel the pebbles crunching under your feet, the smell of the rose bush you're passing, and hear the wind rushing past you. Feel the coolness of the minty toothpaste in your mouth, taste it, the circular motions of the bristles. Just pay attention to life!

Meditation works to reduce symptoms of anxiety by reducing or eliminating mind clutter and slowing your thoughts so you can process emotions and experiences better. It puts you into a deep state of relaxation which results in a feeling of peace and harmony between mind and body. And this state of practiced tranquility becomes almost like muscle memory which you can pull from during stressful times. It's a healthy and effective long-term coping mechanism.

◇ **Therapy.** If your social anxiety is severe and nothing you try to implement or do is helping in any capacity, seeking professional help is the only remaining option. A licensed therapist or counselor will provide more specialized and personal insight into your situation. They will work with you to build the tools and skills necessary to overcome social anxiety and even help you find the right medications if needed.

✧ **Positive affirmations.** Yes, I know I've mentioned this before; I'm telling you again for good reason. Positive affirmations are a popular cognitive behavioral therapy tool used to treat mental disorders such as depression and anxiety. It involves looking in the mirror and rehearsing a list of nice things about yourself. And while it sounds silly and embarrassing, it has a surprisingly high success rate—the mind is a very powerful thing.

Do you know why positive affirmations work so well? Because if you tell yourself something over and over again, eventually, you'll believe it. But this works in reverse, too. Meaning that negative voice in your head that has been there since you can remember has been bamboozling you this entire time!

This is also how your brain creates biases. When you don't see yourself as worthy of love, respect, friendship, or support, you're less likely to value your existence and your contributions. You don't see why there's a need to look after yourself, so you don't. You think no one would value you, not because of their actions, but because, in your mind, you're not worth the effort in the first place. Every small and potentially innocent gesture from someone else gets twisted in your mind and serves as further evidence that you're simply not enough.

Overcoming Social Anxiety

I don't know if you've ever looked at a word and thought you misspelled it. And then you look it up and you actually didn't, but it still looks wrong. It's called "wordnesia" and the psychology behind it is interesting. When we read, we don't focus on the individual letters; rather, our brains automatically interpret it as a unit (i.e., a word). But when you become hyper-focused on the individual letters, you temporarily lose the ability to see the word as a whole. So, in your mind, it's no longer a word you recognize, if that makes any sense.

My hypothesis is that this is more or less what happens when you hyper-focus on a specific trait, attribute, or feature of yourself. Your brain blows it out of proportion and you're left with the result: anxiety.

The first step to overcoming social anxiety is to identify your triggers, and the second step is to find the techniques that help reduce the symptoms in both the short and long term. But in order to overcome it, you will have to face it. Unfortunately, there's no way around this one. In fact, the more you avoid your triggers, emotional reactions, and physical symptoms, the stronger they get.

Avoiding the things that cause an adverse negative physical and emotional response within us is encoded into our DNA. It's as much a part of you as the color of your eyes and the thickness of your fingernails are. It's a survival instinct.

Challenge Your Beliefs

The only constant in life is change. Your thoughts, beliefs, assumptions, and expectations are always changing. Or at least, it should. That's why public opinion, laws, legislation, and the status quo have continuously changed over the course of human history. Because we are constantly learning and discovering new information through studies, philosophers, and medicine. Because it's good to question things, consider alternative perspectives, outcomes, impacts, and decide to do better–be better.

We can look at some ideologies of our ancestors, the beliefs and behaviors that were considered "normal" in those times and grimace. We use that knowledge and information to change the way we do things, the way we see things, and we use it to literally change the world!

But won't actively challenging every thought and belief you have cause even more self-doubt and therefore lower your self-esteem even further? No, but it is a slippery slope. *Challenging* your beliefs (if you're going about it the right way) can strengthen and change your opinions and worldview for the better. *Overthinking* it can lead to mind clutter and self-doubt.

This is why I'm going to tell you how you should go about challenging your thoughts in a way that stops the cycle in its tracks instead of just branching off, making everything worse.

What is the difference between knowledge and belief? Knowledge requires evidence; it's rooted in reality; it's objective. Belief is conceptual knowledge, a strongly held opinion, meaning that even though something might be true, it can't be backed up with proof, and–more often than not—it's subjective (it can be influenced by thoughts, emotions, and assumptions).

An example that might help differentiate the two can be as simple as this: Imagine you're at a store, and you know this store very well. Based on your *knowledge*, you know they have cool ranch Doritos because you physically see it on the shelf, you can pick it up, and you can rip open the bag and eat it (assuming you're going to pay for it). However, that's not to say they're going to have it in stock the next time you come to this exact store. You may *believe* they have it based on your past experiences of buying it, but that doesn't necessarily make it true.

Being able to identify whether a thought is actual knowledge or just a belief is important because it will help you sift through your inner dialogue to find the limiting or negative beliefs that should be challenged in the first place.

Let's take a singular limiting belief that you may or may not have on a regular basis and go through the process of challenging it together. You can obviously swap out the context of the belief if you already have a different one in mind at this moment.

The limiting belief is: "No one likes me; that's why I have no friends."

Step 1: Pause. Let the thought resonate for a second. Really consider the words, the implications it has had on you, and the consequences.

Step 2: Determine whether it's knowledge or belief. Correlation doesn't equal causation. Ask yourself questions about your belief, such as: What proof do you have that this thought is objectively true? Can you read minds? Has every person you've ever met outright told you that they didn't like you, or is it merely a conclusion you drew based on their behavior? Just because you have no friends doesn't automatically mean it's because no one likes you.

Step 3: Consider the alternatives. Could it be possible that maybe people don't interact with you as much because you seem standoffish due to your belief that no one likes you? Could it be possible that other people are unsure of you because your fear of judgment makes it so you never reveal who you truly are? Could it be that your unwillingness to be vulnerable makes you look unapproachable?

Step 4: Gather new evidence. Now that you're considering alternative reasons for your belief, determine which ones are actually true. Think back to when you were in a setting where your belief seemed to be stronger than ever and find proof that supports the alternative reasons for the belief. Using our example, you can try to remember (in as much detail as you can) what your body language was like. Were you huddled in a corner, too scared to join the conversation? Were there opportunities to join the conversion that you didn't take? Did others maybe try to get you to join in by asking questions but your responses were short and detached? Did you maybe seem disinterested and only gave one-sided responses without throwing questions back at them?

Step 5: Experiment. You can test out your new-found beliefs and theories to solidify them. The next time the opportunity presents itself, change one small thing in the way you approach the situation and see if it makes any difference or supports your alternative belief. With our example, you can be more engaged in a group conversation by nodding along, expressing opposing opinions, and asking questions. Even if you're not in a group discussion, maybe you overhear someone say something to someone else that interests you and you—politely—pipe in with a question, statement, or simply agree with the person.

Step 6: Move on to the next limiting belief. Don't try to conquer all your limiting beliefs at once, as this can be overwhelming. It might take some time, practice, and courage, but one by one, you'll discover, debunk, and rectify the limiting beliefs that are holding you back in life. And even make a few friends along the way.

Focus on breaking down complex thoughts into one sentence and then deconstruct them using the steps outlined above. Write down your limiting beliefs as well as the process of dissecting and rationalizing them; when you try to do it in your head, things can get jumbled or spiral into different directions resulting in overthinking and additional mind clutter.

It could also help to start with thoughts that are a little less triggering and also do it while you're in a neutral headspace. Trying to change your perspective is hard on a good day, so make sure you're able to confront uncomfortable truths that come from challenging your thoughts. It could also help going over this process with someone you trust and who won't judge you; they could even answer some questions you may be stuck on or help you uproot personal biases (we all have them and it can be hard to spot them ourselves).

In the beginning, challenging a thought can feel forced or inauthentic. Like you're gaslighting yourself. But that's the thing; the whole reason challenging your thoughts is necessary is because you gaslit yourself into a limiting belief in the first place!

Try to give your mind some time to process all the new information and epiphanies that come up after challenging a belief. Do something that temporarily distracts you, like playing a video game for a couple of hours, helping your mom with dinner, or playing with a pet.

Exposure Therapy

How do you overcome a literal disorder that makes you believe and react as though making small talk with a stranger is equivalent to coming face-to-face with a grizzly bear? You slowly convince your brain that the threat is not as severe as it thinks or believes it to be.

It's called gradual exposure therapy or systematic desensitization. What it does is build your tolerance to triggers and emotional reactions by facing something, starting with the least fear-inducing situation and working your way up once you're ready and comfortable.

Basically, taking itty-bitty steps at a time and making gradual progress. Gradual exposure therapy is used in conjunction with relaxation techniques to help you stay regulated during the entire process.

The goal of gradual exposure therapy is to condition you or to help you build resilience so you're able to eventually face your fears—or in this case, social anxiety—without getting overwhelmed or inducing a panic attack which can be very traumatic and worsen your fear.

When implementing this desensitization technique, it helps to think of your fear in terms of levels. A level one fear is something that makes you feel the least amount of discomfort or anxiety, and obviously, a level ten fear would be something that causes the most adverse reaction.

The first step is to identify your personal level one and level ten fear. For example, a level one fear might be raising your hand in class, and a level ten fear is being at a party surrounded by mostly strangers and not knowing what to do with yourself (just the thought of it makes your stomach flip).

The next step is to identify all the levels of fear between one and ten. So level two could be seeing someone you know in public, level three is meeting someone new, and so on. The levels of fear get progressively more anxiety-inducing. Once you have your list, phase two can commence. Phase two is when you start exposing yourself to those fears in a controlled way.

What I mean by facing your fears in a controlled way is imagining a scenario of your fear taking place and then keeping yourself calm with your preferred breathing or relaxation technique as you do it. Rinse and repeat until the thought of your level-one fear no longer induces a physical or emotional reaction anymore.

Only once you're able to visualize or imagine yourself doing the thing you fear while being able to stay calm do you move on to real life. Using the example of a level one fear being raising your hand in class, the next time the opportunity presents itself, try to calm your nerves and do it. If the anxiety gets too bad and you're unable to keep calm and actually do it in the moment, it's okay! Go back to simply visualizing it while practicing your calming technique. Try again when you feel ready to.

Eventually, you'll do your level one fear for the first time. Then you'll do it more confidently, and then you'll do it without fear at all. At that point, you're done; you've overcome your level-one fear. Now you'll repeat this process for your level two fear until you reach level ten.

Some fears, however, might be hard or illogical to try and face or recreate in real life. For example, falling down or tripping in front of people. Please don't purposely trip or fall. Instead, what you can do is stick to the visualization practice while practicing staying calm, and if it does happen at some point, try to remember your training. Just breathe; it's going to be fine.

Daily Task

Gradual exposure therapy is, as the name suggests, gradual. Meaning it can take weeks—if not longer—until you're able to face a single fear in real life. So your task for today is to graze against the boundaries of your comfort zone in other areas of your life that may not be directly related to your social anxiety.

Stepping out of your comfort zone will translate or bleed into other areas and build your confidence and self-esteem. Get creative with it. Here's a list of things you can do to push the boundaries of what you're comfortable with (in a good way). Challenge yourself to do one of them today, or pick a few and do all of them over the span of a month:

- ✧ Take a cold shower.
- ✧ Change the route you take to school.
- ✧ Visit a new place (park, street, shopping center, etc.).
- ✧ Write using your non-dominant hand.
- ✧ Listen to a song you've never heard before (or don't like).
- ✧ Try out a new recipe.
- ✧ Go vegan for the day (if you're not already).
- ✧ Film yourself dancing or practicing a skill.
- ✧ Take a picture of yourself every day for a month.
- ✧ Change up your morning, evening, or workout routine.
- ✧ Ditch social media for a day.
- ✧ Start that creative project you've been meaning to do.
- ✧ Rearrange your room furniture.
- ✧ Sit in a place you've never sat before (a different couch, an ottoman, or a specific spot on the floor).
- ✧ Pick up a new skill or interest.
- ✧ Do something differently from how you've been doing it before.
- ✧ Change the scent of your shampoo, deodorant, lotion, body spray, or perfume.

◇ Order something you've never had before from a restaurant or fast food joint.

◇ Introduce yourself to a stranger (who you'll likely never see again).

◇ Reach out to someone you've fallen out of touch with or haven't spoken to in a while.

◇ Take on volunteer work that has to do with interacting with other humans.

◇ Eat at a restaurant by yourself.

◇ Ask someone for a recommendation (their favorite book, movie, or video game, for example).

◇ Sign up for a group class or extracurricular activity that you think you might enjoy.

◇ Give someone a compliment.

◇ Tell someone you know how much you appreciate them.

◇ Invite a classmate you don't know that well over to your house.

Get comfortable with change, tension, awkwardness, and the unknown. Someone once said, "If it doesn't challenge you, it doesn't change you." The only certainty in life is uncertainty; once you're able to laugh in the face of discomfort, you can take on the world!

CHAPTER 5

Day 5   CONNECTION

*Be who you are and say what
you feel, because those who
mind don't matter and those
who matter don't mind.*

–Bernard Baruch

✦ ✦ ✦ ✦

ll the small talk in the world isn't enough to establish
a genuine, deep, and meaningful connection with
someone. That's because the connection is based
on mutual respect, trust, commitment, interest, and value.
All of these are difficult to accomplish when you have social
anxiety, lack certain social skills, or have some form of past
trauma or negative experiences that you feel you need to
actively protect yourself from.

Again, it's not your fault, but it is your responsibility to improve yourself, learn, and heal from your past. You can't force deeper connections with people, but you can place yourself in a position where it's more likely to happen.

Empathy and Understanding

Empathy is an interpersonal skill that involves being able to recognize, understand, and relate to others and their emotions and behaviors, even if you may think they're being dramatic or overreacting. It allows you to support others through certain situations and make them feel better.

Just because you're not afraid of frogs doesn't mean there aren't people who find them terrifying. A person with empathy isn't going to shame or belittle someone else for reacting differently than they themselves would've.

The difference between empathy and sympathy is understanding and shared experience. You feel sympathy if you see a stranger crying and empathy if you can relate to why they're crying (and you feel the need to support them in some capacity). So while sympathy can certainly turn into empathy, ultimately, they are separate things.

There are three stages of empathy:

1. **Cognitive empathy.** When you can identify someone else's emotional state (you see them crying and recognize that they are sad).

2. **Emotional empathy.** The ability to share or engage with the emotions of others (their emotions affect your own).

3. **Compassionate empathy.** When you actively try to reduce the emotional turmoil of others (you ask what's wrong or try to cheer them up).

There should obviously be some boundaries around the amount of empathy you are capable of showing at certain times. If you are going through a rough time, you can't always be there and support others to the best of your abilities. But empathy, along with body language awareness, does play a big part in human connection—and it should be reciprocated.

Body Language Awareness

I feel like it's appropriate to start with being able to read someone's body language or at least be aware of it and what it might indicate. It's important to note that reading body language is not an accurate way of determining someone's thoughts or feelings. Many people take reading body language way too seriously.

Reading body language is subjective, and a lot of the meanings overlap or even contradict each other. What I mean by this is that someone could scratch their nose, which, in body language lingo, means they're being insincere or dishonest when in reality, they just had an itchy nose at the wrong moment. For this reason, you should never 100% rely on body language alone to try and figure out what others are thinking or feeling.

Here's a breakdown of the most common body language cues and what they could potentially mean when they happen during a conversation:

✧ **Eye contact.** There's no correct amount of eye contact to give or receive. Too much eye contact can leave you or the other person feeling uncomfortable, and too little might mean you or the other person is distracted, uncomfortable, uninterested, or trying to hide true thoughts or feelings. The eyebrows are also typically pretty involved with emotions. For example, upturned eyebrows (think cartoon-style sadness) only happen during genuine sadness, empathy, or concern and are hard to replicate without real emotion tied to it (unless you're Amelia Clark, she manages to pull this off quite flawlessly).

✧ **The mouth.** Pursed lips usually signal disagreement, disapproval, or disgust. Lip biting could mean the person is stressed or anxious, and covering one's mouth can be a way to hide certain emotions from showing. Then there's the obvious: smiling. A genuine smile is one that "reaches the eyes," which is just code for when the eyes are engaging in it as well (narrowing and creasing in the outer corners). When the eyes are not actively participating in the smile, it could mean that the person is just trying to be polite; it doesn't mean that they're being fake—especially if they do this when they don't really know you very well.

✧ **Hands, arms, and legs.** Crossed arms or legs can be an indication that someone is defensive, dismissive, or disinterested. While clasping one's hands behind the back could signal boredom. Fidgeting is typically a sign that someone is nervous, frustrated, or impatient. Clenched fists signify unity or anger. Personal space also goes hand-in-hand with this; the more space a person takes up, the more confidence they tend to have. But if they're invading your personal space, it could mean they're trying to intimidate you.

✧ **Posture.** This is how a person holds themselves in a general sense. A closed-off posture (hunched over, taking up the least amount of space possible, crossed arms or legs, avoiding eye contact) could mean someone is generally an anxious or anti-social person (or they're just shy and uncomfortable), while an open posture (body takes up the necessary space, arms and legs are relaxed, the torso is exposed, not avoiding eye contact) typically indicates that someone is more confident and willing to engage in friendly conversation.

Again, I want to reiterate that body language is not the end-all-be-all of dissecting what someone might be thinking or feeling. However, if someone's words are not lining up with their body language, that is—more often than not—a sign that they are not really someone to be trusted. Chances are your subconscious will pick up on this anyway and your instincts will warn you of this to some degree.

The body language or "social cues" explained above are only the metaphorical tip of the iceberg. Don't get too caught up in learning everything there is to know about body language and using only that to figure people out. Body language is just too complicated, ambiguous, and multifactorial to rely on accurately.

Healthy Relationships

Relationships, whether it be romantic, platonic, or familial, enrich our lives and fulfills our need for belonging, support, and love. But not all relationships are created equal, some look, feel, and function differently than others. The important thing is that any relationship you cultivate should be healthy and happy.

This doesn't mean that you'll never argue, disagree, or unintentionally hurt each other, but it does mean you're able to respectfully and reasonably work it out and return to equilibrium.

But how do you know whether a relationship is healthy or not?

A healthy relationship is one where both or all parties involved are mutually supportive, trusting, accepting, supportive of personal growth, and adaptable to change. Overall, it *feels* good. You're never left questioning whether or not this person's intentions or behaviors are real and virtuous.

How To Spot a Toxic Person

The best cure is prevention. Toxic people will drain the life out of you, and while it isn't always possible to avoid interacting with toxic people, you definitely want to avoid giving off the impression that you're open to it.

General signs that someone might be toxic include selfish, hostile, and manipulative behavior. But here are a few more specific traits or behaviors that a toxic person might exhibit:

- ✦ always negative
- ✦ quick to judge
- ✦ lies and deceives
- ✦ general rudeness
- ✦ lack of empathy
- ✦ always thinks the worst of others
- ✦ being reckless
- ✦ argumentative
- ✦ gets aggressive or goes on the offense very easily
- ✦ controlling
- ✦ self-centered
- ✦ arrogant
- ✦ greedy
- ✦ disruptive or spiteful
- ✦ impulsivity
- ✦ apathy
- ✦ selfishness
- ✦ perfectionistic

It's important to remember that our actions don't always define who we are, but recurring negative themes and behaviors from people without taking accountability usually means they lack self-awareness. And without self-awareness, they won't change—or even admit that they're the problem in the first place.

Bear in mind that toxic traits can also exist within ourselves, so if you relate a bit too much to some of what was mentioned here, you're not a bad person. As long as you're willing to take accountability for it and work on changing for the better, you're already doing more than most people are!

How To Build Healthy Relationships

If you're someone who's particularly withdrawn, shy, or has social anxiety, building true, deep, and meaningful relationships has probably been a struggle for as long as you can remember. The truth is relationships of any nature are hard to grow and take effort to maintain, like a well-manicured garden.

Your garden might look sparse and overgrown right now, but once you take care of the soil (build self-esteem and social skills) and trim back the weeds (overcome social anxiety or fear), something is bound to sprout if you sow the right seeds and remember to water it every now and then.

Here's how to cultivate relationships and build connections that last:

- ✦ **Be authentic from the start.** If you're the type of person who is always looking for validation or approval from others (in other words, a people pleaser), it might be challenging to break out of this behavior. But pretending to be someone you're not so others would like you is simply not sustainable. Eventually, you'll burn out. Not to mention the other person might feel confused or betrayed because your behavior is inconsistent, which leads to distrust and suspicion on their end.

Fight the urge to pretend you like something, know something, or believe something you don't. Avoid acting in a way that doesn't feel true to who you are.

✧ **Be thoughtful and empathetic.** It can be awkward or uncomfortable when someone shares something deeply intimate or personal with you. Unless they specifically ask for advice, don't give any. Sometimes people just need to vent, and someone venting to you is usually a good sign that they trust you. Simply acknowledging their feelings with a "that sucks, I'm so sorry" or "I don't know what to say, but I'm here for you" is all that's necessary. Thank them for sharing their feelings with you because it usually takes a lot of courage to do so.

Being thoughtful can look like a lot of things, but paying attention and being present in a conversation to pick up what they might like or dislike is a good start. Not only can it give you a pretty good idea of what to get them for their birthdays, but it shows you really care about what they're saying and that they're important to you.

✧ **Be reliable.** Following through with promises or commitments you make to someone lets them know you're someone who can be trusted, and trust is a very important element of any relationship. This doesn't mean there won't be times when you have to cancel plans or tend to something urgent that came up instead, but being upfront and honest about it when it happens is key to maintaining any trust you've built.

✧ **Set boundaries.** Boundaries are like invisible lines—usually regarding behavior, but they can also apply to more ambiguous aspects—that you enforce in any relationship. It's like personal expectations and limitations.

Boundaries allow all parties to feel safe and comfortable, and adhering to each other's boundaries is a sign of mutual respect. Having boundaries is non-negotiable, and being able to both communicate your own and respect the other person's is the epitome of a healthy relationship.

Someone might question your boundaries, and you can certainly discuss why you have that boundary in a respectful way (if you feel comfortable doing so), but if someone judges, protests, or outright ignore it the first chance they get, that's a telltale sign that someone is toxic.

✧ **Communicate.** Okay, duh! Obviously, if you want to build a relationship with someone, it will require some form of continued communication. But bonding with someone isn't going to happen at a constant rate. Some moments will be raw and vulnerable, and others might be more superficial.

Enjoy the good moments because those make the best memories, lean into the vulnerability when it happens, and communicate openly when there are issues or tension for whatever reason.

It goes without saying that all of the points mentioned above should be reciprocated or mutual. Relationships are give-and-take, sometimes compromises are warranted and life happens. Don't be afraid to be vulnerable and express your feelings; in the grand scheme of things, it's unlikely that you'll ever regret it.

Respectful Expression

Everyone has their own idea of what respect means. The official definition of respect as a noun in the Merriam-Webster dictionary is: "To consider worthy of high regard." And, not surprisingly, that description is pretty spot on.

The way I define respect for myself is by treating others like human beings regardless of their age, race, culture, health, or status because we all have intrinsic value. The only thing that can influence my respect for others is a lack of reciprocity thereof.

I once saw a Tumblr post (yes, I'm that old) where someone compared the respect of personhood to the respect of authority. What it basically said was that people share this ideology of respect, meaning: If you treat me like a person, I'll treat you like a person. But there are some people—usually people in power—who, when they talk about mutual respect, really mean: Only if you treat me like an authority will I treat you like a person. And that has really stuck with me.

Entitled people aside, respect is a virtue that we all have the ability to grant to others. It builds trust, prevents conflict, and shows emotional intelligence and maturity. This doesn't mean that you'll never be in situations where someone is disrespectful to you or that you should never disagree with someone. But disagreeing with someone and being able to express your thoughts and feelings in a respectable way is an important skill to have in all forms of relationships.

Unless someone is just an awful or immature person, being respectful when setting boundaries, calling them out for their behavior, and disagreeing will actually strengthen a relationship. And knowing how to deal with receiving disrespect can help you feel more confident and assertive—you deserve respect, don't settle for less.

Here's how to express your opinions, thoughts, needs, and emotions in a respectful manner:

✧ **Be assertive.** You can express yourself confidently and respectfully at the same time. And yes, this will take practice. You have to believe that you're worth standing up for and realize that the only person who's going to stand up for you *is* you. People can't read your mind, which is why you have to tell them when they've said or done something that has hurt you, or when you disagree with them, or when they're being unfair or rude.

Being assertive doesn't mean you should be aggressive, rude, confrontational, or disrespectful. It means you value yourself and your rights while also acknowledging the rights of others. It's about being fair to yourself and others regardless of how they might react to it.

✧ **Reframe the statement.** When you want to express your needs, thoughts, opinions, or emotions, outright telling someone that they are the reason you feel a certain type of way can cause them to feel attacked. This might lead them to become defensive or even start an argument, and that will not yield productive results. Your goal isn't to argue but to resolve.

Instead, you can reframe your statement. So, instead of saying, "You always expect me to drop everything and clean my room when you tell me to," you can say, "I feel frustrated when you tell me to clean my room when I'm busy. I know it needs to be done; can I do it later?"

✧ **Understand their point of view.** We're quick to disagree with someone if they're doing or saying something we don't approve of. But unless they're being rude or disrespectful, take a moment to process whatever it is that you don't agree with. Try to see things from their perspective, taking into consideration what information is or isn't available to them.

If you still can't understand where they're coming from, you can tell them how and why you disagree without attacking or making fun of them for their views and opinions.

✧ **Be considerate.** Talk to people the way you want to be talked to. Again, this doesn't mean that others will return the favor. However, a hallmark sign of being emotionally mature and respectful is leading by example. By considering the other person's feelings, you can prevent them from lashing out and causing an argument.

There are ways to go about expressing your feelings, thoughts, or opinions without being rude or judgmental. Some people will defend their direct rudeness or disrespect by saying they're "brutally" honest. I find that to be a lame excuse; you can be honest while still being kind and considerate.

For example, let's say someone you're talking to has something stuck in their teeth; the only options here are telling them or ignoring it. Not telling them isn't the kind thing to do, in my opinion. Think of it this way, if you had something stuck in your teeth, would you prefer it if someone told you or left you to go the whole day without knowing?

Being considerate is all in the delivery. Saying, "Oh, you have something in your teeth," without making a big deal out of it versus pulling a face and saying, "Ew, what's in your teeth?" Both scenarios display honesty, but only one is being considerate.

Daily Task

I get it. It seems daunting and scary to meet new people. Not every person you meet will become a permanent or important fixture in your life, and there's no way to know which relationships are built to last. But that's the name of the game; life is just one big gamble, really.

But you can't let the uncertainty stop you from trying, and you can't let the fear of wasting your time and effort stop you from participating at all. And you can't let your fear of rejection, embarrassment, or awkward moments dictate everything you do for the rest of your life. So here's what you're going to do today:

You're going to make micro-commitments. These are low-risk, medium-reward actions that might or might not result in an opportunity to get to know someone just a bit better, such as:

- ✧ Add someone from your friend recommendation lists to Snapchat, Facebook, or Instagram.
- ✧ Greet someone when they walk past you.
- ✧ Give someone a genuine compliment (their shoes, an accessory, their outfit, or skills are all safe options to go for).
- ✧ Ask to borrow something, but remember to give it back (an eraser, a pencil, white-out, etc.).
- ✧ Make that comment, either on social media or in real life, given that it's polite and appropriate (bonus points if it's funny).

✧ Ask someone for their opinion or recommendation.

✧ Agree (or disagree) with someone—respectfully, of course.

A lot of things can be an opportunity to start or join in on a conversation; you just have to take a chance sometimes. People are like flavors, some complement each other, and some don't mix, but it takes a certain level of risk and experimentation to figure it out.

CHAPTER 6

Day 6

HANDLING DIFFICULT SOCIAL SITUATIONS

> **"**
>
> *I am not afraid of storms for I am learning how to sail my ship.*

–Louise May Alcott

✦ ✦ ✦ ✦

No matter what you do, there will always be conflict in any relationship. In fact, conflict is a sign of a healthy relationship. People have this idea that conflict is a bad thing that should be avoided. But that's simply not true. No two people are going to see eye to eye on everything all the time. It highlights the beautiful uniqueness that exists within all of humanity.

That being said, conflict isn't a sign that two people are incompatible, and it's how you handle the conflict that matters. It can strengthen and help the relationship grow, or it can burn it to the ground.

Conflict resolution is a necessary soft skill that is unimaginably important in most areas of your life, both now and in the future. You will use it with your future romantic partner, your colleagues, your boss, your friends, and even your children (if you decide to have them).

What Is Conflict?

Conflict is more than a disagreement. However, disagreements can certainly turn into conflict if it's not resolved properly. Conflict is a situation where someone feels threatened or becomes emotionally triggered due to the actions or words of someone else (usually someone they consider a friend, but can also be an acquaintance or stranger).

It doesn't go away when you ignore it. In fact, unresolved conflict will only become worse over time. And as crazy as it sounds, conflict is an opportunity to build trust and security in the relationship, but that will depend on your (and the other person's) ability to overcome it.

Your perception of conflict will tell you a lot about your conflict resolution skills. For example, if you're the type of person who avoids arguments, doesn't uphold your own boundaries, or defends or ignores others' negative actions toward you instead of bringing it up to them, you're probably not very good at it—no offense.

But you have to admit it makes perfect sense; if a person avoids conflict at all costs, then that means they haven't had much (if any) experience dealing with it. Hence, their problem-solving abilities go down the drain or never develop fully in the first place.

The good news is it's never too late to learn.

Conflict Resolution

How you handle conflict comes down to your ability to stay calm and alert when emotions are running high. This means that even when someone has said or done something that has triggered an adverse emotional response, you're able to re-regulate and continue to engage and even face the conflict head-on.

There are two main skills of conflict resolution: Emotional awareness and emotional regulation.

Staying calm during a stressful time allows you to still be aware of social cues and body language so you can assess the situation properly. It's important to regulate your emotions during conflict, so you're able to communicate your needs and feelings in a way that won't escalate things but rather resolve them.

Strategies

There are five main strategies for resolving conflict, but they're not all equal and the method you choose will depend on the importance, impact, and consequences it will have on everyone involved. The five conflict resolution strategies are:

✧ **Avoidance.** This is when you try to sidestep or ignore the issue at hand. And while it's not recommended in most situations, there are some cases in which this strategy can be effective. Avoidance can be used in cases where whatever conflict exists isn't really important to anyone involved and doesn't impact you or the other party in any major way (has no consequences).

✧ **Accommodation.** Resolving conflict with accommodation usually means you'll try to satisfy the other person's wishes, concerns, and needs— usually with some level of effort on your part. The thing to remember with this strategy is that it should only be used if the consequences (or effort you're putting in) don't infringe on your personal boundaries or requires you to ignore your emotions.

An example of this would be to make a commitment to do something that you don't really want to do, say, go to a concert of an artist you don't like with a friend, but you value their friendship, so you're willing to accommodate their desires so you can still spend time together.

✧ **Compromising.** This strategy focuses on finding a way to partially satisfy the needs or concerns of everyone involved. Compromising is usually the best resolution in situations where it's impossible to meet everyone's needs, so each person has to be willing and able to compromise on or forfeit certain things.

For example, you're working on a project with a classmate, the due date is in two days and you're not going to be done in time. You want to ask for an extension but your classmate wants to pull an all-nighter and get it done in time. A potential compromise here could be to meet up after school for the next two days to work on the project more than you were planning to and then decide if it's necessary to ask for more time.

✧ **Competing.** This is the opposite of accommodation. Someone who uses this strategy will do everything they can to satisfy their own needs and desires without considering the needs and feelings of those around them—it's usually done at the other party's expense.

A clear-cut example of this is when you get mad at your friend and give them the silent treatment for not doing what you want to do.

✧ **Collaboration.** Collaboration includes finding a way to fully meet the needs of everyone involved (similar to compromising, only it's a win-win situation for all involved instead of needing to give up in some aspects).

An example of this would be if you want to go see a movie and your friend wants to go ice skating, instead of choosing one, you do both (either on the same day or not, either way, everyone gets what they want in the end).

There are many ways to quickly re-regulate your emotional state, such as breathing and grounding exercises. Emotional awareness can be improved by working on your emotional intelligence, which allows you to accept your emotions in real time instead of ignoring or suppressing them. It also allows you to understand yourself, your needs and emotions, as well as those of others, so you're in a better position to negotiate or mediate a resolution.

Emotional Intelligence

Emotional intelligence is one's ability to understand, use, and control your mental state in order to relieve stress, understand where others are coming from (even if they might be going about it in the wrong way), and empathize with them, as well as communicate effectively to avoid misunderstandings.

It's an important aspect of building strong and healthy relationships, achieving personal and professional goals, and making constructive choices with regard to what's most important to you.

You can improve your emotional intelligence by working on self-management, self-awareness, social awareness, and relationship management.

Emotions are like little blocks of information that help us understand ourselves better. But at times, it can also overwhelm us and make us lose control over ourselves. There's a fine line between managing your emotions and suppressing them. Managing your emotions (or self-management) involves accepting and processing them without letting your actions be controlled by them; suppressing your emotions means avoiding them altogether.

Take a moment to think of the relationship you have with your emotions, and this will give you an indication of how well you handle them. Ask yourself the following questions:

- ✧ Do your emotions flow?
- ✧ Do you pay attention to your emotions?
- ✧ Do you sometimes feel your emotions physically in your body?
- ✧ Do you experience individual emotions, and can you name them effectively?

If your answer to any of these questions is "no," it most likely means that you're not aware of or in touch with your emotions. There are many potential reasons for avoiding strong feelings, such as past trauma, extreme negative experiences with emotions, and the inability to self-regulate.

Dealing With Disrespect

As mentioned in the previous chapter, your peers or even authority figures (such as your teachers, guardians, elders, or even your parents) might treat you disrespectfully at times. Which is quite honestly ridiculous since they're the ones who should be modeling what it looks like to treat others with kindness and respect. Some people are truly so delusional that they believe they deserve respect without having to respect others in return.

But what exactly is disrespectful behavior? What does it look like? How do you know if someone is being disrespectful?

Disrespect can come in many forms. Disruptive behavior such as angry outbursts, threats, throwing objects, swearing at someone, or even physically hurting someone. Demeaning behavior such as shaming or humiliation, degrading comments, censorship, insults or inappropriate jokes, condescension, or faultfinding (nitpicking everything one does). Intimidation tactics like abuse of power, controlling behavior, arrogance, intentionally ignoring or overstepping boundaries, or bullying. Passive aggression or any insidious behavior such as staring, pointing, rude gestures, lying, belittling, taunting, or exclusion.

The circumstances don't matter. No one has the right to disrespect others, no matter how bad of a mood they're in. One could argue that sometimes disrespect is justified. Being disrespectful to someone who was disrespectful first can feel righteous, moral even. But where does it end? All you're doing is creating a perpetual cycle where you feel justified in disrespecting them back, and then they feel justified in continuing to disrespect you.

By refusing to participate in this snowball effect, you give the perpetrator a chance to think about their actions. Retaliated disrespect is expected. So at the end of the day, everyone focuses on defending their actions instead of reflecting on them and becoming a better person. Granted, some people are so stuck in their ways that no amount of self-reflection will help them be a better person. Don't let that be you.

Here's what you can do when dealing with disrespect from others instead of feeding into their narrow-minded delusions of grandeur:

⋄ **Give them the benefit of the doubt.** Disrespect has to be intentional to count as such. So, it's possible that someone's actions might seem disrespectful when it's not actually meant that way. Some forms of disrespect are way less obvious than others. For instance, if someone yells at you, that's obvious and intentional disrespect, but someone not waving back at you when you could've sworn they saw you is less obvious.

It might be possible that they did see you and chose to ignore you; however, if you're friends and have no reason to believe that they don't want to talk to you, chances are they just didn't see you (even if it looked like they did). Giving someone the benefit of the doubt might sometimes mean you let it fly without much thought until it happens again and only then start to investigate or deduce whether they are being disrespectful or just ignorant. If it does continue to happen, or you start to recognize other ways in which they're being disrespectful, you should bring it up and have a discussion about it.

⋄ **Call them out.** Another thing someone who is actively and intentionally disrespecting you is not going to expect is someone calling them out on it. "What do you mean by that?" is a simple, non-confrontational question that's pretty effective.

The beauty about this is that it's so low profile; if someone makes a rude remark about you or even about someone else, ask, "What do you mean by that?" This almost forces them to admit that they're being a walking red flag. Ask the question in a way that makes it seem that you're really curious as to what they are trying to say, don't come across as accusatory. You can ask them to elaborate by repeating the question or saying you don't understand, especially when someone is making a joke at your expense.

But it also works to clear up misunderstandings; if they didn't mean something in a bad or disrespectful way, they'd have no issue explaining themselves. And watching them stumble over their words when they realize that they are, in fact, being a soggy pop tart is just an added bonus. It's really a win-win situation; either they clarify what they meant and you realize they were not actually trying to be disrespectful, or they're forced to tell on themselves.

Other ways you can directly call out someone for being openly disrespectful is by saying, "That's a rude thing to say," "Why did you feel the need to say that?" or "That's not that funny though, is it?"

✧ **Try not to take it personally.** Impoliteness of disrespect is more common than you may realize, especially coming from strangers. Someone who's known for their bad attitude isn't going to change their stripes just for you, and a random person pushing past you without so much as an "excuse me" isn't a personal attack on you. So try not to put too much weight behind their rotten personality. Don't let someone who's insignificant to your existence ruin your day or take up mental energy that could be spent doing something more productive.

This will also prevent you from taking your bad mood out on others who don't deserve it. It makes sense; when someone is rude or disrespectful to you, it might disrupt your mood for the whole day leading to you being unfriendly or even rude to others. It might help to think of strangers' disrespect as an isolated incident. Don't let an event that lasted a couple of minutes throw you off for hours.

Now, when it's someone you do know or that you *have* to deal with every day, like a parent, guardian, teacher, or teammate, and you can't avoid interacting with them, and their behavior is causing you distress, that's when you take matters into your own hands by looking at everything else on this list—and decide on a plan of action.

✧ **Remain calm.** This is where many people fail, myself included, sometimes. It's a perfectly reasonable response to lose your cool when someone is continually disrespecting you. But sometimes that's exactly what they want. They want to get a rise out of you. However, this doesn't mean you should just roll over and take it, either.

Staying calm when someone is being disrespectful accomplishes a few things. It shows them that they're not in control of your behavior and that they can't phase you. Even if this is the furthest thing from the truth, even if you're on the verge of throwing hands, try to stay composed. Yes, this is easier said than done, and you might even have to excuse yourself to calm down elsewhere, but the disappointment they will feel afterward when they realize that they were the immature one is worth its weight in gold!

When you do respond or engage (because you have a right to defend and stand up for yourself), don't raise your voice or resort to insulting them. Simply act with tact. Respond with clarifying questions or the classic "What do you mean by that?" Repeat their words back to them and ask them if you understand correctly. Tell them how or why you disagree with what they're saying.

And if you need to, remove yourself from the situation and take some deep, calming breaths—or punch a pillow. Whatever you need to do to let out the frustration (in a healthy, controlled, non-vandalizing way) so they don't get the satisfaction of knowing they'd upset you.

✧ **Vocalize boundaries, and follow through with consequences.** There are certain behaviors that are simply not acceptable. What you deem as unacceptable will vary, but someone screaming and cursing at you is one fairly universal boundary, I feel. So we'll use this as an example.

When someone oversteps a boundary of yours, in this case by yelling or cursing at you, you are well within your right to demand—not ask—them to stop, regardless of who they are. "If you don't stop yelling at me, I'm going to remove myself from this situation," or some variation of this. And if they do continue, be prepared to follow through with the consequences.

✧ **The power of intentionally misunderstanding.** This kind of ties in with asking them to clarify what they meant by whatever they said. When someone is being sarcastic, passive-aggressive, or gives you a backhanded compliment, take it at face value. Thank them or agree with them and move on. If they correct you by saying it wasn't a compliment or that they meant something else, they look like a bad person, and you can then call them out for it. If they ignore it, they are less likely to engage in that behavior around you.

✧ **Snip snip.** In some cases, it won't be possible to cut contact with someone who's constantly disrespectful toward you, but minimizing your interactions (or cutting them off completely) where possible will save you so much mental energy. And staying around people who are disrespectful is never worth it, no matter how cool you think they are.

One thing I've learned in life is that if people tell—or show—you who they are, listen up. It's not exactly a big jump in moral ethics for someone to talk badly about someone else to you and then talk badly about you to whoever is willing to listen. Rudeness is contagious, and it's up to you to decide if it's worth getting infected.

Surround yourself with people who are respectful, and your chances of being disrespected decrease exponentially.

I want to reiterate that it's not possible to avoid being disrespected, especially from people who believe they're superior and deserve respect, simply because they're an adult and you're still a child. And even as an adult, you'll still encounter disrespect from time to time, so getting comfortable with calling it out in a mature way (and even acknowledging and apologizing when you might be the disrespectful one) is an essential life skill.

Daily Task

Emotional intelligence is an important element in fostering strong connections with people, but it's also necessary for conflict resolution and expressing your emotions, needs, and boundaries in a respectful way—and also respecting the emotions, needs, and boundaries of others.

It allows you to stay calm in times of high stress, take responsibility for your own actions, express your emotions rather than simply unloading them, make others feel heard, and genuinely care about other people and the impact you have on them.

Practicing self-awareness will automatically improve your emotional intelligence, but here's another approach to take on a more proactive role in it:

- ✧ **Allow yourself to be bored.** Get rid of all the distractions for a bit, even if it's just ten minutes a day. Sit with yourself in the present moment without having something to do. It's a scary thought, but it will allow you to connect with and understand your thoughts and feelings better. Just be part of life for a short while every day, no screens, no music, no internet, no games, no hobbies, just you and your brain.

- ✧ **Pay more attention to your emotions.** When simply going about your day, pay attention to how your emotional state changes, and embrace and acknowledge the emotional rollercoaster. It might be unsettling to discover that you feel more sad, angry, or anxious during everyday life than you may have realized—and it can be shameful to admit that sometimes we're not very nice to the people we care about because of it. But it's only through admitting our anger when mom asks us to unload the dishwasher, our anxiety when walking past a group of our peers, or our sadness when thinking of an ex who broke our heart that we understand what makes us tick. And react accordingly.

✧ **React accordingly.** Here's a hard truth to swallow: we can't control our emotions; we can only control how we react to them. So what many people really mean when they say you should learn how to control your emotions is that you should learn how to control your reactions to your emotions.

✧ Recognize what you're feeling and decide if the emotion is warranted or appropriate for the situation, and then react to that emotion accordingly. This doesn't mean the feeling is going to go away. It simply means you're not hurting yourself or others because of it.

✧ **Redirection.** It's easy to look for scapegoats when trying to pinpoint the reason for our emotions. No one wants to be blamed for something, especially when it doesn't feel like it's our fault, but your emotions—regardless of who or what caused them—are your responsibility to deal with. Yes, they're acting like an a-hole, but you can choose to walk away and redirect your emotions elsewhere (in a healthy, non-harmful way).

Your task for today is going to be meditating. Don't worry; it sounds more intimidating than it actually is. You can choose to set a timer for at least five minutes (with a soft and gentle ring to let you know when you're done) or just meditate for as long as you need to. You're simply going to be in the present moment and do a body and mind check-in following a few simple steps:

Step 1: Get comfortable. Either sitting or lying down, settle into a position where your body can relax and be comfortable for the next few minutes. It may help if it's somewhere where you feel at ease and won't be disturbed until you're done.

Step 2: Focus on something. You can keep your eyes open (but your gaze softened, not focused on any particular object in front of you) or shut. A common thing many people who meditate choose to focus on is their breathing, but you can also focus on a sound or smell.

Step 3: Stay in the present. Your mind may drift away; it's normal. Don't get frustrated; simply redirect your attention back to whatever it is you are focusing on (your breathing, a taste, a smell, etc.).

Step 4: Feel. Pay attention to any sensations that may be happening in your body and acknowledge them. Feel the way your clothes are touching your skin, feel the couch you're sitting on (or the bed under you). Maybe a soft breeze makes its way through the window and causes your hair to tickle the back of your neck or your face. Maybe you're a bit hungry or thirsty. Maybe your hands are cold. Accept any emotional reaction that might be making its presence known, lean into it and feel your body react to it, allow it to happen. Invite it all in and then submit to it.

Step 5: Return. Start by bringing your attention back to your breath, and slowly open your eyes. Move your fingers and toes, then your arms and legs. Do a light stretch if it feels good. You can choose to say a few affirmations or journal your experience. Or just move on with your day from here.

Emotions are neutral, and there's no such thing as good or bad emotions. Yes, anger doesn't feel good, while happiness does, but that doesn't mean anger is inherently bad or that joy is inherently good. They all need to be experienced, processed, and accepted.

Day 7 SOCIAL SUSTAINABILITY

Confidence doesn't come out of nowhere. It's a result of something... hours and days and weeks and years of constant work and dedication.

–Roger Staubach

✦ ✦ ✦ ✦

I t's a lot to take in—everything we've discussed so far. I want to remind you that building your social skills, working on self-awareness, establishing connections, and improving your self-esteem is going to take time. Much longer than seven days. However, this book is meant to guide you so you can isolate each of these things and work on them separately.

And while some of them do complement each other or interlace at certain points, if you stick with the program, you will create momentum and stay on track for making progress. Because that's the true goal: progress, no matter how slow.

Maintaining Momentum

If you've been following along and doing all the daily tasks since day one, you might've already gotten into a slightly different routine than usual. You might still be journaling every day, saying your affirmations, working on improving your social skills in certain areas, stepping out of your comfort zone, making micro-commitments, and having done your first ten-minute "no distractions" exercise.

You're doing the most here. Sticking to a routine that incorporates all of this to some degree—as well as taking care of your physical and mental well-being—is key to sustaining your progress in the long term.

Basically, you need to make habits out of it. I'm sure you know what a habit is; it's a set of actions that—the more you do them—the more ingrained they get and eventually become automatic. Meaning you don't even pay attention to doing them anymore; you just kind of do them without much thought.

There is a three-system loop that's responsible for creating a habit: the cue, the action, and the reward. Once your brain has made a strong connection between the cue and the reward, the action becomes automatic. And while it's hard to form a habit, it's even harder to break out of one (or rather replace it, since established habits don't ever really go away, they get replaced).

So yes, if you're in the habit of avoiding uncomfortable social situations, it's going to take some work to replace that habit with one that's completely new and scary to you. But it's necessary if you want to improve your social skills and connect with people.

The Routine

A good routine is one that incorporates activities that maintain self-care and promotes personal growth on a daily basis. Remember, the actions you take don't have to be big for results to occur. And whatever your current routine is (even if you don't think you have one), you should never try to change everything all at once because you will lose motivation and fall behind. This will leave you feeling defeated, which will further demotivate you, leading to you giving up on the whole thing entirely.

Self-Care

There's a lot of debate as to what self-care means. But, if you take it at face value, it means taking care of yourself, as the word itself implies. It's things you do to ensure your future self is well—which includes your mind, body, and spirit.

You take care of your body by leading a healthy lifestyle, eating a balanced diet, getting regular exercise, getting enough sleep, getting annual checkups with a doctor, and having healthy hygiene practices (like taking a shower semi-regularly, brushing your teeth daily, etc.).

You take care of your mind by doing things that bring you joy and get rid of stress and mind clutter, such as journaling, art, music, and other hobbies or activities. This can also include things like spending time with friends, being supported and surrounded by people who mean a lot to you, and even playing video games or watching a movie.

You take care of your spirit by doing things that make you feel like you're a part of something greater, something that makes you feel like you have a purpose. This could be helping others in need, volunteering, practicing mindfulness, connecting with nature, or praying to whichever higher power you believe in.

Self-care can also include things that you might not enjoy doing in the moment, but it makes you feel good about yourself afterward. Exercise is a great example of this. You don't enjoy sweating and being out of breath, but you feel a sense of accomplishment and fulfillment knowing every time you do it, you get just a little closer to your fitness goals.

Personal Growth

This includes things you wish to improve about yourself, whether it's your self-esteem, your social skills, your emotional intelligence, or all of the above. You need to implement and practice it as much as you can—preferably on a daily basis as part of your self-care routine where possible.

Life can get pretty crazy; everything happens so quickly in the era of the internet that our minds sometimes have trouble keeping up. Personal growth can mean a lot of things; it's up to you to decide what your goals are and how you're going to achieve them.

Goal Setting and Tracking for Personal Growth

Your self-discovery and self-improvement journey will look different depending on what exactly you would like to achieve. There's no communal list where everyone progresses at the same rate or even starts at the same level, which is why it's important to define your goals early on so you can work out a plan of action for achieving them.

Making progress is what gives you the motivation and encouragement to continue, and since self-improvement is very subjective and happens so gradually, you'll need a way to track your progress.

Think of it like this: You need to demolish a house; that's your goal. But not just any house, a brick house. It's a humongous task, so you focus on one thing at a time. You were only given a hammer, so you start chipping away at the mortar, and inch by inch, the bricks underneath get exposed. It feels like you're getting nowhere. Only after an entire day's work do you step back and see that you managed to complete an entire room. After a month, all the mortar on the walls of the entire house is gone, just by you repeating the same action day after day, by being consistent.

The house is still standing, and you still have a long way to go before you achieve your goal, but the work you have done so far was both necessary and meaningful. You might even stumble upon another tool that can get the job done quicker, or at the very least easier, but that doesn't minimize your previous efforts. Similarly, there might be days where all you have is a toothpick and can't get anything done, but again, that doesn't take away the progress you've already made so far.

But determining progress on something that can't physically be observed or quantified is a bit different than simply stepping back and having a looksie. And relying on your subjective memory or intuition to confirm or deny whether you're objectively moving forward or improving is not reliable.

Goal Setting

Look, the SMART method is a good guide for setting goals: Your goals *should* be specific, measurable, achievable, realistic, and time-bound. And if you want to use the SMART system, be my guest. I'm just personally very bored of it. It's everywhere!

This is why I want to introduce you to a slightly different approach. Starting with determining what your ultimate self-improvement goals are. Think of three of the most prominent challenges in your life right now (that you have control over) and write them down, for example:

- ✧ I don't have friends.
- ✧ I don't take care of myself.
- ✧ My GPA is 2.0.

There might be more, but we're going to focus on three of the challenges that affect you the most first. You're going to look at each of these and conjure up a unique goal based on what you want the end result to look like. Based on the above-mentioned examples, let's go with the following:

- ✧ Become part of a friend group.

✧ Get into a consistent self-care routine.

✧ Raise my GPA to 3.0 (so I can at least get into college).

This is your metaphorical brick house. You're going to craft a plan of action for the most important one and make a start. In my opinion, a self-care routine is the most important goal to achieve out of all three on the list. Because when you're taking care of yourself, you feel better, and when you feel better, you'll have the mental and physical capacity to tackle the rest of your problems.

I'm going to start by evaluating my current self-care routine: Doom scrolling social media until two a.m. in the morning, yes. Haven't had a glass of pure water in six months, check. Forgets to brush teeth—oh, don't you dare judge me! This is a safe space, remember?

So, it's not… ideal, but we know what we're working with now; we have a starting point. I would do some research and figure out what a healthy self-care routine generally looks like. Getting enough sleep, eating a balanced diet, drinking enough water, keeping up with personal hygiene, and moving your body are the bare basics of self-care. Simple enough.

What I'm *not* going to do is completely up-root my daily life and overwhelm myself by trying to change every single unhealthy habit at once until I inevitably give up and go back to square one. Instead, I'm going to isolate one factor, in this case, increasing my water intake.

My initial goal is to drink a single glass of water every day for at least a week. I'll set a reminder if I have to, or combine it with another task so I don't forget (like drinking a glass of water right after I take a hot shower since that is when I usually feel thirsty—and I would ignore it). I would reward myself every day that I manage to drink a glass of water and be kind to myself if I do happen to miss a day here and there.

After I have taken to the habit of drinking a full glass of water every day, I would move on to the next milestone: Drinking two glasses of water a day. Once that habit has been established, I have significantly increased my water intake from what it was—which was zero. By this point, I'd be pretty chuffed with myself, call it a win, and move on to a different factor of building a healthier self-care routine.

Your goal is your desired result; your milestones are how you get there. Jumping from drinking no water a day to the recommended amount, which is eight, is unrealistic. And honestly, even if you stick to two glasses of water a day for months before you try to increase it again, it's still an improvement!

You should also only focus on one, maybe two, manageable milestones per goal at a time. For example, drinking one glass of water a day and going to sleep half an hour earlier than I normally would. Only once I've gotten my water intake and sleep to where it needs to be would I move on to the next ones: Diet and movement. Again, small changes and milestones that are sustainable are the way to go.

Instead of only having chocolate as a snack, I'd have chocolate-covered strawberries; instead of only having Cheerios for breakfast, I'd also have some full-cream yogurt alongside it. A healthy, balanced diet is more about adding beneficial foods rather than taking 'unhealthy' stuff away, but

I digress. For more movement, I'd add a five-minute walk around the block to my daily routine, obviously while listening to music, an audiobook, or my favorite podcast.

After months of consistent effort, I'd have gotten to a point where my self-care routine was solid. Sure, there might be days where I skip breakfast or don't take a walk, or still forget to brush my teeth, but 80% of the time, I nail it. I'm happy with a B minus, and you should be, too!

Now, whatever goal you choose to start with next will depend on the priority, importance, and effect it has on your life. Let's say I have less than a year before I need to start applying for colleges or universities. And I'm definitely going to need a scholarship. In this case, I would prioritize my goal of raising my GPA over my goal of becoming part of a friend group.

While still maintaining my new self-care routine, I would brainstorm what I could do to raise my grades. Summer school, online classes, and getting a tutor are all feasible options. On top of this, I can revise my textbooks (maybe going over previous chapters and highlighting what I'm struggling with) and ask for extra-credit assignments. I might do weekly study reviews to make sure I understand the work that was covered and make notes as I go so I have summaries of the important stuff when studying for tests. I would put more effort into homework, assignments, and projects and ask for help if I needed it.

There are plenty of YouTube channels dedicated to breaking down the high school curriculum content for any class so it's easier to memorize and understand. I would take full advantage of this resource, too. But I would also schedule rest or off days, days where I do the bare minimum, and make sure I have time for self-care as well as things I enjoy, like hobbies. Burnout takes years to recover from; you don't want that before you even start college or enter the workforce.

Last but certainly not least, I would sprinkle in small steps toward making friends while pursuing my other milestones relating to self-care and raising my grade. For example, my first milestone would be to do some introspection (as discussed in the previous chapters) and figure out who I am, what's important to me, the type of friendships I want, and the type of people who I want to be surrounded with.

Then, I'd observe my peers and identify who I'm most interested in being friends with, the kind ones, the non-judgmental ones (they're rare, but they exist), the ones who have the same interests and values as me, the ones who are applying to the same colleges as I am. This information will help establish an initial connection—albeit a rather superficial one. It will take time and effort to nurture the connection so a friendship can grow from it.

In the meantime, I'd also work on my self-confidence and self-esteem so I'm better able to showcase who I really am and not be so afraid to open up to and trust other people.

Goal Tracking

We are constantly changing, whether we're actively trying to or not. Our experiences, thoughts, and emotions create our perspective. A simple example of this is to think about something you didn't know when you were younger and how it has changed or shaped your current understanding of the world.

For example, when I was younger, I thought turning the car light on while driving was illegal because, well, my dad told me so. As an adult, I know that it's not actually illegal; it just drains the battery. My dad told me it was illegal because I wouldn't have been able to understand the consequences otherwise. He was just trying to avoid being stranded on the side of the highway with a dead battery.

We don't keep track of these little changes and bits of information we learn or figure out on our own. Until one day, you take a general knowledge quiz at 12 a.m. out of boredom and you realize that you didn't even know a lot of the things you know or remember where you learned them from. Personal growth is just like that, you hoard and implement little changes and habits until you're a completely different person, and yet, you didn't even notice it while it was happening.

How do you keep track of a concept such as self-improvement? How do you measure whether your self-confidence has leveled up? It's not like you have a stats menu where you can see your progress on a bar. Maybe Elon Musk can add that as a feature or app for his brain chip once it passes human trials.

Tracking your personal growth is as simple as finding a way to document it. Journaling can be a good way to do this, but while it can give you an overall idea of how your inner monologue and perspective have changed, it's not very specific.

You'll need to look at your goals and determine what the best way to track them would be—using my three goals from before, I'd say that for my self-care goal, a daily habit tracker is a good idea. For improving my grades, a spreadsheet that documents my progress in a line graph is straightforward and sufficient. And for building and tracking personal relationships, I'd add it to my daily habit tracker and put a symbol or draw a little smiley face every time I initiate a conversation with someone.

With regard to a timeline, I'd be lenient with it and not be too hard on myself if I don't complete milestones within the given timeframe. You really can't put a time limit on personal growth since you can't possibly know how long it's going to take. In most cases, with regard to personal growth, a due date is more so to keep yourself accountable. The only thing on my list that will need a set timeframe is raising my GPA before college applications open.

Your emotional health or mood can be tracked through a week/month/year in pixels: That's where you give all your feelings a color key and color in one square per day based on your most prominent mood for the day (red is anger, yellow is happy, blue is anxious, and so on). Your skills can be tracked by means of having a sketchbook for tracking art skills, recording yourself practicing, or anything else that allows you to physically see your improvement over time.

Another, more "out there" way to track your progress is by putting yourself to the test and seeing whether you would fare better now than you would've previously. This is for things like social skills, where there really is no other way to track your progress and new knowledge other than to just go out and try it out.

And obviously, you'll record your milestones and goals so you can celebrate once you've reached them!

Motivation

Your goals, milestones, and the approach you take to achieve them will look completely different to everyone. But any goal has to be important to you because if it isn't, you don't have any reason or motivation to complete it or make progress with it. So go ahead and ask yourself why, "Why is this goal important to me?"

Using my three example goals of being part of a friend circle, improving my self-care, and raising my GPA, the reasons are pretty self-explanatory. Having friends who support me is important for my mental health and it would make me feel less lonely. Self-care is equivalent to self-love, which will raise my self-image and ensure I stay healthy. Raising my GPA means I get into the college of my choice, which will allow me to pursue my dream job.

However, even when your goals are important to you, it doesn't mean your motivation will last. Motivation is just excitement rebranded. And since excitement is just an emotion, it's not enough to keep you going in the long term. I'm telling you now that you will inevitably lose motivation, probably quicker than you realize. Whether it's because you forget your motive behind them or get bored or distracted, it's how the cookie crumbles.

This is why you shouldn't rely on motivation to fuel you. Don't get me wrong, motivation is a great thing to have, but it shouldn't be the driving force behind your actions. If you wait for motivation to show up in order to take action, you will go long periods of time without making any effort toward progress at all.

It might help to think of motivation as the effect and not the cause, meaning that motivation isn't necessary for action but rather the result of action. And sure, in some cases, you might see something online or even in real life that inspires or motivates you, but I would say that's the lowest form of motivation that exists.

No, what's truly motivating is seeing the fruits of your labor—sticking to the plan even though you don't feel inspired or motivated to do so. The feeling you get when you realize you have been severely underestimating yourself all this time. Motivation *is* the reward. It's a release of dopamine—the feel-good hormone.

So, what *should* you then rely on to stay consistent?

Commitment.

Yes, it's hard. Losing sight of a goal, taking longer to reach a milestone than you anticipated, and backtracking by skipping multiple days are all things that will make you feel bad about yourself and just revert back to your old ways, giving up on the whole idea of self-improvement. It all comes down to commitment.

The journey to self-improvement is not linear. And what many people fail to understand is that commitment doesn't guarantee success. It means staying committed to a goal even when you regress or fail altogether. It means trying again no matter what others might say or think, or even what you might say or think of yourself.

Have the commitment of a toddler. It takes roughly two years before a child starts walking confidently, without support, and without falling down every two minutes. At no point has any physically-abled toddler decided that walking isn't for them because they have stumbled one too many times. It takes even longer for them to start talking fluently, but they don't give up. Why? Because they don't judge themselves— mainly because they don't yet have the mental capability to do so yet, but that's beside the point.

What would happen if you let go of the shame, guilt, or judgment that comes with perceived failure? What would happen if you completely redefine what failure and success mean to you?

Is failure the act of not meeting your own or others' expectations, or is it the lack of taking action in the first place? Does failure determine your value and worth, or does it simply mean that you need a different approach? Is failure a destination? And if it is, wouldn't that mean that you can only fail when you stop trying?

Failure can't be measured. Not in a way that's substantial or objective, anyway. It's purely based on opinions and imaginative social constructs. Your own included! Change the way you determine and view failure because nothing destroys commitment quite like the belief that you have already failed.

Daily Task

Your daily task for today is going to be about your daily routine and what small changes you can make so you can achieve your goals. You're going to start by mapping out your current routine. Think about what you do on most days from the moment you wake up to when you get back in bed, don't worry about time stamps; just keep it as detailed and accurate as you can.

Can you identify anything you're doing (or not doing) that's holding you back from achieving your goals? Maybe you try your best to fly under the radar at school, have no hobbies or extracurriculars, the only two places you go are to school and back home (even on weekends), and you spend more hours on your phone than the amount of sleep you get per night.

Now you're going to find one small thing you can do differently that will result in a slightly better outcome in the future. For example, sacrifice ten minutes of your screen time every day to do something that either includes self-care or self-improvement, like sitting in the sun, going for a short walk, or self-reflection. Or having a breakfast meal that consists of something other than a single cup of coffee. Or blocking out time to spend with people in your life who you value and care about.

You'll continue to accumulate all these little habits one at a time that make you feel better about yourself, and eventually, you'll be resilient enough, confident enough, and strong enough to face and recover from all the discomfort and curveballs that life throws at you—because sometimes life is simply unavoidable.

CONCLUSION

One thing that you learn quite quickly as you grow up is that no one—regardless of your social or economic status—makes it through life without getting a few scars along the way. In the hypothetical war zone that is life, some may lose limbs while others only end up with bruises, but getting hurt to some extent is inevitable.

We can't control our emotions, but we can learn to control what we do about them and how we express them. And how you react to your emotions will change your perception of the world in the long run by rewiring your brain. This is why every journal entry, every thought you challenge, every positive affirmation, and every milestone you achieve counts. Every effort and any amount of progress is worth celebrating.

Low self-esteem (and, as a result, low confidence and social anxiety) has many roots and can take on many forms. But I can tell you this: It's never your fault. Having unsupportive parents with unrealistic goals, narcissistic friends, having gone or are going through a stressful period, exhibiting signs of a mental health disorder, or doing poorly in school are all circumstances that are not in your control—and they create the perfect breeding ground for self-doubt and resentment.

Maybe you avoid conflict because it never ends well and leaves you triggered and emotional for days. It never feels like you're wanted or included, so it's easier and less painful to simply remove yourself from the discussion before others make the decision for you. You're so scared of failing and what the consequences would be that you can never take accountability for your mistakes or learn anything from them—because the fear of punishment overpowers the lesson behind it. You never seem to do anything right, so you avoid doing it at all, or you lack the motivation to even try because every time you do, you hear that little voice in your head telling you you're not good enough, not smart enough, not funny enough, not talented enough.

You look at what others your age have been able to accomplish and you feel angry, jealous, or spiteful. You're being compared to others by the people who are supposed to love and encourage you. How can you be happy for them if their success is being used against you? How can you be friends with them if they're a constant reminder of your incompetence?

It doesn't always take extreme circumstances to affect your self-image. And while a lot of it comes down to how you were raised, that's not always the case. The seed of doubt can be planted by a random comment from a teacher, a disappointed sigh from your father, or a bad grade on a test you actually studied for. If enough of these seeds are sowed, eventually, one will break through the soil. From then on, you'll look for any and all justifications as to why you keep on watering it:

"Why would they want to talk to me?"

"It's not even worth trying."

"I'm the only person I can trust."

It happens so gradually that you don't even realize it until one day, someone asks you why you're always so quiet and withdrawn, why you never come out of your room, or why you choose to be alone. It's because the world is a scary place for an impressionable young mind. It's because your assumptions and past experiences keep you hidden and scared to show the world who you really are. As a result, no one will know who you really are—not even you.

This unstable sense of self will follow you around until you've addressed it. You're at the age now where you're expected to know what your ultimate goals and dreams are in life. Only, you've been so focused on what you're *not* that you forgot to pay attention to what you *are*.

Here's the thing, though, when your brain has convinced you that no one likes you, you avoid others to avoid the emotional turmoil. When you don't practice social skills, they don't develop or strengthen.

So, you don't see yourself as worthy; you assume others think the same, and you don't know what to say or how to react in certain social situations. You're afraid you're going to embarrass yourself, and you're overthinking others' reactions, doubting their intentions, and going above and beyond to avoid spending time out in public. You might even break out in a sweat, experience heart palpitations, or have full-blown panic attacks during social events, or even while talking to someone you know well.

It's hard to connect with someone when it feels like you're fighting for your life. But by taking small steps at a time, using my version of the seven-day system, you can overcome your insecurities and build your confidence until nothing anyone does or says can shake the ground beneath your feet.

And as much as none of this is your fault, it's your life we're talking about here and, ultimately, your responsibility to take the reins. But do me a favor and try to smell the flowers along the way because as much as life can suck sometimes, there will be moments when everything is worth it. Savor those moments when they come.

You might be thinking that you have such a long way to go still, and you're right. But don't focus on the end goal because when it comes to self-improvement, there really isn't one. Don't look too far into the future either; just focus on your next step, and once you've taken it, the next one after that.

You don't have to be the best; you just have to be slightly better than you were last week.

CAREER PLANNING

FOR TEENS

How to Understand Your Identity, Cultivate Your Skills, Find Your Dream Job, and Turn That Into a Successful Career

EMILY CARTER

INTRODUCTION

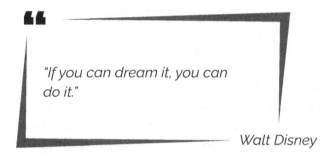

"If you can dream it, you can do it."

Walt Disney

How many times have you looked at yourself in the mirror and thought, "What am I going to do with the rest of my life?"? Or how many times have you noticed your classmates and the people around you constantly working on themselves, leaving you feeling like you are falling behind? A certain level of panic might set in as you realize you don't have much time to prepare for the future. Fortunately, you can always turn that around – and today, you're starting to do just that!

The winds of change are coming as your secondary education ends. It is time to start thinking about career paths.

As you walk through the halls of your high school, the terms career counseling and career planning become terms you meet more often. What does that mean? Do you suddenly have to think about tomorrow?

The short answer is yes. When you are a teenager, time is of the essence, and time waits for no one. Instead of starting to browse the options aimlessly, you took the logical first step and you purchased this book.

The importance of career planning during your teenage years will set the pace for how your career path will develop in the future. I am not saying that you can't thrive at a later age. However, during the crazy times of uncertainty that we live in, the best approach to the world of professional development is an early one. It is important to gain early access and exposure to help you achieve career awareness. But not only that. Through career planning in your teenage years, you enable a firmer and more harmonious career path that aligns with your wishes and goals.

Up until now, you may have used the classroom as an environment similar to the workplace. This is the perfect way to begin. It sets the tone for what you should expect in the future and helps you become more aware of your skills and interests. Nevertheless, it is still a classroom at the end of the day. It is still a closed and safe space where you can make mistakes and not be as involved as you should be.

This book can help you step out of your comfort zone. It can help you utilize the brainstorming bit and use it to your advantage. Once you take the first step, you will notice endless possibilities. The practices you get to learn and the experiences you are about to undergo will help create individualized access to a brighter tomorrow.

How does it sound so far? Convincing or not?

There is a second important aspect of choosing career planning during your teenage years, and it includes all the benefits you get from it.

Going through the process of choosing your career can help you identify your interests. It is okay if you weren't quite aware of your likes and dislikes up until now. This important aspect can help you choose the field that will make you happy in the future. Every person in the world has a "true calling," so why not figure out what yours is from an early age?

Another benefit you will gain is knowing how to make an informed decision. After all, there are all these factors to contribute; you might have difficulty navigating through it all. That is okay. That is what career advice is for. You can always rely on a mentor or a role model to help you get through the challenging period. Ultimately, they will motivate you and help you set goals that will lead you to a satisfying career option. Depending on the fields you are interested in, there is so much information to gather. Avoid losing yourself in the process. Understand the requirements, skills, and qualifications needed to succeed. Once you arm yourself with the appropriate knowledge, you will have all the power in the world!

But there is no knowledge without training, so surround yourself with the best options that can help you enhance everything you know. Training opportunities, volunteering opportunities, internships, shadowing people, and part-time jobs are all key points in your quest to thrive professionally. Consider this a two-way street – you get to advance your skills and learn many new ones, but you also get to identify the skills most employers require. I can teach you how to keep in mind all the future training that will act as a catalyst for your bright tomorrow!

Many of you have big dreams and want to achieve them but are scared of the outcome. Have no fear. All you need is to stay focused and keep working toward your goal. Considering everything, you will slowly start to enjoy the benefits of your careful career planning. Here are only a few of them to get you started:

- ❖ You will learn that this is your journey only. Being surrounded by adults, starting with your parents, teachers, relatives, counselors, etc., you might lose yourself. Starting to think that this is a decision that will affect anyone but you – meaning you need to take a step back. Instead, you will embed this in your brain – the journey is yours alone – enjoy it.

- ❖ There is a benefit to change. Change is something that will happen to you either way – why not take charge of it? Reading this book will give you exclusive insight into how to manage change and flourish every time you do it successfully.

- ❖ You will learn how to make mistakes and fix them as well. The decision-making process is the important part, but make no mistake about it, you will fail at it – at first. Every decision comes with the possibility of making a mistake. But every decision is also a valuable experience – you will teach yourself how to enjoy the good decisions and quickly fix the bad ones.

✧ You will learn how to make up your mind and if needed, to change it too. Career planning comes with a lot of twists and turns. You may start at one point with one goal in mind and end up in a completely different place. Your road to success will be filled with twists and turns and challenges wherever you look. It is essential to accept that, depending on everything you discover about yourself, you might need to change your plans (sometimes even completely).

✧ Keep learning – from everything. Every step you take comes with a lesson. The same goes for this book – every chapter is filled with lessons for you to remember. It all comes down to reinforcing your connection while seeking out new experiences.

✧ There is also always time to celebrate yourself. Don't forget to have fun while discovering everything you can about yourself. Above all, you are a teenager, and this is still your time to shine and have fun! Just remember to work hard during the process and celebrate every milestone you complete. This way, you will boost your confidence and maybe, some magic in the air!

Throughout this book, you will learn how to set up a system that works for you. The structure allows for being flexible and persistent and learning how to tackle every obstacle that comes your way. For starters, being true and honest with yourself is the best way to begin your journey toward professional success.

Other than that, I am also covering various topics such as how to explore career options and to broaden your horizons. Learning how to leap into the future by uncovering some potential job prospects that represent the future. But never stop working on yourself. Using your technical and transferable skills is a part of all job experiences – together, we will see how you can utilize them best.

It is not all about the technical part – you will also learn how to develop a fantastic support system filled with people you can trust. Allow me to enter a hidden part of your mind and explain the importance of role models. After doing that, you might realize you have had a role model all this time!

As the planning continues, you will also gain an understanding of what it means to have some practical experience before you dive head-first into the job world. I am covering all topics – from building the perfect portfolio and resume to successfully being a part of a job interview. Moving on, you get to discover how to recognize the available professional options. Weighing in the factors and knowing how to decide on your career is essential.

Once you understand how the market works, what types of job prospects are right there at your fingertips, and how to improve your skillset constantly, you will become an invaluable part of the force that drives the world.

Let me empower you to make an informed decision about your future. There is only one bridge between your dreams and reality, so take a walk with me. Today, we are commencing an amazing journey of career planning.

Today, your dreams are waiting – let's start chasing them together!

CHAPTER 1

UNDERSTANDING YOURSELF

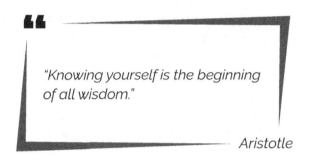

> "Knowing yourself is the beginning of all wisdom."
>
> — *Aristotle*

E ven though we live in a different era, this timeless truth continues to echo throughout the centuries.

But let's be honest for a moment – finding and understanding yourself can be incredibly tricky when you are a teenager. Driven by hormones and emotion, you wander through life's corridors while external factors try to sway you from your true self. And in this modern era, where the comparison to influential people can easily seduce you to build your interests around someone else's norms – the road can become even more challenging. Top it off with family expectations and other influences from your society, and voila; you are officially in the *"I don't know what I want"* maze. Oh, and the fact that so many career choices mount while you are already overwhelmed doesn't help either.

But how can you possibly get out of that maze and come face to face with your true self?

In short, the answer is within. You just need the right tools to guide you, which is what this chapter is all about. With self-assessment and personal reflection as your compass, you will uncover your inner landscape of interests, values, and skills. In addition, you will also learn how your personality traits play a major role in making the right career choice. By understanding who you are and where your interests and passions lie, you will not only define the first step toward your career but also unleash your full potential.

Now, prepare to see yourself from a different angle. Uncover the truth within, and relish how complex, unique, and beautiful you are.

Self-Assessment and Personal Reflection

The first step towards choosing a career path that resonates with you is the act of self-assessing and reflecting. You need to be able to decide on something you will genuinely enjoy and be passionate about.

As a teenager, it is easy to be influenced and distracted by many external factors. That is why it is essential to simply find a quiet place, sit down, and think about all that makes you, YOU.

Let's start with your general values and motivations. Ask yourself, what truly matters to you? What do you value? Do you live and breathe in the name of a team spirit, or do you value a quieter and more individual approach? Is the support and presence of your family the motivation you need, or maybe you wish to become more independent and carve out your own path somewhere else? Are your relationships built on trust, and that kind of support motivates you to achieve any goal? Maybe accountability and responsibility are the pillars of your actions. Or maybe, you find that honesty and transparency are super important for progressing through life.

Whatever questions and thoughts arise, try to self-reflect and write it all down. Grab a piece of paper, a journal, or a notebook, and allow every answer to flow into it. I don't recommend typing on your phone or computer; a good old-fashioned piece of paper and a pen would do perfectly. This is because the writing process is slower on paper, and it allows you to savor every thought. It allows you time to think twice before you write something down – do you really want it or not? While composing your words, you will paint a visual image in your mind and have time to really mull things over. In addition, it is a fantastic exercise to gain clarity and open your path toward discovering yourself even further.

Only some things may be clear from the start, but by gradually working your way inwards, you will understand what shapes you as a person. Take a peek into the hidden nooks within – you just might be amazed at what you will find!

Plus, by defining your values, you will gain the confidence you need to become empowered. After all, your beliefs are part of choosing a career path that reflects your principles. Slowly but surely, these principles will give you a purpose that will silence any external factor. Finally, you will see how a sketch of your persona emerges on what previously was a blank page. Trust me, as the days pass and you reflect more and more, that sketch will become more clearly defined.

The next step is to identify your talents, skills, and passions. It is the part called adding color to the sketch. But before you start pondering on that, I want you to throw aside any high expectations. Just forget about what you are supposed to be or what your society prefers. Even if you don't have the answers immediately, give yourself time. And let me assure you, not all talents revolve around being creative! You don't have to be a virtuoso to succeed in life. There is beauty and potential in everything.

That being said, in the next part, I will further help you narrow down your core values, identify your interests and skills, and even uncover some hidden talents just waiting to see the light of day.

Identifying Your Values, Interests, and Skills

Through the part of self-discovery, you find out how to best utilize your interests and skills. However, you have to define them first before you can move any further. In this part, we will put focus on your self-discovery through immersing yourself in practical activities, revealing your interests, values, and skills.

Values

Values are the pillar of every human being. A clear-cut set helps you define who you are, what your core values are, and how they help you shape yourself into a confident young person.

Values can even boost your decision-making skills. So, for the sake of your bright future, try to outline them.

Once you have your general values mapped out, it is time to dive into something more specific. As I already mentioned, what you stand for needs to be aligned with your career. You cannot be one person privately and someone entirely different when it comes to your professional progress. Not only will you be fooling yourself that it is what you want or need, but it will be draining to go against your values. Simply put, your career path should complement your personality rather than go the opposite way.

With the help of these questions, you will gain a clearer idea of what matters and motivates you the most:

- ✧ Is being a leader important to you? Or are you entirely okay doing your thing in the background?
- ✧ Are you comfortable working and expanding on someone else's ideas, or maybe you wish to cultivate and "grow" your own?
- ✧ Is creativity something you excel at and a big part of who you are?
- ✧ Are you someone who wants their actions to benefit society?

✧ Do you perform better when you have clearly defined rules or when you are free to experiment?

✧ Is gaining more knowledge a priority?

✧ Does being under pressure motivate you, or does it have a reverse effect?

✧ Do you wish to advance or thrive in your comfort zone?

For some of the questions, you might need more time to decide what to answer – which is normal! If you find yourself struggling to answer, you can do some of the interests below and then get back to answering these. Sometimes one aspect may fill in the blanks in the other.

Interests

It goes without saying that your interests should also be aligned with your career. But this is also important in the long run – your career choice should be engaging and satisfying. As a teenager, it is easy to indulge in many activities or have periods when you are entirely passive. That being said, it is not really easy to immediately think of everything that interests you. And that is perfectly okay because I have the solution for that too. Here is an interesting exercise you can do that can bring you a step closer to answering your question.

As you can see below, all you need to do is think of a few past and present experiences. Dive in!

Think of experiences from your past:

✧ List up to ten notable things that brought you some satisfaction, made you feel like you've accomplished something, or pushed you out of your comfort zone – in a challenging yet exciting and enjoyable way.

✦ Feel free to write one sentence that will explain why you found it satisfactory.

✦ Read them out loud and begin noticing some patterns.

Think of current interests and activities (out of school):

✦ Would you rather read or watch a movie? Or both?

✦ What are the genres that you enjoy the most?

✦ What was the theme of your most recent enjoyable conversation? Do you talk about that subject often, and how do you feel about it?

✦ Do you have a role model? If yes, who and why?

✦ What is your ultimate travel destination?

✦ What are the topics that often grab your attention – both during conversations and when watching the news?

✦ What entertains you the most?

✦ Do you feel like you are more of an outdoor or an indoor person?

✦ Whenever you had to choose between watching a documentary or playing a video game, which one captured your attention more?

✦ Have you noticed yourself unconsciously doing something (writing, drawing, or maybe playing guitar)? Is there a thing that so powerfully draws you in, you lost yourself in time and space?

Even though some of the questions may seem unrelated at this point, I promise each has its own purpose. Your favorite movie might not pass your exam or land you a job in the future, but it will open other doors like what your mind is drawn to, which genre, and how it relates to your life, etc. It provides a path towards introspective, creativity, expressing yourself, finding empathy, or maybe even confidence. Whatever you discover, it will benefit you in more ways than one.

Skills

Last but not least, the part most teenagers dread – the skillset. Now, you might be terrified by the fact that you need to show a certain set of skills (even if it is only for yourself), that you freeze. That's okay! It is okay if your mind wanders aimlessly for a little while as you compose yourself. Give it a little bit of time, and then start doing this next exercise!

For this part, we will go over the activities and skills – to draw out potential hidden talents.

Think of what kind of activities you enjoy and the skills that come with them:

- ✧ List up to 10 activities you enjoyed. This can be absolutely anything!

- ✧ Next to each of those activities, write which technical skills you cultivated. These can be problem-solving, organizing, writing, narrating, debating, leading, helping with a specific aspect, etc.

Did you notice that you easily came up with your list of skills?

Every skill can be an arrow pushing you in the right direction. For example, if you are a good writer, this can serve you in multiple careers like publishing, journalism, teaching, book writing, etc. If you have a knack for solving challenging problems, your future can revolve around management and other areas like social jobs or politics. If you've always been good with numbers and technology, then your future area of expertise may be in the field of math, physics, technology, or something else along those lines! In essence, even a single skill can set the sails toward your ideal goals.

After finishing all three aspects, you will have plenty to think about. As you've never approached your goals from this perspective, you might also be surprised to rediscover your passions and interests. In essence, all of them will help you carve not only your career but also your overall future academic and job satisfaction. Moreover, some of them will reflect your personality traits, which is another factor to consider. All in all, they will help you fully shape yourself.

But how can you connect these traits to your professional life choices? If you can't quite make the connection yet, allow me to elaborate.

Take a look below at how they are important for navigating your way toward what you want and need.

Personality Traits and Their Relevance to Career Choices

While your values, interests, and skills are essential to get an idea of your passions and abilities, your traits will complete the whole picture. Research shows that your future academic and job performance can be directly affected by your unique personality characteristics (Wille et al., 2010, 2012; Bakker et al., 2012). In a way, the better they complement one another, the more productive and happier you will be. For example, we can take the most general categorization of introverts and extroverts. You can easily see how an extrovert would fit in a career that revolves around being social, and an introvert would feel more comfortable doing something independently.

Simply put, by defining your traits, you can pinpoint your strengths and weaknesses, achieving better career satisfaction and maximizing your performance.

Where do you see yourself thriving the most? Naturally, you wouldn't be comfortable plunging into a career that doesn't align with your personality. No worries, I got you covered! If you need to know yourself better and highlight your personality traits, you need to look inward and do some work. For that reason, I suggest doing several tests such as the ones below. You can easily find each of them by doing a quick Google search:

- ✧ Myers-Briggs Type Indicator (MBTI) – This questionnaire is based on C.G. Jung's principles and shows the uniqueness of how your personality traits help you in your decision-making.

- ✧ The DISC test – This behavioral test dates back one century, and it was established by the psychologist William Moulton Marston. It represents four aspects: Dominance, Influence, Steadiness, and Compliance, which explain your day-to-day behavior and attitude toward others.

✧ The Hogan personality inventory (HPI) – I love this one as it describes the bright side of your personality. It basically shows your attitude toward others when you are at your best.

✧ Gallup's Clifton Strengths Assessment – Another amazing tool that will help you identify your emotions, thoughts, and how you behave. It is a fantastic way to discover your talents further.

✧ Enneagram Personality Test – Finally, we have the Enneagram, which will depict how you see the world and, naturally, how your emotions are shaped based on those horizons.

You can decide to do one, two, or all! If you feel like all would be too much for you, that's okay! Even getting one score can serve your purpose and enrich the journey to self-discovery and awareness.

I hope that you have started working on creating a better version of yourself because this is only the beginning! By working on this chapter's elements, you should have no difficulty doing the following:

✧ Self-assess your motivation and values and further reflect on them.

✧ Become inspired by your interests and skills.

✧ Acknowledge your personality traits and discover your strengths and weaknesses.

I believe that now that you have discovered so many things about yourself – both new and old – you feel excited to see where it can take you! From this point of view, yes, the possibilities are endless! So, without further ado, let's explore your career options in the following chapter.

CHAPTER 2

EXPLORING CAREER OPTIONS

> "At the center of your being, you have the answer; you know who you are, and you know what you want."
>
> — *Lao Tzu*

A s we move on together to the second chapter, there is no bigger truth than this.

You hold the power within to answer your most difficult questions. You know yourself best, and if you are honest with yourself, then you will start thriving! In this chapter, we tweak the saying from one of the greatest minds in the world – Lao Tzu, to fit our needs.

When exploring career options, it is natural to start thinking about two very important core questions; "Who am I?" and

"What is my life purpose?" Answering these two questions can help you get a step closer to getting the true sense of who you are.

Don't skip this step, as it is an important process to go through. As an individual teen, it can help you better understand yourself and your place in the world. At the moment, there must already be something that appeals to you more than anything else. That is a great starting point for you. As I guide you through some steps you can take, remember that the world is your oyster! The possibilities are endless, so keep an open mind.

Broadening Horizons: Introducing a Wide Range of Career Paths

Broadening horizons or overcoming obstacles? Depends on how you look at it! It is natural for you to enjoy doing various things at your age. You may enjoy drawing, painting, writing, the news, insects, animals, technology, cakes – literally anything! At this stage, your future is bright and filled with adventures, so you first need to grasp that as a concept.

Broadening your horizons does not mean stepping into the uncomfortable but rather stepping out of your comfort zone by simply enhancing your best features. At your age, it is important to broaden your horizons and allow your opinion to change as many times as you need.

If you have been interested in, say, becoming a doctor as a young kid, that does not mean you need to keep following that path by any means necessary. Every once in a while, it is okay to stop and reflect on what you have done until now and how well you have developed.

This is where all your options come in. There is always a wide range of career paths for you to consider. In essence, broadening your horizons means growing and developing. For example, about 5 years have passed since you last said you wanted to be a doctor, and now, both your interests and perspective have shifted. You feel a little uncertain about your decision – many other driving forces pull you apart from medical school rather than push you closer.

During this period, you have developed some new skills and uncovered a few hidden talents that change everything. So then, why not change everything? Your speaking and listening skills have significantly improved, and you have sharpened your wit and are detail oriented. You started loving how society develops and want to be a part of changing it for the better. Law starts sounding like the better option with each passing day.

Here is where I empower you to go after what you want and after what your set of skills allows you to go after. There is no need to abandon your potential for anything just to complete the goal you (or your parents) set for yourself long ago.

The key is using your skills for something you will enjoy doing. Remember that your whole life is in front of you, and with a little bit of your help, it can unravel in the most magical of ways. Using the tips from the first chapter, outline the interests, values, and skills you are best at, and then take it from there!

Self-assessment is important. Ask yourself, "What do I enjoy the most?" – it is how you will identify the potential career paths that align with your personality and interests.

Researching and Gathering Information on Different Industries and Professions

Next stop, you start your research! After you have collected the information about yourself, it is time to start implementing them. One of the most critical aspects of finding your true calling is looking into organizations and companies (even entire industries) and searching for someone with your specifications. Anything from thorough research on the internet to going to some networking events will do. Research allows you to thoroughly understand a potential professional path – requirements, expectations, and further developments.

This is how you identify career options and branches that perfectly fit you.

Also, think of it as an essential part of your journey toward becoming an adult. The time and resources you invest in this end up assisting you in choosing the right career prospect for you. So, set yourself up for a bright and happy future!

There are many ways you can begin pursuing the career that suits you the best. If you have never done research until now, have no fear! I'm equipping you with a complete guide on how to do it and make the best choice for you!

Start by determining what you want – the first step toward creating a bright future for yourself is being honest. Think about establishing your preferences and goals. You can go as specific as you like! Write down everything – from working hours to whether you would relocate for a career (at a certain point in life).

Prioritize the elements you feel the strongest about. Some of them are certainly more mandatory than others. These are your starting points.

Do you have any skills? – continue with listing all the skills you deem essential to your professional life. If the list is smaller than you expect, don't be discouraged! You are young, and time is on your side. Work toward developing some new skills you find interesting. After a while, you will be amazed by how long your skill list will get.

Your potential career options – write down the potential career options you have thought about. Yes, you can add more than one! Allow yourself to browse through the vastness of options – I encourage it! Having a few options will not only give you a sense of stability but it will also help you to open up your mind to something that you haven't even thought about before.

Career requirements – when it comes to expectations, it is a two-way street. Just as you expect something from a certain field or organization, they will expect something back from you. Are you ready to meet the expectations? Sit down and do your online research. Learn as much as possible about the career prospects, including experience and educational requirements. Learn about the most common responsibilities in the workplace.

A fresh point of view – following a certain profession or industry requires taking a peek into the future too. From all the ones you have lined up, which one seems like the best option for the future? As a young adult, you should consider this too. Society progresses, and as it does, it opens up new doors to the future, and at the same time it closes the ones to the past. Make an informed decision on the right option for you – one that will blast you into the world of tomorrow!

Talk to a few experienced people – you can start with the ones closest to you. If you have any relatives, or if your parents are involved in a field that you have taken an interest in, pick their brains a little bit. Remember that your research can be as extensive as you want, but it is a good idea to get some insight directly from the field too. A job can sound complicated on paper but simple in real life, and vice versa.

Do you have the option to visit their workspace? Jump with both feet to such an occasion!

Start outlining your professional life – it is all about managing your expectations while getting what you want! Outlining your professional path can help you create a solid strategy that will last you for years to come. It can give you the freedom to revise it whenever it is needed, possibly every one, two, or maybe even five years – it is all up to you. Project your needs onto the paper and see what it comes up with!

While I am on the subject, there is another thing you can do.

Emerging Careers and Future Job Trends

I only touched upon the subject above, but I believe it piqued your interest. So far, we have determined that you might have one or several careers lined up – depending on your skills and requirements. As choosing a career is one of the most important aspects of life, young people are more and more keen on taking their time before deciding what they want (instead of jumping the gun and regretting it later on).

Yet again, we return to the question, "What do you enjoy doing?" to help you get to the desired destination. The wide range of options spans from one side to the other and keeping the future in mind is a good idea. As with every other teenager, you probably want to do a good job and enjoy doing it for a long time.

This leads me to the next section – start exploring some future job trends.

At this moment, you have little to no experience and limited knowledge of what makes the world go round. All that can change in an instant. Right now, everyone (not only young people) is in an uncertain environment where things can change just like that. Navigating through the challenge of searching for the perfect professional path in a constantly evolving society is a challenge – but not an impossible one!

There is always one good place to start, and that is beyond the voice of reason! I'm not saying that you should look for something completely unreasonable, but rather expand your horizons just a little beyond the reasonable choices you have made until now.

A factor of certainty is what you should include while doing this. Add that to your skillset, and you might end up uncovering a whole new world of emerging careers.

Just to get you started, here are a few of the most promising innovative job prospects of tomorrow.

Software developers/computer managers – the tech era as we know it is in full swing, and just at the right time! Gen Z is all about technology, paving the way for new emerging careers that will shape the world of tomorrow. For this particular one, you will become a valuable asset on the market. From writing codes to analyzing and maintaining platforms, there is nothing that you can't do with this job!

To give you an estimate, currently, the job market is open for people who have a bachelor's degree, and +5 years of experience.

Coursera has listed this as one of the most promising future jobs.

Web developer – another programming heaven for all you computer lovers! Nowadays, any brand or company needs to have its own website – and as a web developer, you can make that come true. Front-end, back-end, webmaster, and full-stack developer – these are the four main options to choose from. If programming languages are your biggest interest, then this might be the perfect option for you.

To give you an estimate, at the moment, the job market is only looking for people who have a degree, no experience is needed.

It requires a simple skillset, and since first created in the 1980s, the nature of this field has changed a few times. First, with the creation and vast use of the Internet, and then with the usage of mobile phones.

Financial manager – if numbers seem like the better choice, then achieving financial stability for a company must be a part of your dream, right? Profits and expenditures, strategizing about all the bigger decisions, and utilizing your planning and organizing skills to the fullest are what a financial manager is all about.

Are you looking into this? Companies are hiring – you need a bachelor's degree and +5 years of experience.

It is estimated that this particular job will achieve growth of about 17% in the next five years.

Medical assistant – providing support in hospitals is the dream of many young people. Do you consider yourself to be one of them? If a part of your skillset includes communicating with clients, if you have always been keen on pharmacy, and if you love helping doctors, then becoming a medical assistant is the perfect choice for you.

To become a medical assistant, you need professional training and a high school diploma. This is always a growing branch, with an estimated job growth of 18% in the next few years.

Teacher – since almost every aspect of today is moved online, why not this too? The future of teaching is online. Have you noticed you have the potential to lead a class rather than be a part of it? Spreading knowledge can be a wonderful thing and preparing the new generations to come for the world sounds like an excellent idea. So, why not add the online teacher option to your list too? Consider this a great way to utilize your abilities and grow your own business from scratch. There is a wide market for anything you are looking to offer. As it is increasing with every passing minute, you could share your knowledge with people from all over the world!

Did you know that there are more than 51 million YouTube Channels, and an average visitor spends about 40 minutes a day on this platform? That has to give you some boost to try creating something useful and uploading it there!

Personal trainer – more and more people are becoming aware of their body image, mostly due to social media. As a teenager, you must have witnessed that in your surroundings too. What you are probably not familiar with is because of the fast-paced life of today, not many people can keep up with their physical activities. This is where you come in. If your people skills are honed to perfection, if you love being active, and nurture a fondness toward the human body, have you thought about being a personal trainer?

A few things you should know here – you need certification, but not a degree, to become a personal trainer. You can choose to work inside or outside the gym. You need to nurture effective communication and an encouraging attitude. As a relatively new field, you can get as creative as you want. And finally, personal trainers are not dietitians or nutritionists.

These are some of the highest trending jobs that you can consider working toward. However unconventional it may sound, one of these might be the perfect fit for you.

When it comes to discovering more options for your future, I recommend first exploring your high school resources and what programs they offer. Plus, you can reach out to a school counselor and gather opinions.

No matter where you are in the world, I would recommend searching through various career groups on social networks, like Facebook, and connecting with other young individuals – both locally and globally. Or you don't even have to connect, just gather information and analyze the latest career trends. Not only do they share many tips and websites that can be of great help, but some may inspire you to discover your own path.

When it comes to leading global websites that can help you shape your journey and be inspired career-wise, LinkedIn should be on top of your list. Other useful sites are Indeed (one of the most popular job search engines worldwide and it is easily accessible to 53 countries), Monster (with a comprehensive database of career advice and tips), and CareerBuilder, etc.

In addition, career magazines like Harvard Business Review (HBR), Forbes, and Entrepreneur can prove to be valuable assets in your quest.

Simply Google any of these, and you will easily find them.

Considering Non-Traditional and Unconventional Career Paths

Speaking of unconventional, I can notice the slight crest around your smile once this word is mentioned. So, if you are leaning more toward the creative side, there is a solution for you too! The job market is constantly changing, and the demand for certain skills changes too.

With a non-traditional career path, you might not get the linear progression you hope for, but you are in for a treat either way. As a young mind, it may even be the more logical way to shape your brain and delve deep into the professional world by choosing an unconventional path. Many industries allow for this due to the diverse skills that you can get from it.

Here are a few reasons why you should consider this:

✧ The right approach can help you land unique and adventurous job opportunities.

✧ Exploring many options can help you create a career that fits your lifestyle like a glove.

✧ You get to enjoy the freedom and flexibility that many people can't.

✧ The satisfaction of building something from 0 is immense.

✧ Presenting some new options results in passions that may be worth taking a second look at.

Again, I remind you of the question, "What do I want to do?" Think about what may benefit your future that still aligns with your goals and interests. Write down your passions and think about how to incorporate them into creating a new career path for yourself.

But how do you start looking for the right opportunities? Since people overall are on the rise looking for alternative ways of making money, why not join the club? As a teenager with a fresh perspective, you have plenty to offer. Here are a few ways how you can use your skills and start building your career:

- ✧ Think about having a "side hustle." This is for those who want to take on some freelance tasks. It is a great way to start learning the tips and tricks of successful freelancers. Also, it is a great way to see how your skills have progressed and how proficient you are at finishing certain tasks.

- ✧ Look into start-up businesses. They are the perfect way to start your business venture with a little help. Create a solid business plan that is unique and shows a fresh perspective, and then start researching ways to complete it!

- ✧ Online ventures are on the list too. So far, digital ventures are considered a phenomenon in the global economy. If you have an idea you need to bring into existence, then take a leap of faith! It just might be worth it.

Remember, exploring career options does not have to be a hassle or a task. Make it as enjoyable as you can. I hope that you will consider these notes and start working toward your goal. Consider this a rewarding experience, where every step is equally important. Open yourself up to a whole new world of possibilities – but not before you've reached the end of this book!

That said, in the next chapter, we will go into detail on how to develop essential skills.

CHAPTER 3

DEVELOPING ESSENTIAL SKILLS

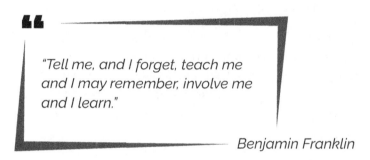

> **"**
> *"Tell me, and I forget, teach me and I may remember, involve me and I learn."*
>
> — *Benjamin Franklin*

Welcome to the chapter where I help you develop some essential skills needed to succeed in the workplace. Now, these essential skills are not necessarily all the ones that you have already written down. For example, marketing, management, technical, or computer skills are all good, but you can't really use them if you don't have (or work on) your soft skills.

The difference is that, unlike hard skills, you display soft skills in each situation where you converse with another person.

447

These are different from the ones you can learn in school. Most of them are typically learned through life experiences and the people you see as role models. Interestingly, as you grow, before you plunge yourself into the job market, you never notice that you are learning them as you go.

The subconscious part of the entire learning process is quite interesting. You do that by mimicking the behavior of a person you admire, by rationally trying to judge a situation based on facts instead of emotions, and of course, my favorite – learning from your mistakes.

All of this means that you are growing. So, when the time comes to determine which skills you excel at and which ones need honing, this is where you become fully aware of yourself as an individual. There is a highlighted importance to these skills that can make you stand out from a crowd (if utilized properly).

Now, I am encouraging you to look upon your past experiences, every situation that has taught you something. If this confuses you, allow me to help you. Let's take a look at how to identify your soft skills.

Identifying and Enhancing Your Transferable Skills

First things first – what are transferable skills? These are the soft skills you can transfer from one job position to another. Most of them are not technical by nature, and they all help you get the job done.

They are also known as soft skills – a group of important abilities that enhance your competence in the professional field. Every employer is interested in them. Even if you want to make it out on your own, you still need them to make yourself more available, presentable, and more successful at what you want to do.

Now, determining your transferable skills requires some introspection. Answer yourself this – is there anything you are naturally better at than the people around you? As you grow, have you noticed that you are better at certain things? Each time you have worked in a group, was there a task that was consistently (and I mean always) done by none other than you?

That is your strong side.

All you need to do is start building upon that. Grab a pen and paper and start writing down every skill that you have noticed about yourself. It can be anything from a good trait (such as good communication with others) to your high levels of empathy and resilience!

Identifying these non-academic skills can help you figure out how well you can adapt to various conditions – in your professional and personal life too. Consider them the tools you need to thrive in a cultural, social, and professional setting.

At some point, while writing these down, you may start wondering what good these skills will do for you. Are these skills really that important that you should focus on them so much? Or should you just look the other way and ignore them? I'm here to nudge you in the right direction and to tell you to stick this one out! There are many reasons why this is important. Any professional setting values them because:

- ✧ By having them, you enjoy support and success in any workplace.

- ✧ You can stand out with them in an interview with an employer.

- ✧ Add them to your CV to make it worth taking a second look at.

- ✧ Whenever you apply for a promotion, having soft skills is perfect for accentuating (how it helped you navigate your position and relationships with others).

- ✧ Even if you want to make it on your own, they are much needed, especially since, all jobs include some form of communication with clients.

The best thing about transferable skills is that they are called that because you can use them at any job! That makes it essential for you to recognize and accentuate them even more!

You have probably managed to create a list of skills by now. Now, let's further break down this exercise into two bits.

The first step is to write down the competence level (it can be a number from 1-10 or 1-5, whatever suits you best) next to each of them. It is important to be realistic about yourself so you can get the best results out of this exercise. Some competencies might get a 10; some might get a six or even a two – and that's okay! Look at the numbers and note the ones with a lower number. That gives you an idea of what you need to focus on. Whether it is a time management skill, or the power to work well in a team, if it needs your attention, do everything it takes to improve it.

There are many ways to enhance transferable skills – some of those ways include:

✧ Taking one or even a few online courses or maybe watching YouTube channels that provide such presentations.

✧ Volunteering someplace that will get you a step closer to working with people in order to develop your 'people skills.'

✧ Put yourself in a teaching position and share your knowledge and wisdom with others.

These are just a few to begin with, but the truth is, once you start looking, you will see that there is a whole world of options that provide you with a way to hone your soft skills.

The next step is to take a good look at your list and find out what is missing. Yes, this is something you might not have thought of until this moment. But there are so many soft skills that you are bound to forget about a few of them. Does your list need to include some literacy skills? Maybe organizational skills? Or some stress management skills? Yes, there is a lot where that came from too!

Do your research and add all the ones you find on the Internet. They can help you widen your horizons and paint a new picture of what you can perfect and achieve within this section.

On that note, I have separated some of the most important ones for you – how to build and make the most out of them so they can help you thrive in a professional environment! Take a look!

Communication, Teamwork, Problem-Solving, and Critical Thinking Skills

According to the World Economic Forum report on the future of jobs, these are some of the most wanted transferable skills! Increase your value by working on enriching them with every passing moment. Here is a straightforward way on how you can do that for each one.

Communication

How you provide information to the people you work with and the clients you work for is a vital aspect of any job. Considering how they wish to receive the information you provide is one of the ways you can be proficient at this soft skill in particular. As a teenager, do you think you have what it takes to master the art of communication?

Sharing and giving information – communicating – is a vital part of life not just in a professional setting either. It is everywhere around us, and it comes in many forms. You have already encountered them – a verbal, a non-verbal, a written, or even a visual form.

The most important bit here is knowing how to give and receive clear and concise information.

As a teenager who has grown up amid the Internet and technology boom, you may know much more about communication than you think. Adults a few decades back used the telephone as a means of communication. Then along came emails, texting, and social media. Nowadays, communication is made easier in theory, but not everyone can do it.

What happened?

Ease of access meant losing the proper dialogue needed to establish a relationship with whoever was on the "other end of the line." In effect, newer generations (including you) lost the ability to communicate effectively. Communication's most essential aspects include patience, listening, understanding, and controlling your thoughts and emotions in order to get the best outcome for your situation. Because of today's culture, like many young people, you may have been neglecting this skill most of your life, it is only natural not to know how to properly establish a relationship in any setting, not just a professional one.

Thankfully, that can be fixed!

It all starts with the simplest thing – eye contact. Whenever you have the opportunity to talk to someone, there are many things you can do to make yourself more presentable and to successfully open up the lines of communication. Here are some other ways you can practice in order to improve your communication skills:

✧ Start paying attention when someone is talking to you. Make a scheme in your mind and pinpoint the essential things so you can reciprocate.

✧ Work on using clear language. You don't have to make your sentences long and complex – sometimes, the simplest answer is the most effective.

✧ Use body language to your advantage. Sometimes non-verbal communication says more than words do. Practice standing up straight, using a calm tone of voice, appropriate gestures, and gentle facial expressions.

✧ Ask for feedback whenever you can. This is an exercise best done within a circle of people you are comfortable with. Ask your parents, relatives, or teacher if they find your communication skills to be improving.

✧ Speak up when something is not clear. Start from the smallest thing – when you see that something is not very clear to you, asking questions about it is a great way to clear the air of any assumptions.

✧ Work on your confidence. Last but not least, consider your level of confidence as a driving force that pushes you forward into the professional world. Invest a small portion of your day to work on it, and soon, you will see some incredible changes.

Communication is great, but once you've mastered communicating with a single person, can you manage to do the same with more people at the same time?

Teamwork

The meaning of Teamwork is communication and navigating several relationships at the same time. It improves equality and the ability to recognize the strengths and weaknesses of each person in the group. An additional benefit is that it provides excellent opportunities to work with various types of people.

Do you consider yourself to be a team player? Do you know that being a good team player is one of the key aspects of success? Taking pride in being able to adapt to change is a good thing, so make sure to accentuate it whenever possible.

But what happens to those that don't have the high level of skills for this?

As a teenager, you might find yourself in a difficult position if you are unable to be a team player. Some of us are followers, others are leaders, but everyone can fit the model of being a team player. If you have written this down on your paper and put a low grade next to it, then it is time to take some action!

Here are some tips to get you started!

Generally, it is a bit difficult to teach a person how to become a team player from scratch, but thankfully, there are a few exercises that can help you hone this skill to perfection. Other than communication being a pillar of a good team, here are a few other things to consider exploring:

⬦ Define the relationship by making clear everyone's role in the group. Any group at the beginning may seem like total chaos, but that is only until responsibilities are divided up. Once that happens, everyone understands their duties and tasks, avoiding confusion and repetition, and thus creating a seamless experience.

✧ Focus on collaborating too. If you don't know how to become an equal participant in a group, then have a discussion. Talking about it can clear the air and give you the floor whenever you want to share an idea or a thought. Also, this way, the entire group promotes compromise and encourages everyone to contribute with their valuable and unique perspectives.

✧ There is no group without trust. Practicing trust starts from something small and develops over time into the biggest support the group will have. If you haven't worked in a team until now, you might not have experienced this, but after working in one for a while, you will start to feel a certain level of integrity that the group exhibits. It becomes a supportive and reliable space where everyone is equal in terms of sharing concerns and ideas.

✧ The team shares the strike or the win together! It doesn't matter if it is a win or a loss; a team always sticks together. When the collective objectives are met because you know that you have worked hard enough as a team to reach the goal, then you also have the grounds for the celebration together as well.

✧ Learn as much as you can. At the end of the day, the team is comprised of many different people. All of them, along with their unique points of view, traits, and responsibilities, can give you a free platform to learn! It is the perfect opportunity for personal and professional growth, so whenever you have the chance, jump at the idea of being a part of a team!

As you can see, being in a team is a continuous process and you can't learn much after only one day. However, spending some time being a part of one may end up with you acquiring many fruitful results.

Every team has its ups and downs. What happens when you reach a low point and need to resolve a certain issue?

Problem-Solving

There is so much happening in the world right now that it is impossible to avoid stress. Unpleasant situations can stand there, waiting around every corner. As a teenager, you might have encountered a lot of them, or you may have only experienced a small amount. Either way, you must learn they are an inevitable part of our day-to-day life.

In the professional setting, a failure or a mistake can bring on a large amount of stress. I have seen this happen many times on various occasions. Sometimes, the situation escalated to become even bigger than it was, and in other cases, it was resolved almost immediately. Do you know what contributes to this outcome?

Having problem-solving skills. The ability to analyze a certain situation (and de-escalate it if needed) is a much-needed skill in every professional environment. Any teenager would be lucky to master this skill, as it is imperative for success in an individual and group setting as well. Developing and presenting problem-solving skills can help you to thrive.

For those that feel stuck...

If your problem-solving skills are not up to par, remember you can always do something about it. Nowadays, plenty of exercises and tips will get you started working on it. Here, practicality is key, so try to push yourself whenever you are in a tricky situation. The following are some practical tips for you below:

- ✧ Try to calm your mind down. If you are a person that doesn't work well under stress, do some stress relieving exercises. It can be anything from slowly breathing in and out for a few seconds, counting back from 20, or anything else that works for you. The purpose is to create a calm and collected environment within.

- ✧ Collect all the facts. If you don't know where to begin, simply follow the trail of information. Whenever you are faced with an issue, start by gathering information about it. What happened, how many people are involved, what's at stake? Look at it as if you were solving a puzzle – you need to tie all the pieces together. Once you do that, the solution usually stares you right in the face.

- ✧ Always look for a pattern. If you are wise enough, you will start looking for patterns at an early age. The mind of the average teenager might not go that far, but I am here to help you overcome that challenge. Each time you evaluate a tricky situation, try to look for a pattern of behavior. Start with yourself and expand your circle as you go, including your peers along the way. Try to find a connection to why something is happening (especially if it occurs repeatedly).

✧ Think outside the box. Yes, you have heard this many times before, but for a good reason. Coming up with alternative and creative solutions for challenges and issues can help you develop in unimaginable ways. Don't try to limit yourself to conventional approaches. Take up the exercise of creating a fictitious problem. Then, think of at least three ways to solve it. It is called training your mind.

✧ After you have come up with a valuable solution – enforce it! The sooner you take action to mend an issue – the better the results will be. This is slightly connected to the previous point. Sometimes, the first solution will backfire. And that's okay. It is why you have a few tricks up your sleeve – use them wisely!

✧ Don't give up. The most important thing to remember is not to give up on this. Take this as a personal note rather than a tip. Building up soft skills such as this takes time, so practice persistence. Learn how to make yourself think better with every challenge you face until your skill becomes next to perfection.

As we move on from the subject of problem-solving skills, I couldn't help but look forward to the last bit. Completing the circle with the last skill – critical thinking.

Critical Thinking

Instilling all of these key skills that scream leadership position means focusing deeply on each of them. The final one includes the art of critical thinking. Have you always found yourself to be a fairly reasonable person that is open-minded, a little bit skeptical, but always with respect toward precision and different points of view? Then, you are a valuable critical thinker.

These individuals tend to analyze any situation, observe, and evaluate it based on their information. The language of Michael Scriven and Richard Paul (2003) defines critical thinking as:

> *"Critical thinking is the intellectually disciplined process of actively and skillfully conceptualizing, applying, analyzing, synthesizing, and/or evaluating information gathered from, or generated by observation, experience, reflection, reasoning, or communication, as a guide to belief and action."*

What happens if you feel like you don't have it?

There is a certain discipline to learning everything – apply that in this situation as well. As a teenager, learn how to use critical thinking to your advantage. It is the last piece of the puzzle from this section that can shape you into a phenomenal professional.

Enhancing your critical thinking skills can be done with the assistance of the following tips:

✧ Evaluation should be the first thing on your mind. Evaluate everything from your sources, to how you filter the information into a relevant and irrelevant pile, and also, whether you challenge any assumptions or leave them hanging in the air. This is the first aspect of critical thinking. Developing a heightened sense of reasoning is key.

✧ Listen to the arguments and sources. As a critical thinker, you need to consider all the arguments you encounter during challenging situations, as well as the sources of those arguments. Again, an excellent exercise is to come up with a fictional issue. Develop the issue like it is a scene from a crime book. Come up with a few peers with various backgrounds and expertise and then think about their claims. Go step by step and explain your thought process to yourself. Consider multiple perspectives, however "out there" they may be. Creating such a scenario can help you develop a certain "voice of reason," where you only conclude based on facts.

✧ Ask the right questions. Have you ever noticed how the most difficult question to answer is… "Why?" Do you know that is the only way to fully explore an issue? You stimulate your practice-thinking abilities this way and you may be surprised by all the answers you get.

✧ Always, and I mean always, broaden your horizons. This is not something you can only apply in this case but in every other aspect of life too. Reading books, articles, and research papers can help you broaden your knowledge on any subject and help you feel like you are doing something to improve your critical thinking skills.

While I am on the subject of books, read as much as you can! For example, finishing this one will give you plenty of insight into what you want to do, be, and achieve in life. So, keep going!

Developing Digital Literacy and Technological Proficiency

After we have taken a good look at the most important skills together, it is time to go through another section that includes transferable skills from the 21st century. So far, I have delved into the subject of skills that have been around for a long period of time. But at this point, after you have mastered the ones above, it is time to look toward the future.

Being proficient in technology is a must for anyone these days. Whether you are a teenager, an adult, or even a senior, you are bound to adapt to the lifestyle of the world we live in now. It involves plenty of technology everywhere you turn. So, how does this apply to a professional environment?

Imagine having your own company and looking to employ a handful of people. The company can be in any sector, starting from IT and finishing up in the fashion field. As you go through the interview process, you come across an applicant with no digital literacy (almost impossible in this day and age but humor me for the sake of argument). Would you consider employing them if you knew how much time it would take to educate them on the subject of technological proficiency? Yes, it does seem like an unnecessary challenge, right?

Being skilled in digital literacy means knowing how to look for and filter relevant information precisely, quickly, and safely. This is more than just knowing how to use a computer. It is the act of browsing safely and being professional while doing it. It is a skill that will help you become a lifelong learner.

If you put your mind to it a little bit, you will realize that digital technologies are ever-changing. Nothing is constant. Even though this results in an array of flexible ways that help you to learn and work, you need to know how to keep up with the latest trends.

Being digitally literate can help you integrate into any field you want. Do you want to know what it takes to make that happen? Be mindful of the following tips:

⬥ You should start from scratch. Yes, as a young person raised in the digital era, I know this sounds kind of weird, but hear me out. You need to familiarize yourself with the simplest of tasks, such as file management, knowing your way around all operating systems, creating spreadsheets, and knowing how to present the information. Many features might have slipped through your fingers, so take a few steps back and explore.

⬥ Learn how to stay safe on the Internet. As beautiful a place as it can be, it is also the place of predators, information thieves, and more. Knowing how to be cautious when sharing information on the web is a part of being proficient in digital language.

✧ Even if you are not into coding, programming, or software development, you still need to stay on track with the latest developments in the field. That way, you can present another way of staying on top of a situation. Participating in a few courses or online forums can help you continuously build your knowledge.

✧ Experiment for creative freedom. Let's face it, eventually, with any work you do, you will want a little bit of freedom for your creative side to shine through. Pick the digital world as the most useful tool to make that happen. Challenge yourself – resolve issues using technology, learn through the trial-and-error process, and make the most out of it.

✧ Talk to people. However out of the blue this might seem, talking to peers that are as equally involved in the digital world as you may open up some fresh possibilities for you. Exchange ideas and discuss projects – it is how you can grow and deepen your knowledge.

Digital literacy will always evolve and grow. Being a teenager, it should not be difficult to adopt a growth mindset and be open to all the opportunities technology can provide you with!

Cultivating Emotional Intelligence and Adaptability

Well, well, well – we have slowly reached the topic that most teenagers avoid – emotional intelligence. But, instead of boring you with details, I am here to tell you that you can express your emotional intelligence in a healthy manner that can also help you evolve in the working arena.

Do you know what emotional intelligence means? *It is the ability to define and take control of your emotions and recognize the feelings of those around you.*

On the other hand, *adaptability is the capacity to adjust to ever-changing conditions.*

Do you know how you can develop both of these transferable skills?

The simplest answer is to create a higher level of self-awareness. The emotions you deal with as a teenager may be overwhelming at times – it is a normal process, as you are still learning how to put them under control. By being a little gentler toward yourself, you can notice which things trigger you and how you react to them, thus getting to the core of you.

Another thing – the people around you (especially in a professional setting) count on you to think on your feet and with a cool head. But that doesn't mean you should quickly dismiss all your feelings and act like a robot. Find the balance where you can validate the feelings of others and show empathy but still act professionally.

Practice active listening skills but learn how to create a barrier where it does not personally affect you or change your opinion in any way. All of this can be a handful in the beginning, so I suggest you take things slow and one at a time.

Showing a healthy and appropriate approach will only result in maturity and success. Calmly dealing with any changes that may come your way is the best way to take full control of a situation and come out on the other side like a true winner!

Did all of this seem like too much for you to handle? After all, you are still very young, and you have yet to expand your knowledge and skills, but with clear guidance, you will tackle this seemingly complex subject. That leads us to the next chapter – finding the perfect guidance!

CHAPTER 4

SEEKING GUIDANCE

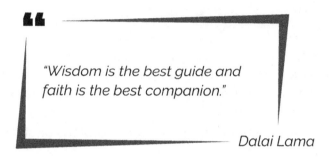

"Wisdom is the best guide and faith is the best companion."

— *Dalai Lama*

B ut what happens in those times when you feel like you have lost any sense of direction? However hard you try, and however clear your goal may be, sometimes you might get the feeling of being stuck. You feel like all the research and theory that you have done is simply not good enough.

This is the time to start experiencing the practice bit, not only the theory bit. After all, by plunging yourself into the professional world you step into the unknown without a safety net. Deciding what you want to be when you grow up is a tough question.

Instead of putting yourself under a lot of pressure by trying to accomplish everything on your own, why not try to seek out some guidance? Take the pressure off and create a safe space for you to thrive. I am giving you some insight on how to pave the road to success with the help of others.

The Role of Mentors and Role Models

Many studies have shown the importance of mentoring. All humans learn as much as possible by watching, then mimicking someone else's behavior. It has always been the easiest way to learn. Being a teenager, it is especially important to surround yourself with people you look up to, people who can positively influence your existence, and help you develop an understanding of the professional world.

Think about what kind of learning experience you want to gain. Also, try to answer this question – who do you look up to the most? Why? The role models and mentors should be people who are active participants in the community. They should be able to thrive in a professional and/or a personal setting, and they should also be able to offer you a plateau of educational and career aspirations.

There is a slight difference between a mentor and a role model. Here is a brief explanation of both.

Mentor – a mentor is a person who has plenty of experience in a specific professional field and possesses the skillset that you lack. As a teenager and a less experienced individual, they support your transitioning process from the safe environment of a classroom to the rollercoaster of the real world.

More often, they provide you with examples of how to think and act in the most common situations. I encourage every teenager to have a mentor – it can be anyone – a teacher from school, someone you admire, someone from your workplace. Ask them if they would assist you and take it from there!

Role model – the role model is not necessarily someone who can show you how to properly act, but rather show you the importance of differentiating between bad and good. A role model often presents positive and negative examples to help you understand both and to choose the right one.

Also, role models can be people you choose unconsciously. This starts from your early childhood, as you are drawn into the behavior of the people you see most often – your parents, relatives, teachers, etc. Who is your role model? Have you noticed something about them you liked so much, you started implementing it yourself?

Both are considered equally important since they can boost both morale and motivation. Their role in shaping your future includes the following:

- ✧ You get inspired. Whether it is a mentor or a role model, they are oftentimes more experienced than you are. Note their stories, their challenges, and the obstacles they had to overcome. Allow them to teach you how to navigate through your work with the help of the knowledge you have accumulated over the years.

✧ Take the advice. Despite how much stubbornness there may be within you, give them some space to help you. A career decision is a challenging process, so once you decide to seek assistance, let them help prepare you for a particular profession.

✧ Deepen your skillset. Having the proper set of skills is the jumping point that will help you stand out from the crowd tomorrow. Most of these skills include the transferable skills I talked about in the previous chapter. Mentors are especially important here, as they give you a better insight into skills such as communication, navigating through a professional environment, the power of a successful presentation, etc.

✧ Write down all the contacts. Both the mentor and the role model can be of invaluable worth when it comes to getting you in touch with the right people. They can help you create a beneficial network and make you more visible to the most important people and companies in the industry.

This is only the beginning – getting a taste of what you want sounds like a dream. But there is still a lot to cover, so let's move on to the next guidance step.

Utilizing Resources Like Career Counseling and Guidance Services

You are a part of the generation that will be the driving force that moves the world forward. Having this in mind, utilizing all the available resources to be the positive change in the world takes bringing out "the big shot" resources like career counseling.

It is a beneficial step that will lead you in the right direction and to the desired career path. Getting in touch with a career counselor is the push you need. As an individual, you are in a transitioning period, because as soon as your teenage years are over, you will become a valuable asset in the job marketplace.

Career counseling and guidance are the steps you can take to identify career opportunities that you are otherwise unable to uncover by yourself. The first step to take is to talk to a teacher, your school counselor, or a career advisor and start gathering information.

All of them may provide you with various tidbits of information, so once you set up an appointment with them, get the most out of your one-on-one with them. In the previous chapter, you created a list of the strengths (your skills) and rated them. Take that list with you and discuss it with them. You won't believe how valuable their input will be.

If you want to get the proper guidance, then you also need to share all your accomplishments up until that point with them. Gather your information about your education, your grades, your hobbies, your interests, and every extracurricular activity you have undertaken such as internships, etc. All this information can provide an insight into who you are, and can be extremely valuable to any counselor who is trying to help you.

They will give you a lot of tips and steps you can take. They will teach you how to explore job descriptions, and they will help you learn how to research multiple occupations. In the meantime, after reviewing every bit of the information you have provided them with, they will let you know if you need to obtain any additional qualifications for the field you have in mind. On top of all that, a career counselor will also guide you through any of the alternatives as well.

Last but not least, they will provide you with some online platforms to help you with your career exploration. They will help you to evaluate the potential for growth, and to teach you how to search for the best opportunities within the salary range.

Networking and Informational Interviews

Have you heard of the term networking? If your core goal includes finding the perfect job field for you, then you probably have. But not all teenagers know what it means. Networking represents getting in touch with any of the connections you have obtained during your time researching the job market. The target of networking is to build a relationship with companies and individuals who can, in the present or the future, give you plenty of advice, information, or a professional opportunity.

An informal interview is a vessel through which you deepen your relationships with the contacts from your network. Consider them as an opportunity to expand and get some useful info from a simple conversation.

Before you begin, you need to know how important this step is. As a teenager, from the informal interview, you will gain:

✧ Information about how you actually do a specific job. You will get the real picture of what it is like to occupy a certain position, rather than learning from your idea about it.

✧ Insight about how it is to work in a real environment, with real issues, and real rewards. Sometimes, the stress can be almost overwhelming, at other times, you may enjoy every second of your time spent there.

✧ Knowledge about how to get to where you want to be. With a few strategic steps, you can get into the field of your choosing.

Now, you have opened the doors of communication and you have set up an interview. You have done everything – from gathering information about the person you are meeting to collecting all the information about yourself. These are all proper steps but, once the interview begins, what are you going to ask whoever is on the other side?

Allow me to be of service. Below you will find a set of questions that you can consider as a starting point. Go over them, think about which answers you want to get, and how you can deepen the conversation on each question. Consider these questions as a way to take control of the interview and to get all the information you need. Here they are:

✧ Ask the other party to describe a day in their life. What types of situations do they encounter, and how do they deal with them?

✧ What are their interests? Is there something they like a lot, and something they strongly dislike? It can be anything from getting up early in the morning, to a special routine.

✧ The steps they took to get to where they are right now. Opportunities, formal education, expanding their skillset – everything it took!

✧ How many mistakes did they make along the way? Did that greatly impact their current position? Would they change something from their past?

✧ Why choose the field they are in at the moment? Are they planning on sticking with it for a long time, and what surprises came with the job?

✧ Ask them to give a piece of advice to a youngster like yourself.

✧ Can they recommend someone else for you to talk to? It is a great way to further expand your network.

Networking and getting information from informal interviews are great ways to get ahead on your quest for a successful professional life. Here is another extra step you can take to make that happen.

Engaging With Online Communities and Professional Organizations

There is another way to gain all the relevant data about job prospects – seeking guidance from professional organizations and online communities. Over the past few decades, these two options have become pillars of the thriving community we live in today. There are many, many options out there, all you need to do is begin your research.

❖ Identify the communities that can help you. It is important to locate the ones you share the same interests and goals with – it is how you will get the most out of the experience.

❖ Being online is easier – you are only a few clicks away from finding a community that aligns with your career goals. Once you find it, become an active member of it. Ask questions and take part in discussions. Soon you will realize you have expanded your network beyond your wildest imagination.

❖ Engage as much as you can. Virtual events, webinars, volunteering, taking up an internship, and sharing your journey with others – establish yourself as a knowledgeable member of the community and open up a path for further engagements and networking opportunities.

Sometimes, when you are too close to a certain situation, you might get caught up in it and set some unrealistic expectations. Guidance from a third party is the best way to tackle the situation. It is your responsibility to set up a support and guidance system for yourself. That way, you can help yourself move further along the path of creating a bright professional future for yourself.

With this, you get some help for the next step, which is planning for education and training. Let's go through the subject together.

CHAPTER 5

PLANNING FOR EDUCATION AND TRAINING

> *"Education is the passport for the future, for tomorrow belongs to those who prepare for it today."*
>
> — *Malcolm X*

P lanning for your future sounds like one of the most exciting things to do. Considering this will be one of your biggest life changes, it is only fair to do it your way. At least mostly, right? However, that still doesn't change the fact that you are a teenager and might not know what you want or how to get it. But don't let this discourage you.

There will be moments when you feel doubtful about your choices. Then it is best to simply take a deep breath and try to remind yourself that you don't need to rush. Put one foot in front of the other at a pace that suits you – after all, these are major life choices, and it is best to be handled with great care and research on your part.

Concentrating on educational and vocational plans may help you identify yourself better and help you reach financial stability. When you focus on all your lists, wishes and plans, and get support from the people around you, you know you are headed in the right direction.

As a starting point, review your options. Do they require special education or simpler training? This act of evaluating the steps needed to get to a certain position is called career planning. As a teenager, you think you have all the time in the world. Be careful here, you should avoid shifting to a slower gear and letting go of your professional dreams.

Instead, it is time to delve deeper into your options. Let's go!

Exploring Post-Secondary Education Options

It is vital to understand that whichever option you choose, you should probably not do it at the last minute. Yes, choosing a career path is a challenge in and of itself, but that does not mean you need to procrastinate until the last minute. Remember, you are getting into a pretty competitive world out there, so start your engine now!

Make sure to have collected all the necessary documents and submit them before the deadline. Check the admission periods for all the schools you are interested in and underline them as important dates!

This is the importance of sticking to a plan. Do you know the answer to the question "What do I want to do after school?" – If not, then make a note of it to answer it before your final year of school begins. During that summer, you can give yourself time to think and research all the options – are you going to college, do you want to undergo vocational training, join the military, or get a job?

It helps to talk with a person that you consider close. This can be your friend, maybe a family member, or even a professional. During this period, it is important to keep focusing on improving your skills, both technical and soft.

Once you become ready to start preparing yourself for the next chapter of your life, it is time to dive deep and take some action! Once school's out, you can start doing plenty of things to prepare yourself for the next chapter. Here are a handful of things that should absolutely be a part of your list:

- ✧ Start visiting trade schools and colleges. Consider it the most important step you need to take, and that is why you are doing it earlier than expected. Planning your future means deep research, so why not start visiting universities beforehand? Explore the different campuses and see what types of degree programs they offer. It will become an invaluable experience. You can differentiate between what they offer in theory and how they achieve it in practice.

✧ Start job-shadowing someone. It kind of sounds like a mentor, but it's a whole other thing. Once you have decided on a particular branch you'd like to get involved in, it is important to shatter the glass ideal of what the job is supposed to look like. Rather than creating your idea of what the responsibilities and workflow will look like, take a more "hands-on" approach. Shadowing a person who works in the field of your interest is a great way to get the feel of it without actually working.

✧ Start volunteering. Extra-curricular activities are just as important as academic achievements when applying to a university (or anywhere else). Also, getting some valuable experience can only enhance you as an applicant and person ready to dive into the professional world. Inquire about some volunteering spots in your town. There is a high chance you'll find one that fits right with your interests and skill set. Help others and help yourself through the process as well.

✧ Take note of what you need to improve. A skill set is something that you can focus on and improve at all times. If you need to boost your creative thinking process – focus on that. If you need to improve your presentation skills – focus on that, and so on. I believe you get the picture on this one, so get to work!

✧ Brainstorm the next year. The last year of your studies will go by in a flash. Thankfully, it is time to start looking into some activities and skills you haven't tried so far. Be mindful that some of them can help you get some leadership skills, and skills to become an excellent teammate. Read about the available courses and choose one (or a few) that seem like a good fit.

Evaluating the Importance of Higher Education for Specific Career Paths

Sometimes, it takes a little bit of time to realize what you want to do in life. And that is fine. There is an undeniable stability in wanting to take the year off and explore your options a little further. Of course, it only works if you truly commit to it.

However, before you immediately jump to the conclusion that maybe taking a year off or focusing on working for a while before you get to your dream might set you back a bit. Why? In most cases, there is a certain importance in higher education, especially if your career path leads you right to it.

For many teenagers, having a higher education means getting into a specific field of work and achieving success.

While there are many professions out there that require no university degree, many of them still do.

Think about this for a while - even if your preferred career choice does not require you to continue your formal education, if you have the chance to go to university, why not take it?

Are you looking for a way to enhance your learning skills? Higher education can make you more prepared, help shape you as a person and provide you with the option of career maturity, adaptability, and a sense of belonging.

Allow me to elaborate further. Some careers require a traditional approach, and here are a few to begin with:

If you are going into medicine. Do you think becoming a healthcare professional without any higher education is possible? If this is one of your choices, then you absolutely need to comb through all the universities that provide graduate programs that will get you a step closer to achieving your goal. Whether it is a nursing program or medical school, you need to be adequately prepared, especially in those cases where another life is at stake.

If you are going for a legal profession. Are you dreaming about becoming a lawyer or a judge? Your dream will only nudge you in the right direction. It requires plenty of work and studying hard. Also, it cannot be achieved without formal training. Every legal professional undergoes a graduate and even a post-graduate program. Through these programs, you get the ability to understand and learn complex legal concepts. You will also enjoy the perk of building your network while in law school.

If you are going into education. There is no way you become a part of the educational system without the proper education, because it will be you that one day shapes the minds of the future. Obtaining a degree in teaching will open up a realm of possibilities for you. It can help you make the transition from a teenager yourself to someone who helps teenagers in the future become who they want to be.

If you are going into science. There are more than a few reasons why going into the field of science requires investing in higher education. You will not only enjoy the perks of the wider network, but also you will gain expertise, guidance, and research opportunities, as well as laboratories so advanced that you'll get to learn some pretty spectacular things! On top of that, gaining better data analysis skills and using scientific methodology while obtaining your scientific research degree will make you feel even more fulfilled!

If you are going into engineering. Due to the fast advancements in technology, it is no wonder why so many young people want to be a part of this ever-growing world. Being one of them yourself is a great idea! If you have always had a knack for building and creating things and have shown a special kind of admiration toward technology, then this is the field for you. But don't be fooled into thinking that a few YouTube crash courses are the equivalent of higher education. Obtain a degree in computer science, information technology, or engineering. It is a field requiring a certain level of specialization to thrive.

These are just a handful of options that require a formal higher education. But if these are not on your list, there is no need to feel discouraged! In the next section, we go through some alternatives that you might find incredibly useful!

Considering Alternatives to Traditional Education

We live in a world where looking for alternatives to college has become increasingly popular, and it is getting more socially acceptable by the minute. Teenagers fail to realize that this practice has existed since the dawn of time. Every generation has that "revelation moment" where they realize there are many alternatives to be considered.

For some teenagers, college is still an essential and wonderful experience. But, for those who wish to take a more alternative path toward creating a bright future, many options are right here waiting for you! Does your teenage intuition tell you that maybe college is not the right choice for you? Before making a long-term commitment that you might regret, pause. Let me help you think outside the box for a bit.

Your career goal should be your main focus, and getting there is only a part of the process. So, look into some of the options that I have laid out for you and see if one of them appeals to your senses:

An apprenticeship – the delicate art of training for a career as a carpenter, an electrician, and so much more lies in the form of an apprenticeship. This is an incredible way to get the most out of your training and enter the workforce as a worker with plenty of skills! After an apprenticeship, you can easily get licensed (granted after you are under strict surveillance and training for a specified time period). Take this as an alternative to traditional education but know that it too takes a while to complete it.

Community college – you might have only heard about this option until now but don't know what it is. So far, this has been the most popular alternative to university studies, mostly because of the accessibility point of view. A community college is a fantastic option that offers various programs – one of which will surely be up to your liking. This is an excellent chance if you are considering attending a school close to your home. The perfect option if you want to take on a job while working. Do you wish to get the feel of a higher education without going through the entire four-year challenge? Community college is the answer.

Online learning – the vastness of the Internet shows no limits! All you need to do is find the right course that fits your needs. Dedicate a few hours of your day to learning what you love. After some time, you will find yourself filled with knowledge and skills that you could have only dreamt about obtaining in such a short time! What I love the most about the Internet is that anyone can use it as an educational tool. Why not do that yourself? View it as a means to improve overall performance and expertise. Take some free courses or pay for a few courses if necessary! Either way, as long as you are determined and pass the classes with flying colors, you will have a list of employers or clients waiting for you.

A vocational education – one of the fastest-growing college alternatives is the trade schools. It seems that although they cost a little less than a more formal higher education, they are still the preferred choice of many. Any teenager wanting a streamlined path toward becoming a part of the workforce should try this. Why waste your time sitting in classes you have no interest in? Instead, spend your time wisely – learning what you are interested in!

An employment – you might be one of those individuals that want to get right into building their portfolio with employment – right out of high school. In today's world, getting a job after finishing your secondary education and working your way up the ladder to a position you choose is more possible than ever. Even though, as a worker, you will encounter many challenges along the way (and during the application process, too), it might be worth your while. Many employers nowadays value the possibility of career advancement through both employment and education, so if you are up for a challenge like this one, I encourage you to take the next step.

Social media – as you can see, in today's world, there are many more options than you can think of. One of those options includes having a full-time career as a content creator or a social media personality. This is an option that was not available 10 or 15 years ago. Even though it is a relatively new field, it attracts more and more people every day. If this is your dream job, then you might want to learn something more about it. Many young people start with this, but only a few succeed. The key is having an entrepreneurial and dedicated spirit, so good luck!

Entrepreneurship – instead of getting a degree or a 9-5 job, you can always focus on building something from the ground up yourself! Turn that dream into reality with the help of some meticulous entrepreneurship. As a young mind, you have a fresh perspective of what the world needs and where it is going, so why not utilize that to create some cash flow? The invention or the business idea that you keep circling back to – focus on that, build on that, and reap the benefits once you succeed!

These are part of your options (to name a few) that can help you determine which professional path you want to take. After narrowing down your choice, we come to the next step of the planning process – finances!

Financial Planning for Education and Scholarships

Fitting your professional future into your budget can sometimes mean making a little bit of a sacrifice. Since it is only for the duration you need to obtain the proper skills or degree, this should not be a problem. As a vibrant young teenager, you have plenty of options – if you don't have the necessary means to finance your next step it does not mean you should immediately quit!

All you need is a solid plan. So, here are a few resources that could get you started:

- ✧ See how you can save some money and make the most out of it. Check the available scholarships and whether you are eligible for any of them. As a student, many benefits and grants serve the purpose of helping you achieve your goals and dreams, so use them to the fullest extent!

- ✧ Create a balance between focusing on your education and your work (mostly if you want to do a good job at both). Many teenagers skip this step, firmly believing that they "got this." Well, do you? Set some time to think and create a plan that can help you achieve all the deadlines, finish all the work, and complete your goals. You can help prevent spiraling down into a hole filled with missed deadlines and opportunities.

✧ Be mindful that things can change in a minute. Understanding that there is a specific extent to which things can go one way if you don't maintain them is key. Upgrade your flexibility and remember to prepare yourself for everything. Because, as much as you give, sometimes, things can go awry. It is in those cases that you need to have a plan B, C, and all the other letters if you need to – make sure you are prepared for the unexpected.

✧ Always be on the lookout for new opportunities. Every new day is an opportunity in and of itself. As much as it sounds like a solid idea to make a financial plan, that does not mean that you should completely ignore some wonderful opportunities that may cross your path. Regularly check any resources that might be of help to you, and don't give up!

Create a stable financial structure that can support your next step in the educational process. Be mindful of those bad days, as they may come easily, but they may also go easily as well.

Now, we are at a crossroads – the subject of planning for your education and the training process to become a valuable part of the workforce is complete. But we are only getting started on the practical aspect of it!

The next chapter encompasses the power of practical experience. Learn all you can about it!

CHAPTER 6

GAINING PRACTICAL EXPERIENCE

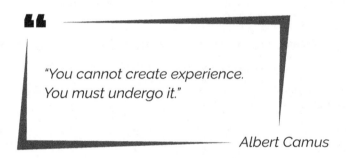

*"You cannot create experience.
You must undergo it."*

— Albert Camus

E xperience is not something that you can obtain by only listening to your classes or courses. For this bit, you need to dip your toes into the professional waters and find out how you can swim for yourself.

The teenage years are the best years of your life. But they are also the ones where you should work the hardest. In the beginning, it might seem like a waste of time to focus on gaining and sharpening your skills. But, if you look at the long run, you will soon notice how, with each passing day, you have a bigger need for them.

So, once you've established your plan for education and training, it is time to start gaining some practical experience. That will help you set a strong foundation for all professional curveballs that life throws at you later.

Do you know where to begin? Do you know your options? This is another confusing aspect on the road to finding the right career path. Thankfully, it is easy to overcome it! I have broken down the most popular choices for you below. Take a look at them and evaluate how they would fit into your situation – one of them will eventually work out for you!

Volunteering, Internships and Part-Time Jobs

It is easy to become a part of the enchanted circle – you need the experience to get a job, but you need a job to get experience! I have noticed that this fact can create a bit of panic for some teenagers. No worries, there are always some pretty good options that can help you get started. As long as you are dedicated to your goal, you can achieve anything!

For a beginner such as yourself, it might confuse you to notice that plenty of job opportunities require a certain degree of relevant experience. This is a normal part of the job-seeking process, but when you are at such an early stage, how can you take control of the situation?

Well, there are many ways you can contribute to building your portfolio. For starters, take a look at the most common ones – volunteering, internships, and part-time jobs.

Volunteering – these are available in almost every field. In today's world, volunteering is the act of being an active participant in the community. When you start doing this at an early age, it sets you apart from the crowd and makes you more prepared for what's to come.

Consider this as an essential activity that will open the doors to finding the perfect job opportunities for you. Are you looking for some experience in the democracy field or maybe the veterinary field? A passionate individual like yourself should only view this as the essential steppingstone into the professional world. It will give you an insight into how your community works, bring some purpose to your life, and teach you some valuable lessons about work. Fun fact – volunteering can also improve your overall well-being and self-esteem!

Why not check out a few companies in your area? Do the proper research (depending on your field of interest) and note the few distinguished establishments you find. From this point on, all you need to do is get in touch with them and start volunteering!

Internships – some of you feel the need to benefit financially as well as professionally on the road to success. That is where internships come onto the scene. As with volunteering, you get to benefit from creating a wide network, get some experience, and help yourself learn about what you want to do later in life.

Even though remote work is becoming increasingly popular, as a teenager, you have more access to an internship than ever before. Think about dedicating a summer or a few hours of the week to this cause and see how it will benefit you in the long run.

After you have completed your internship in whichever field you like, (administration, social media, fashion, graphic design, etc.) you will come out the other end thriving! You might not notice, but through the process, you will not only gain a little bit of professional and financial stability but will also expand your theoretical knowledge beyond your wildest imagination. Plus, you get to amplify your resume!

Part-time jobs – now, you are working toward getting a university degree, and that is your sole goal. So, why waste your energy with working a part-time job?

This is the mindset of a common teenager. You might feel like this would be an unnecessary distraction when in fact, it is the one thing you need! A part-time job can give you a unique insight into what makes the professional world go round. You will get to experience it for a short while and learn some valuable lessons during it.

If your soft skills are not up to par, you will certainly experience a revelation. Besides seeing how specific rules apply in the workplace, you will improve your time management, gain a sense of responsibility, and learn how to work in a team.

Last but not least, this will not only boost your resume but your confidence too!

Remember, these options are only the tip of the iceberg! There are as many options to gain experience as job choices, so buckle up because I have a lot more for you.

Summer Programs and Camps

Now, while I was on the subject of internships, I mentioned that you can spend a summer learning and expanding your skills. If this is stuck in your mind, then this next part is for you.

First of all, let me applaud you for your good thinking! Considering a summer program or a camp is an excellent opportunity to grow, learn, and figure out what you want to do with your life. While many teenagers underestimate the subject of a summer camp, (sounds geeky at first) you saw the possibility of investing in yourself! At the end of the day, that is what matters the most!

On the other hand, if you are still on the fence or strongly against it, allow me to elaborate. What have your summers been like up until now? Going out with your friends, maybe reading a book, playing video games, and spending your time idly doing nothing important. If I am correct, then you probably need a change. As much as you deserve the break after 9 months of studying hard, there is a much better way to use your time and acquire something valuable.

To those of you that have not yet realized the benefits of investing in yourself over the summer, I dedicate this next bit to you:

- ✧ Start using everything you have learned so far – even if it has only been in theory, entering a summer program will give you the platform to try all you have learned so far. Whether it is a technical skill or a soft skill, this is the best place to see if it works, as it is a safe zone that will not lead to some serious repercussions.

- ✧ Go soft and go practical – you will be placed in a unique environment – a learning one. This is not only your time to shine but your time to also be a creator of a better self. Practicality is key here, so once you browse the plateau of available summer camps and programs, choose the one that will give you the best experience.

✧ It is about all kinds of skills – you may not have thought about this until now, but entering a summer program can help you plunge into a world without any kind of safety net. Deliberately place yourself in a position where it is obligatory to learn many life skills. It all starts from the smallest and simplest skills and builds up to the challenging ones you are looking to obtain. This can be a way for you to learn both how to make your bed and practice leadership skills. Sounds like something you'd want to experience, right?

✧ A summer program is not a place of anarchy – but a place of understanding and learning accountability. Yes, you will be left to your own devices, but you will be under the constant observation of professionals who know how to handle any situation. Consider them your mentors and let them guide you. These are usually a handful of counselors who are there for you to learn from them. They will hold you responsible for your actions to the fullest extent, thus giving you the trial, you need for a professional life.

✧ Learn without the stress of – school, exams, talking in front of your entire class – all of which can make you feel high levels of stress and anxiety. Everything changes the minute you are a teenager, so the important thing is to give yourself time to grow. But also, the space to grow. A summer program is a great way to learn without the added stress of classmates and grades. It is about letting go of your fears and fully committing to the tasks at hand.

✧ Make life-long connections – I know that expanding your network is the last thing on your mind when starting a summer program, but it is one of its most incredible benefits. When you look at it – both the counselors and your peers may end up being excellent and very valuable to you in the future – and vice versa!

I hope that I have helped you make up your mind on this one. Speaking of mind, this next one might be the perfect fit if you want to sharpen yours in a more competitive and challenging environment.

Shadowing Professionals and Job Shadowing Opportunities

At this stage, you must wonder what various jobs look like. Is the stress level the same in any field? Is there a different level of responsibility depending on the type of work? Also, how do you know you have reached a stage where you are ready to become a professional or an expert in a particular field?

If there is one thing that can help answer all of these questions, it is a job shadowing opportunity. You are a teenager, which means that most of these vacancies where you can shadow someone are designed specifically for you.

Having this opportunity to shadow a professional means you get to have someone introduce you to the vast business world and what it encompasses. Additionally, it has proven to be a successful approach to bringing successful individuals into many fields, and it has become an acceptable – no, preferable course of action.

This can help you determine your major in college, realize what you want to do after you finish high school, and give you an idea of what the rest of your life would look like. Remember that question grown-ups always asked you? "What do you want to be when you grow up?" Well, after this, you should be able to answer it satisfactorily.

Do you know what you need to do to get there? Other than being polite and professional, you need to choose a company that can provide you with one of their employees as the best example of what you want to be. Request a shadowing appointment where you introduce yourself. Share your interests, which school you're attending, why you are interested in shadow work, and whether they have someone on the dates you're available. For this last one, keep in mind that not all will have someone available for the first dates you request, so showing some flexibility is a plus.

Once you make all the necessary arrangements, it is time to start the shadow work! It is key to realize that you are in the observer role and won't have much to do. In contrast, you will have much to see and learn. Even if you don't have any background in the field, use this as the groundwork upon which you will build a better understanding of the workplace as a definition.

There are many things you will learn on your job shadowing journey. The small tasks you get will result in you gaining the following:

You will learn how the job you want works – shadowing a professional will give you direct access to your future – you will see how you should function and witness a typical day that includes all the responsibilities, challenges, and issues.

The connection with the other positions – any job you choose to take up as a career path will have a close connection to another branch. With job shadowing, you will learn how to connect with various branches and form successful relationships. You will learn how to be a part of a well-oiled machine that works impeccably.

Expand your network – however long or short your shadowing experience may be, it is crucial to start networking. You are a teenager now, but the connections you coin will be the ones that can help you spread your wings in full glory once you become a part of the workforce.

Learn how to learn – don't be afraid to ask questions and take small matters into your own hands (when possible). This is how you can develop a more accurate representation of yourself and the job you want to do.

Note that, depending on the job shadowing program you find, the tasks may vary – substantially. Making the most out of it can only mean one thing – flexibility. Keep an open mind, whatever the situation, trust your gut, and think independently. Circumstances may change at any moment, so here are a few tips to help you out during those times:

- ✧ You don't need to focus so much on leaving a good impression, but you should always be polite and professional.

- ✧ Keep in mind that your mentor might have some demanding responsibilities and provide the space to finish them.

- ✧ Not everything will look interesting – a part of the experience may be incredibly dull – that is normal.

✧ Appreciate everything your mentor says to you – remember, they dedicate a valuable portion of their time to teaching you how things work.

✧ It is okay if, by the end of the shadowing process, you realize you don't want to pursue that particular career – consider it another lesson you have learned.

After you have gained all the necessary practical experience, you should be ready to write it all down – as a part of your resume! Do you think you got what it takes to create a successful one?

Building a Portfolio or Resume to Showcase Skills and Experiences

It takes the skillful act of putting words together and doing it in a way that accentuates your capabilities to the fullest extent. However active you may have been with all the internships, volunteering, job shadowing, etc., you may not have the proper skills to put all your experiences into words.

More often than not, teenagers get confused when they come to this section, and not only because it poses quite a writing challenge, but many need to recognize the difference between a portfolio and a resume.

Before we go much further, help yourself – learn the difference.

Portfolio – the portfolio is a visual representation of your practical work. It should be filled with examples of your work. You might think that only photographers use a portfolio (due to the visual aspect of it), but anyone can use it. A portfolio can be filled with links, videos, texts, various illustrations, and so much more.

A typical portfolio includes an originality statement (a small paragraph where you write that the work included is yours and confidential). Furthermore, it should have a summary of your career, a brief biography, and a small paragraph that will serve its purpose as a belief statement. Here, you include your motivations, values, likes, and goals.

Resume – on the other hand, a resume is a more concise and less creative way of showing a company who you are. There are many formats for you to choose from, but all in all, it should contain the following – a summary of your working experience (as a beginner, you should list all the practical experience you have gained, including starting and finishing dates and contacts, in chronological order), add your education in chronological order too, and list all the skills you have (these include soft skills and technical ones, relevant for the position you are applying).

Before you start applying for the jobs you have found, you need to create an impeccable resume and portfolio that will set you apart from the crowd. There are a few ways how to do that:

Research the role you're applying for – there is nothing worse than giving your potential employer a bunch of information they're not interested in. Put some time and effort into researching the role you are going for and customize your resume to fit their needs (to a certain point). Remember, you still need to keep the information within reasonable and truthful boundaries.

Add all your accomplishments – gather all the recommendations, achievements, extra-curricular activities, internships, and programs you have undergone. Demonstrate to your future employer that your education and investment in yourself have been your primary goal up until then.

Keep it short but include everything – I know this sounds a little complicated, but you need to keep your sentences short. Include all the info you need, and especially for your resume. Keep it within a page.

Promote yourself – language is not the only thing that matters while creating your resume and portfolio. It is imperative to know how to promote yourself too, so further enhance it with color. You can even go as far as creating an online portfolio – that's always a showstopper!

By the end of this chapter, you've made it easier for yourself to become a person that has some participation in the practical section, not just the theoretical one.

As we close the chapter on gaining some practical experience, we open the next one – deciding what you want. Toward the end of the job shadowing part, I mentioned that you might not like what you see. Have you thought about what to do if that happens? Either way, see for yourself in the following chapter.

CHAPTER 7

MAKING INFORMED DECISIONS

> **"**
>
> *"Nothing is more difficult, and therefore more precious, than to be able to decide."*
>
> — *Napoleon Bonaparte*

N apoleon's decisions may not have always been right, but he is definitely right about this one. It is finally time for you to decide what you want. However scary it may sound, bear with me – there are ways to exclude your emotions and make a choice based solely on facts (ones you have gathered so far).

From knowing the current and future job opportunities to knowing how good or bad you would be at each of them, it is all about considering the info you have. That said, there are a few steps you can take that can help you pick a successful career alternative.

Weighing the Pros and Cons of Different Career Options

You are a teenager, so don't be surprised if you find it very difficult to exclude emotions from your decision-making process. After all, this may be the most challenging step you face. Thinking logically, you must already have a few alternatives lined up, and now, all of them seem like good options! So, which one to go for?

Start enjoying the power of making a list with pros and cons. If you are unable to do it yourself, ask for help! Get your mentor, a friend, a relative – anyone whom you trust, to assist you. Making a decision this large requires your full attention and the need to analyze all the factors. I recommend you use all the deep research you have done so far, as well as some soul-searching.

It might be difficult at the moment, but *picture yourself ten years from now.* What do you see? Do you see a role where you can thrive and constantly move up the corporate ladder, or do you maybe see yourself as running your own business, making the rules as you go? Try answering this question truthfully – you will gain an excellent starting point for your career path.

You have a very big decision to make, so get your pen and paper out and start writing! Lay out all the options in front of you. Underneath each, make a division into two sections. One will be for the pros and the other one for the cons. Remember, you are making this decision based on your priorities and needs! Start writing things down. While you do that, do some further investigation of your own – down to the last detail! Take a look at the working hours, take a look at the experience needed for each field separately, and take a look at the benefits that are mostly offered for each position. Also, see if there is a possibility for growth in every field. As an inexperienced individual, you may overlook this, but some job positions can become generic over time. That being said, after a few years, you may find out there is no room to grow. It is much better to be aware of it before you are already deep into the work.

Consider this as one of the best aspects of your decision-making process. Right now, all opportunities may seem equal – when in fact, they are not. Instead of leaving it all to your gut, you are doing the right thing by filling out the negative and positive sides of every alternative you have.

In reality, when you look at the situation on paper, you will see that some concerns you thought were incredibly large can be handled in a minute. On the other side, you may uncover some potential opportunities or new concerns that will completely shift the focus of everything.

Trust the process – that is the most important thing to do. Find the thing that is the driving force that would pull you forward into professional success and discover what your breaking points are. For some, it might be the generic work I mentioned earlier. For others, it might be the long hours or maybe, the long commute. *For you, it will be anything that does not fit your wants and needs.*

The pros and cons list is just a plan where you prioritize your needs and goals and align them with the job opportunities on the market. I am explaining the market demand and how to understand it better below. Read it so you know how to make an even better and more informed decision.

Understanding Market Demand and Job Prospects

As a teenager, you might not be able to identify what skills are necessary for the job market of today. During all this uncertainty, you might be panicking and unable to take a step in any direction. However, when your future employment is at stake, you need to understand both the market demand and the job prospects.

The uncertainty that is arising in the *market demand* at the moment is due to its dynamic nature. Things progress faster than usual, and it is all thanks to the help of technology. Many job opportunities considered solid and necessary about a decade or two ago are now slowly diminishing. Contrary to that, technology paves the way for many new prospects to emerge and promises these will be the exact ones that will lead society into the future.

What you might notice here is that the job prospects for you (based on the specific and soft skills you have) vary from the market demand.

Let's talk a bit about disruptions.

In a perfect world, as soon as you finish high school, go to university, and get a degree (or not), you start working within the field you want. Everyone gets the training and fulfills the requirements during high school, with almost no extra-curricular activities, and the transition from a schoolbook to an office desk is as seamless as possible.

In reality, things cannot be further from this. Nowadays, the world is facing a global skills gap since the market is constantly looking for a vaster skillset than anyone can achieve with traditional education. I cannot imagine how it is for a teenager such as yourself to face this kind of situation.

Fortunately, however limited your skillset is, understanding the market demand and looking into future job prospects can help place you a step ahead of everyone else.

Noticing a gap or a lot of inequalities between what you want to do, and your level of expertise is the first step in the right direction. This means that you have realistically evaluated the prospects and are ready to face whatever challenges may come your way.

You are now standing on the edge of a certain change. Instead of holding back and pushing your potential down, try doing the exact opposite. Embrace change, become change. The transition from studying to working can either make you or break you. Try to focus on the making bit.

Making yourself better for future *job prospects* comes from the ability to invest in your career development. That is what we have been learning about together until now, and that is what you will continue doing long after you read this book.

Do you need some tips to help you set up for the future? On top of all you have done until now, here are a few tips that can catapult you to the top of your employers' job lists!

1st tip – it is essential to stay on top of all the recent changes in your field of interest. All the recent changes equate to adding some new skills to your resume. As long as you are aware that change is constantly happening, you can stay on top of the situation and become a life-long learner. Consider this as a primary tip that will help you increase your employability. While you regularly update your skills, you will become more in sync with what employers want and what the market needs.

2nd tip – signaling that you are the best candidate for the job in any field requires having some professional validation beforehand. I have mentioned this many times before. Consider this as an extracurricular activity. Getting an extra certification or undergoing a seminar is somewhat of a precondition for entering the workforce. Many courses vary in importance, duration, etc., which can signal to employers you have taken the extra step to become eligible for a certain job position.

3rd tip – focus on positive development (and I don't mean this in the sense of making yourself presentable). Expand your views and interests as much as you can, and always have this in mind – *you are doing this for yourself.* Yes, showing a certain level of diversity is important, especially as a young person just entering the workforce. But at the end of the day, it is you who must be happy and fulfilled by it.

That leads me to the next aspect to consider – and that is the overall quality of life based on the career path you choose.

Considering Lifestyle Factors and Work-Life Balance

Enough about technicality. Let's talk about practicality! By now, you must already have a system set in place and a certain lifestyle. You have your wants and needs, your goals, and your routines. You have your friends, your relatives, the people you are closest to. You have your hobbies and interests and things that help you pass the time. You have an entire life set up.

You have a certain lifestyle that, up until this point, has been supported by your parents/guardians. Suddenly, it is time to start thinking that you need to survive by yourself. It is time to let go of the training wheels.

Now, it is time to face the music and start thinking about how to make it on your own. Transitioning from a teenager to an adult feels like it's happening faster than a heartbeat. As soon as you turn 18, you're not a child anymore. On top of choosing a career path now, you also need to be extra careful about it so it can fit into your life and not change it as much.

Considering the balance between work and life is another one of the most important factors when choosing your preferred field of interest. It is not all about technical and soft skills and how to upgrade yourself. It is also about the overall quality of life and whether the subject you choose fits right into that.

If you are still looking at the pros and cons list you made earlier, remember to focus on choosing a career that helps you lead the life you want. Today, anyone, even a teenager, can notice that the lines between professional and personal life have become blurred, almost non-existent. The many trends, including flexible hours, working from home, being constantly available for work because of your smartphone, etc., have resulted in more of a negative response than a positive one. People who have been working for years have noticed how they bring their work home more frequently than before, and the shift in working hours is actually a shift in their entire day. That can lead to plenty of frustration and stress.

As a fresh mind who is only entering the world of work, remember that you have all the power to create the lifestyle that will suit you the best.

It is important to maintain a balance between professional and personal life.

It is important to understand how valuable of an aspect this is.

It is important to strive toward creating a life for yourself that you like.

I am hoping that I can help you reinforce this as soon as possible so you can enjoy the outcome for many years to come. If you weren't aware until now that life is full of choices, here it is. You are in front of one, a very important one. Any call you make will influence your life.

There are a few perks that come with choosing to make a balance between your work and your personal life. Take a look at them below:

✧ You will have some time to focus on your physical health. It is important to maintain an active lifestyle, especially if the career path you choose tends to lead to a more sedentary lifestyle. Keeping your body active can help you remain focused, happier, healthier, and thus enjoy a good work-life balance.

✧ Never neglect mental health too. Being a workaholic may be a challenge for you now – you are young, full of energy, and have a lust for life. But what will happen in 10 or 20 years from now? Constantly focusing on your work without having time for yourself or your family and friends can result in a significant mental decline. You should be able to work without having any difficulties, so eliminate them from the start.

✧ There is a lot of stress in the world, don't let it consume you. Imagine taking up a career path that requires you to be available nonstop, gives you little to no freedom to do something for yourself, and makes you constantly feel under pressure. Eventually, you will start slipping, and you will be unable to manage your workload. Being under a lot of stress for a long period will only have a negative effect. This is why you need to opt for a job that teaches you how to manage your workload within working hours and allows you to leave something for tomorrow.

✧ When you have the time to focus on personal activities, you are more productive at work. This is a fact that you might not be aware of yet. Having some personal time for yourself, instead of only focusing on your professional engagements, can help you feel more fulfilled, thus be more productive and present while working.

All of this sounds excellent on paper, but once you are part of the real deal, it can significantly change your viewpoint. Sticking to a schedule you have set beforehand may be more difficult than you have imagined. It is at those times you should focus on the following:

✧ Start your work, and then set a goal. Try to be as realistic with your goals as possible. Understand that you can work both on a personal and a professional goal at the same time and make some room for both during the day. Doing this can help you maintain a better balance.

✧ While you work, work productively. Come to terms with the fact that you will only have a certain amount of time in the day dedicated to work, so make the most out of it. Increase your productivity levels by managing your workload and ensure that the extra tasks you may get from your work will not affect your personal life.

✧   This leads me to the following – separate state and church. Work is one thing, home is another, and while you are at home, refrain from using your work laptop or checking notifications after hours. If you want to maintain a balanced lifestyle, then stick to the schedule you've prepared for yourself.

✧   Last but not least, put stress management as your priority. Every job comes with its obstacles and challenges. Learn that while you're still a teenager. Also, find a healthy way that helps you cope with stress. It can be anything from taking a 5-minute break to developing a new hobby such as running, writing, listening to podcasts, etc.

Achieving a balance between work and life is essential. Instead of looking for a job that has long working hours, create stability by growing and enjoying more aspects of life than just the work one. Learn how to best evaluate where the biggest potential for growth is.

Evaluating the Potential for Growth and Advancement in Chosen Fields

There is a sort of dramatic point to it all, but if you are not growing in life, then what are you doing exactly? The potential for career growth comes from the fact that you need a sense of purpose to start this journey. It is the path that separates you from the bigger picture and the career of your dreams.

Looking at that piece of paper with all you've written down on it. Can you easily spot the career paths where you'd have the biggest progress?

Important note – *career growth and career development are entirely different things. If we have focused on career development and transferable skills until now, career growth shifts the focus to entering a field that can help you thrive.*

Career growth has the option to advance in a particular field. In the long run, it helps you unlock a higher level of your potential, ultimately reaching the top! If you choose an area where, after a while, you will hit the ceiling of developing your skills and will start doing generic work, would that bring much satisfaction to your life? Contrary to that, choosing a field where one thing constantly changes will give you a plateau of options – ones you'll never be bored of.

After all, it is all about growth. Right now, the power is in your hands – you can shape your future life and add this secret ingredient in every aspect. You may not believe it, but in all cases, the possibility for career growth is the catapult that will move you forward. Essentially, it is highly beneficial to your well-being and will make you happy. So, choose career advancement, choose a better life, and choose yourself!

There is a balance in everything, isn't there? I applaud you for being able to stop and look within, weigh in all the factors, and make an informed decision. From all the steps we have gone through together, this might have easily been the most difficult one – so brava!

Consider this as a chapter where you need to take a breather from all you have done so far and rest your body for the next bit that is coming – taking some swift actions! We're going from a passive to an active exercise – let's see what you need to do there!

CHAPTER 8

TAKING ACTION

> **"**
>
> *"Now is no time to think of what you do not have. Think of what you can do with what there is."*
>
> — *Ernest Hemingway*

I t is time to start acquiring the career of your dreams. You have done all this planning, researching, and investing in yourself. You are more than ready. You got this. These are the last steps you will take toward creating your bright future.

Taking action does not mean aimlessly running around and doing everything you can until "something sticks." It means being strategic about your future, striving toward the achievement of your goals, and of course, having a backup plan.

Are you excited to get started? Your own chapter in life is almost ready to unfold.

Setting Short-Term and Long-Term Career Goals

There is a certain importance behind setting goals for yourself. It amplifies the importance of being a part of society, and for many teenagers, it gives the much-needed self-boost. Career goals are the motivation that can drive you forward and keep you jumping out of your bed, filled with excitement every morning.

You are a young person, so learning how to set goals properly is a skill you should possess. The trick to knowing what you want is being completely honest with yourself.

By learning how to set short-term and long-term goals, you create a mood board. Fill it up with everything you want to achieve.

It is important to note that it is not all about the destination. This is about the journey along the way as well. As a teenager, you need to stop to realize what resources you have at hand, determine that what you want to achieve is really your goal, not someone else's, and identify all the aspects where you might need some help. So, when you look at it, it is a simple thing to do. But it requires your full attention!

All of us have goals. They can be small, large, personal, or professional. Nevertheless, many teenagers confuse the action of setting a goal with the plan to achieve it. Daydreaming and thinking about what you want to achieve without doing anything about it will only get you somewhere, but not necessarily where you intended. It is a nice sentiment, though. Do you want to achieve everything you put your mind to? In that case, you need a solid plan to make it happen.

Actually, you need a **smart** plan to do it.

Are you wondering why the word smart is accentuated? SMART goals are a concept that can help you achieve wonders, especially with your career. It is the guidance many teenagers aren't aware of but find useful when they stumble upon it. This exercise can help you map out the steps to achieve your goal. It is probably one of the best exercises you will utilize, mainly because many people of all ages use it – constantly!

SMART is the acronym for the process you are about to undergo. Each letter represents a significant course of action you should take to achieve a successful career. Here is a short representation of what they mean:

S – stands for specific. By this point, you should have more than just an idea for your future self. Don't be afraid to go into a detailed plan – it might give you a clearer view of the big picture!

M – stands for measurable. This means tracking your progress. Take small steps toward achieving it, but ensure they are measurable. Take learning a new language as an example. Dedicate an hour of your time every day to understanding it – that is a quantifiable way of achieving your goal.

A – stands for attainable. Be realistic with yourself. We have covered the aspects of what you can and can't do, underlining your strengths and weaknesses. Now it is time to use that. Don't push yourself too hard – instead, create an attainable goal (one you know you can achieve).

R – stands for realistic. Just like the previous letter, a realistic goal will help you develop your skills instead of creating a cloud of insecurities around you.

T – stands for time-bound. When you set up a goal, you should have a specific timeline. This means tracking down your progress until the process is complete. Breaking down the long-term goal into smaller milestones can help you prove there is constant progress and help you easily reach your goal.

You know what SMART goals are. Do you know how they support you? During the time you dedicate to fulfilling your dreams, this exercise provides you with some silent support along the way. Regard it as your fuel.

The process of setting a goal can have a positive impact on your overall lifestyle. After putting some time and effort into the plan, it can help you become better, stronger, and more successful. Ultimately SMART goals are shaping you into the person you want to be.

Take the lead as soon as you set your plan. Create some long-term or short-term career goals. As an exercise, it can provide you with many benefits, not only because it will give you the confidence you need (and open doors for you). Also, this is ultimately a rewarding experience. Working to achieve your dream results in picking up an extra skill or two on your way there. You will start feeling more independent and will learn from all the challenges you meet along the way.

Also, every time you set up a goal (be that a short-term or a long-term one), remember it can change at any time. Keep your mind flexible at all times. Give yourself a break every time you feel like you need one. Finally, don't forget to celebrate all the little milestones! It may seem insignificant, but success is made out of a lot of the small things you do every day. Pat yourself on the back after every milestone you achieve.

However, this is only the beginning. After all, you should know how to create a proper plan filled with strategies. For that matter, I will go over all the necessary details to do that in the following section.

Creating a Strategic Action Plan

It is all about creating a professional development plan. Through this door, you will enter right into the professional world. Depending on your goal, you can outline some objectives. Create a solid plan on how to achieve them. There are numerous opportunities out there for you. You can dream of becoming an art director, a graphic designer, a party planner, someone who runs their own business, etc. You have so many available options; you just need to choose and start walking your path toward success.

That is what a strategic action plan is for.

The bottom line is - be aware of everything. When I say everything, I mean – start from yourself. Knowing where to begin means fully understanding what you are good at. This is your jumping point and the strength you hold when times get tough. There are a lot of factors that weigh in here. So, take a look at the outline I have prepared for you below – you might find it incredibly useful!

Analyze Your Strengths and Weaknesses

We have mentioned them at the beginning, but as you can see, they are such an important part of creating a career path that we are constantly going back to them. Through them, you outline who you are.

As I pointed out before, these include both the soft and the technical skills you currently have. Once you finish evaluating yourself, you start outlining which ones you excel at, and which ones need improvement. The ones you are good at are the force driving you toward achieving anything you want. The ones that need improvement are the ones that are currently holding you back.

On the other hand, the list might lack a thing or two, so you might consider adding them and working on them – that's a great option too! Think skills, think traits. Any one of them can be polished to perfection through formal education or training. You may even achieve perfection by working on them without any help!

Write Down the Values

As you start working toward making some progress on a professional level, you will see there will be many bumps in the road. Some are minor, such as tight deadlines or an argument with a colleague. But others are of a more considerable significance. These include when the workflow interferes with your decision-making process – when working under a lot of stress every day and doing a lot of work that you are maybe overqualified for, but without the proper compensation.

It is time to reconsider things when what you do interferes with your professional development plan. Before wasting 5 or 10 years at a job you don't like, outline your core values and find a workspace that aligns with that.

Think About the People Who Can Help

When creating a strategic action plan, finding your weaknesses is an inevitable part of the process. Instead of letting it put you down, rise back up. I feel like there is no such thing as too much networking. It is essential to building your professional portfolio and ensuring you are noticed in the job market.

All the connections you can make with both offline and online networking can contribute to a flourishing career. Make it a part of your action plan to attend as many events and seminars as possible. Try to make a variety of it too – some of them can be events for improving your transferable skills, and others may be informal events where you reach out to people from your chosen industry.

Either way, the networking plan can be your ultimate jumping point to where you want to be.

Work on Your Image

Another significant aspect of a successful career plan is presenting yourself in such a manner that employers can't say no to you. This means a presentable and decent style and having one all over your internet presence. Let's face it; everyone leaves a digital footprint, so make it count while you are working on yours!

What I mean is making sure your professional and personal online platforms are thriving. For example, create a LinkedIn profile, and showcase all the work you have done so far. Let future employers know that you are a dedicated and qualified individual.

Constantly add to your accomplishments. This includes everything from attending conferences and seminars to workshops and academies. In this way, you will demonstrate that you are dedicated to constant improvement.

Keep an Eye on Job Openings, and Don't Be Afraid to Make a Selection

After all, you have come all this way and worked so hard on yourself – you should not allow yourself to be swayed into a job option that does not check all the boxes for you. Being flexible about it is one thing – completely changing your mindset, goals, and vision just to fit a profile is another thing. Appreciate all the work you've done so far and only consider possible employers who would do the same.

These are the handful of important things you should note when you are creating an action plan. Every step matters – so step into the land of opportunities with a solid plan.

At the end of the day, it is all about feeling capable and confident with who you are and confident with what you know. Once you reach that point, there is nothing you cannot overcome. The more honest you are, the more bullet-proof the career action plan you make will be.

Overcoming Obstacles and Staying Motivated

Earlier in this chapter, I mentioned that sometimes, plans can change. The teenage years are filled with challenges and obstacles. These are an inevitable part of life. In fact, they complete life and give it fullness, representing the magnificent experience of being alive.

That often translates into the professional field. When you work on a goal for a longer time, you may get caught up in the process. That can ultimately bring some dissatisfaction and lack of motivation. It is a part of the journey. It can happen to anyone.

Do you notice this starting to happen to you? In the beginning, you were doing great, but something happened, and suddenly, you are feeling lost in the whirlwind of information and the next steps you're about to take. Suddenly it all seems like too much. Suddenly, you need some time to breathe.

Sometimes, when working toward a goal, you start struggling to find motivation right before you cross the finish line. The reality of the situation is that getting motivated is the most challenging part of the process. When you transition from high school into the real world – that is the biggest change. Being a teenager, you may feel like you don't have enough time to do everything in time.

Any transition process is difficult. Every action you will take in life may come with more than a few obstacles. If looking for the motivation to continue working on you seems too much, this section is designed especially for you.

Did you know you will come face-to-face with a few snags on your way to success? Did you know that about 80% of teenagers end up not following their primary career path? Something comes in their way of achieving their dreams, and they simply give up. That does not mean that they are unhappy with their current career paths. It only means they have encountered a change.

Whatever happens in your quest for the career of your dreams, you need to remain flexible and open to all possibilities. The process can be overwhelming but remember that it's not over until you get what you want and feel accomplished, happy, and satisfied with your choice. Curveballs will come and go, but instead of giving in to the pressure and the low motivation levels, try doing the opposite. Powering through is the best way to persevere.

Here are a few tips to help you get back on track.

Remember, it is all about finding the best approach for you. When you start feeling like your motivation levels are going down, it is time to switch it up. Don't be afraid of change – that only means that you are adapting and acknowledging yourself in all your glory!

Learn to Remember Your Goal

There are so many things you need to do on your path to greatness. Starting with the big picture, then breaking it down into smaller bits, setting some short-term and long-term goals. You are constantly figuring out your next step – and that can be a lot. Any human could get caught up in the process and lose the necessary motivation to continue. When this happens, stop, take a minute to breathe. Remind yourself - what is your primary goal?

But try not to get too attached to the initial concept that you've developed. Also, do you repeat to yourself what you need to do every day? If you need to remind yourself what your daily goal is, is it the right choice for you?

It is Okay if You Slip Up

As I mentioned, change can happen at any time. Once you are working on a long-term goal, it is natural for you to feel like your batteries are drained. Even if you miss a task or two, there is no need to be disappointed in yourself. The important thing is to get right back up and recommit to your goal. Did you manage to get off track because of your grades or a hobby? No worries, you got yourself!

Think about it this way – every person on the planet who had wanted to make a change eventually slipped. Everyone who has worked on themselves have had a minor or a major setback. Don't let that make you feel discouraged. Change and fluctuations are a natural part of the process – it means you are on the right path.

Get Some Extra Support

Talk to your family, friends, or mentors and seek additional help. You would not believe how much of a difference a sound support system makes. Surround yourself with people who are familiar with your goals. These people would give anything to support you every step of the way.

This way, whenever you feel down or start feeling tired of pursuing your dream, you can turn to any one of them. Their job is to make you feel secure in yourself while reminding you to push your limits. They are here for you, so don't be afraid to share.

Visualization and a Positive Attitude

This is the power couple you need to succeed! Start visualizing yourself – how you overcome any obstacle that comes your way, how you achieve your goal, and how that makes you feel. Use the happiness you feel each time you picture yourself succeeding and allow it to be the force that moves you every time you feel like stopping.

Positive self-talk can change a lot. It is not only an excellent way to keep your self-acceptance and self-motivation up. This practice also improves your overall attitude and mood. You deserve to achieve greatness, which is what you aim at – every day.

Embrace every barrier that comes your way. Refresh your memory – you are bigger than anything that stands in your way. Losing motivation can happen to anyone. Ultimately, your goal is a constant and positive change – and that doesn't come without a few challenges!

Continual Learning and Adapting to Changing Career Landscapes

Adapting to change is just as important as overcoming obstacles. Another aspect that we have only touched upon is the subject of tomorrow. Every field – be it technology, biology, engineering, or writing – is led by experts, respectfully, and these people are improving the course of the future career paths of everyone that follows.

Right now, you are in the place of a follower – someone still learning and slowly applying the rules. Becoming a part of a workforce that is changing by the minute can feel like entering a race mid-way. Thankfully, this is not necessarily bound to happen – especially if you come prepared.

The key to becoming a part of the future is your mindset. Think as if you are already there. Up to this point, you have only been a high school student. Until you realize the best way to thrive is to become a lifelong learner, you might not get far with your career goals.

The ever-changing career landscape is what will nudge you in this direction – you weren't expecting this, right?

All of the skills that I have mentioned before are a great starting point. Your soft skills, such as time management, problem-solving, critical thinking, the ability to successfully communicate, etc., are the perfect ground upon which you will build yourself up. Combine that with the technical skills – but remember you constantly need to upgrade them too.

Ten years from now, you may have to face the fact that your career choice is now obsolete or a dying branch – what then? To avoid this from happening to you, choose a wide range of sources for improving and broadening your technical skills. If you allow this to become a continuous learning habit, you might end up as a part of a flourishing collaboration in a field you never even thought to be a part of.

Keeping an open mind when it comes to career searching can be a stretch for some, so here is a successful way to deal with it:

✧ Try to give some new skills a chance – you might end up liking them.

✧ As you do that, remember there is no need to try something extremely different from what you are doing at the moment. Be diverse but selective.

✧ Before entering the workforce, you have the unique position to look at things from a different perspective – from the outside. Analyze and look for weak spots – this is the commitment to lifelong learning.

✧ Once you become a part of the workforce, bring the outside – inside! Provide a unique point of view and help develop the creation of a steady stream of genius ideas.

Nobody can do this but you – you have the distinctive opportunity to rise to the occasion of always being a few steps ahead. Achieve that with the power of continual learning, and you will have no worries adapting to the ever-changing career landscapes.

Learning to recognize an opportunity is something you will practice for a lifetime. But, preparing to seize an opportunity you find is something you practice every day. By taking action and giving it your best to shape everything you have learned so far into an impressive representation of who you are, you will be ready to plunge deep into the next step of your life.

Finally, it is time to make the transition into the professional world. Don't worry. If you have done everything we have covered up until this point, you are more than prepared for it!

CHAPTER 9

TRANSITIONING TO THE WORLD OF WORK

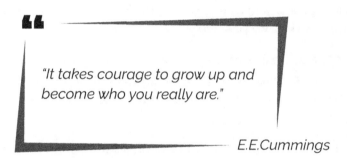

"It takes courage to grow up and become who you really are."

— *E.E.Cummings*

Congratulations on reaching the final stage of this book! You are almost done with your secondary education, and it is time to turn over a new page! Now comes a time in your life when you will discover the endless possibilities of job professions.

Soon enough, you will have a crisp degree in your hand and a head filled with knowledge and useful information. After a successful secondary education, it is time to continue your learning process through another channel – work.

In this process, you become yourself. Now, learn how to utilize all available tools and make the most out of your working experience.

Job Searching Techniques and Strategies

There is a difference in approach every time someone thinks of a job opportunity. Some people create opportunities and grasp them with both hands. Others have a more laid-back approach and wait to see when a new job opportunity opens up. Both methods are good, but it is time to think about which group you belong to more. Are you proactive about it or are you more passive?

My advice is – to be the former instead of the latter. Yes, you can still wait for an opportunity to open up, and you will meet it with arms wide open, but in the meantime, why not put some effort into it?

There are many aspects to consider as soon as you start looking for a job. Approach the situation from any angle – see that you have made the right connections. Make sure you've undergone all the extra training and academies, and mentally prepare for when that day comes – and you are employed.

I am talking about strategies and techniques. There are multiple ways of how you can approach the job market, and some of them are known to be very effective. As soon as you spot a job opening, thoroughly evaluate it before applying for it. For those who still need a nudge in the right direction, here is a detailed list of what you can do.

1. Make a Selection

Once you get out of school, you might become overwhelmed with all the possibilities out there. This is where you need to make a selection. Review all the open options and only apply to those that made the cut. How to make the proper selection? That's easy – all you need is to ensure the job opportunity aligns with your skills and interests.

2. Digital Footprint

The digital presence is the first thing your future employer will look at. Even though, for almost every vacancy out there, you need to send out a resume and a cover letter (sometimes even a portfolio), they are bound to Google you. Your online presence is what leaves a first impression long before they contact you for an interview.

Teenagers nowadays rule the social media platform, so why not use it to your advantage? Create a profile on a job-related social media platform (such as LinkedIn) and showcase yourself as a strong candidate.

You can even take an extra step. Depending on the field you are interested in, you can create your website and show your area of expertise. Think of it as the extracurricular activity that will set you apart. Through your digital footprint, you let your employer know your area of expertise, skillset, and work.

> A tip for those just entering the workforce: for example, if you are a graphic designer – pick a few subjects and make a few templates. This is a great way to show your abilities and provide the employer with a portfolio.

3. A Specific Set of Skills

The job you will apply for will require a specific set of skills. This is why you should constantly tailor your application. Many companies out there need a particular level of expertise and knowledge, so when applying, let them know you have it. Re-evaluate your skills each time and accentuate the ones that are of the most significant importance for the vacancy. Visit the company website and see what they focus on and what they promote. You may even find another opening for a job that suits you better!

4. Referrals Are a Power Tool

As long as you remember this, you are good to go! Until now, you must have done a plateau of extra activities, including internships or part-time jobs. Ask for a referral because you are more likely to get hired for the job of your dreams once your future employer sees that you have done very well before. You can even get a letter of recommendation. This is the additional step you take toward achieving your career goal. It works like a charm!

Making a career move can be easy if you know how to use all the tools at your disposal properly. And, while we are on the subject of tools, we talked about building your resume. Did you manage to create one that would capture the attention of your future employer?

If not, the next section is dedicated to all the details that make up a successful resume and cover letter.

Crafting a Compelling Resume and Cover Letter

You may be good at many things, but writing is not one of them. The thought of sitting in front of your laptop and writing a resume and a cover letter scares you. Yet, you know that getting the job you want is right there at your fingertips. All you need to do is create a compelling cover letter and resume.

There is a certain importance to the application you send when applying for a job opening. These documents are a representation of who you are. Naturally, you want to make yours so good that they accentuate you as the best candidate. Every young professional should implement this. But gathering and writing down all your knowledge and qualifications is not enough.

So now, you sit in front of a blank page and ask yourself – how to create a successful professional resume that captures the essence of who I am?

Here is how.

Resume – it is a vessel through which you can prove you have the knowledge, skills, and expertise to tackle any challenge that comes your way. The moment you start writing your resume, you stop being a student and become a young professional. Present yourself in that light. Add all your relevant educational achievements to the position you are applying for (remember, I mentioned earlier that you need to tailor your application documents to the vacancy).

It is all about including relevant information. However, there are a few steps that are a must. Maximize the power of your resume by adding accurate information. Start by including your contact info (email, telephone number, etc.). Let your employers know that they can contact you at any time. Also, the beginning of a resume should include a summary. It can be short, only a few sentences, but make them count. Highlight your achievements that are related to the job you're applying for.

Working your way down, you should add your educational accomplishments (chronologically) and your work experience. The chronological order will reveal your age, so you can include any internships, part-time jobs, volunteering – anything you have done to accentuate your skills.

Next stop, you have the technical and transferable skills. Accentuate them. Let your future employer know you hold all relevant knowledge for the position. Use active language when describing your achievements and focus on important keywords. When tailoring your resume to a specific job, use concise language. Open their website and find a few keywords. Include them in your resume.

Prioritize the content that is relevant to the vacancy. You can exclude anything unrelated to the job you are applying for. Finally, proofread, and you're done!

Cover letter – the thing about a cover letter is that it should read like an essay, but it should be brief and to the point. A cover letter is not more than half a page, and it should speak directly to your employer about how your set of skills applies to the job you are applying for.

I advise you to avoid any fluff content. Instead of talking about what you want to achieve and how unique and original you are, talk about how you can use your skills to excel at the job. The cover letter should let your employer know you are a terrific hire. Here is how you can do that.

First off, you can use a cover letter template, but write a new cover letter each time you apply for a new job. Tailor it to the organization or company you're applying to and avoid being generic about it. At the very beginning, address the cover letter to the hiring manager. Using "to whom it may concern" or "dear Sir or Madam" does not show that you are very interested in the job, so avoid these salutations.

A good opening is everything. Make the hiring manager want to know more about you by hooking them from the first line of your cover letter. Make it snappy, passionate, and witty. Also, this is a great way to include the word "why." Why are you applying for the position? Why are you the best candidate? Let them know that you have a lot to bring to the table.

With the help of your qualifications and a few strategically placed examples, show why you are the perfect candidate for the job. This is the backbone of your resume. If you have a few experiences, accentuate the ones that present you the best.

Last but not least, finish off with a bang! The last paragraph of your cover letter is your last chance to make a memorable impression, so use it wisely. Sign off with a professional and positive attitude instead of loosely selling yourself. Create an appropriate closing, and hint to a CTA (call-to-action). Oh, don't forget to sign it with your first and last name too!

As with the resume, proofread it, make the necessary corrections, and you are done.

After you've successfully drafted and sent out your application documents, you come to the waiting period. Depending on the company, this period varies from a few days to a few weeks.

This is your chance to prepare yourself for the interview.

Navigating Job Interviews and Professional Etiquette

When the waiting period is over, and you get the call that you are invited for an interview is when it all suddenly becomes real. The interview is your chance to make a good impression and learn more about the company and its people. The interview's success depends on how you prepare for it, what you say during it, and what happens after the meeting. The three stages are essential to cover. On top of that, there is the factor of professional etiquette, so let's see how you can make the most out of it.

The first stage – the preparation stage is the process that will help you execute a flawless interview. You have a goal, and that is to show that you are the perfect applicant. Practice confidence, capability, modesty, and perseverance. Shift your focus from only leaving a good impression to presenting your true self in the best light possible. Come prepared because the interviewer can ask you some tricky questions. Know how to let them know your weak points but point out how you are working to improve them. Practice how to answer every question they have skillfully.

When I said to come prepared, that meant you should have a question for them too. Browse through their online presence and see what they are all about. If their vision and mission seem unclear, ask them what it is. It would help clear the air right from the start and leave a long-lasting impression that you are genuinely interested in the vacant position.

Work on your body language too. Remember to be polite with everyone you meet and have professional yet natural and open body language. Practice how to keep your back straight and your head up.

The second stage – the second stage is what happens during the interview. Leaving a good impression is important, so I advise you to show up on time (that means at least 10 minutes early). Through this, you show your interviewer that you respect their time and appreciate the time they've taken from their busy schedule to fit you in. Let the professional attitude shine through, both inside and out. Dress appropriately, showing that you are ready for a successful start. Right before you enter the room, turn off your phone – you should have a smooth interview without any interruptions.

Take your portfolio with you (if needed). For those job options where you have to present a summary of your work, take your portfolio with you. It shows the recruiter that you are more than prepared. Use a pleasant and positive greeting and begin. During the course of the interview, be a good listener and answer all of their questions. Allow them to finish their trail of thought and show that you can be an excellent team player.

Table manners are everything, so if your employer is conducting an interview with you over a meal, then remember the basic table manners and refrain from any alcoholic beverages.

The third stage – the interview is coming to a close, and everything went as smoothly as you expected. You have made an excellent connection with your interviewer, and now you want to express your gratitude for this opportunity. Follow up with an email and wrap up the entire experience with a positive attitude. Even though this is a small detail, it will make you more memorable than anyone else. On top of it, it says plenty about your personality and accentuates your attention to detail.

Having professional etiquette and working your way through a job interview takes a lot of work. There are many aspects to consider and look out for – curveballs are everywhere. Thankfully, with my help, you can easily overcome any challenge that stands in your way.

Embracing Continuous Professional Development

Continuous work and self-development are the only ways to keep thriving in a constantly developing professional landscape. Things evolve as quickly as possible, leaving almost no chance for workers and employers to adapt. In such an environment, it is of absolute importance to keep refreshing your skillset and elevating your experience.

That is when Continuous Professional Development takes the floor. Also known as CPD. This is a program that is specifically designed to offer benefits to everyone who is a part of the workforce. As a young individual, fresh to the job market and ready to learn, CPD provides the best benefits to help you reach higher ground in your career. The best thing about it is that you can constantly upgrade yourself through the program!

The fast advancements in the professional world mean you should be ready to improve within minutes of entering the workforce. That is why you should focus a little bit on the CPD. Once you start taking an active part, you will see how your skillset will be constantly refreshed.

Do you know what you gain through a CPD? You put a little bit of effort and time into sharpening your skills, but you come out the other end like a winner! During a short period, you have the unique chance to work on specific skills you need to hone (or learn from scratch) and advance in your chosen field. Continuous professional development acts as a platform through which you are given a safe space to learn, develop, and improve.

The main goal of a CPD is gaining a wider palette of skill sets that will ensure the profession of your career. However, it comes with many other benefits.

- ✧ You keep up with the latest trends. There are constantly new trends out there, with the latest one being working from home. The norms change from one day to the next, thus creating the need to adapt. An increase in following the working trends has developed a sense of reason, community, and the demand for a CPD.

- ✧ You create a higher value for the profession. Take up a part in a CPD that is all about your profession and see how much you are missing out on. The constant development (especially if it is a field connected to technology) requires someone who keeps up – so be a step ahead!

✧ A boost in morale is always appreciated. CPD holds the power to make you more effective in the workplace. Through the program, you can open the door to career advancement and finally utilize your leadership skills.

✧ Refresh your memory as to why you chose this career in the first place. Even as a young person, you may find yourself in a dull position with only a few years of working experience under your belt. Enroll in a CPD program and refresh your interest in your role.

It is all about staying ahead of the curve and making yourself relevant. Enrolling in CPD programs and courses is the best way to do that. Look at it as the indispensable tool that will grow your career and expand it in every direction. Make yourself the best lifelong learner, unlock your hidden potential, and remain relevant in a dynamic environment.

A high level of responsibility comes with taking up a new job. Becoming a part of the workforce has never been easier and more challenging at the same time. But, despite that, you have grown so much and developed in unimaginative ways during these chapters. This was the final chapter – the cherry on top – that helped shape you into the strong professional of tomorrow!

CONCLUSION

> " *"The only person who is educated is the one who has learned how to learn and change."*
>
> — *Carl Rogers*

C hange is an unavoidable part of life. It is the only constant thing in this life. My dear reader, my lovely teenager, you have come a long way since you started reading this book. Evolving from being a high school student to becoming an active participant in the community falls under the category of the largest shift in life – ever.

If you are still unaware of what you have done, why not look back and review the road you've traveled? After all, you have been focusing on completing the milestones one by one. Whenever this happens, every human is bound to pay attention to the task at hand, not noticing the change that happens all around.

As a teenager, so far, you have been exposed to a limited number of experiences. All of them have been great, and most have also provided a lesson you'll need in the future. But, after completing all the exercises we worked on together, you should have a clear path about how to proceed in life.

You started with your interests and your skills. You also unraveled some of the most important dilemmas of a teenager. It takes a lot of courage and self-reflection to find out the answers to questions about your future self. No wonder many of you may have even been scared about taking the next step of discovering yourself. Some of you may not have had any idea how to proceed. After all, preparing for your future career and exploring all the possibilities can be a confusing time. But thankfully, you have come out the other side shining through!

The most important thing you have extracted from your journey to discovering your future career path is reflection. Thinking twice before taking a step in any direction is better than aimlessly wandering back and forth. You learned how to harness and direct your energy toward something important to you, toward a field you'd thrive in.

Thanks to this book, you did not lose sight of all that is important to you.

Through careful planning and a few conveniently placed steps, you managed to build the future you. Now, who do you see when you look at yourself in the mirror? Do you see an accomplished individual ready to take on everyday challenges? Do you see a person who is more than capable of tackling a situation and completing tasks with flying colors? Here's to hoping for a positive answer, but either way, you have done an amazing job.

From reflecting upon your character, your strongest and weakest traits, to working toward creating a bulletproof resume, even to exploring the career options and researching the market of tomorrow – that is all you need to do to find out what you want to be.

But, most importantly, you learned two things.

The first one is pinpointing all the weaker spots using deep self-reflection. You have learned how to be honest with yourself because only a truthful approach can help you unlock your full potential. After making many lists with your interests, goals, and skills, you have learned how to differentiate them. Also, you learned how to rate them and how to improve them. You have even discovered the power of lifelong learning – something that can help you become a professional in any field you choose!

The second one is discovering what is good for you and properly researching the job market to get there. What you might not have been aware of up to this point is that exploring career options and analyzing the market in a way where it could provide some valuable information to you is difficult. Through this book, you learned how to do that with ease. Whether it was a traditional or a non-traditional approach, you marvelously tackled the act of gathering info on many industries. It is one of the greatest skills you will ever develop!

Remember, you did a lot of planning - and a lot of research too. You worked on yourself as hard as you could. Now, it is time to dive deep into the professional world.

There is one last lesson to be learned here. Throughout the book, I continuously mentioned that you need to put your dreams and needs first. Whichever path you choose to walk in life, make sure it is one you have chosen yourself. Even though you might need to manage your expectations as things unravel, I strongly advise you never to give up on your dreams.

Writing this book, even though it is filled with many logical steps and instructions, still has a very important undernote – believe in yourself and work to achieve your dreams! It would be my greatest pleasure if you use all the steps, I included here to get the career of your dreams. Manage your expectations but try to exceed them every time! At the end of the day, it is all about obtaining the career of your dreams! It is where you can make a difference! Become a part of a field that has always been your passion. That is why, throughout this book, I have constantly mentioned your beliefs and goals and their high significance. Because, in many ways, your uniqueness and all your talents make you a valuable part of this world. You need to utilize them to make the most out of it and bring some positive change into something important to you.

At last, you will feel a sense of completion – the work you've done to get to where you are right now is only a starting point, but it is still so much! Hopefully, I have helped you learn how to pursue whatever makes you feel satisfied and happy.

So go out there and start serving your purpose – I am confident you will always thrive.

THANK YOU

Thank you so much for purchasing my book.

The marketplace is filled with dozens and dozens of other similar books but you took a chance and chose this one. And I hope it was well worth it.

So again, THANK YOU for getting this book and for making it all the way to the end.

Before you go, I wanted to ask you for one small favor.

Could you please consider posting a review for my book on the platform? Posting a review is the best and easiest way to support the work of independent authors like me.

Your feedback will help me to keep writing the kind of books that will help you get the results you want. It would mean a lot to me to hear from you.

Leave a Review on Amazon US →

Leave a Review on Amazon UK→

ABOUT THE AUTHOR

Emily Carter is an author who loves helping teens with their biggest turning point in life, adulting. She grew up in New York and is happily married to her high school sweetheart. She also has two of her own children.

In her free time, Emily is an avid volunteer at a local food bank and enjoys hiking, traveling, and reading books on personal development. With over a decade of experience in the education and parenting field she has seen the difference that good parenting and the right tips can make in a teenager's life. She is now an aspiring writer through which she shares her insights and advice on raising happy, healthy, and resilient children, teens, and young adults.

Emily's own struggles with navigating adulthood and overcoming obstacles inspired her to write. She noticed a gap in education regarding teaching essential life skills to teens and young adults. She decided to write comprehensive guides covering everything from money and time management to job searching and communication skills. Emily hopes her book will empower teens and young adults to live their best lives and reach their full potential.

To find more of her books, visit her Amazon Author page at:

https://www.amazon.com/author/emily-carter

REFERENCES

The Big Book of Adulting Life Skills for Teens

Adulthood quotes (546 Quotes). (n.d.). Www.goodreads.com. Retrieved May 18, 2023, from https://www.goodreads.com/quotes/tag/adulthood?page=2

AdventHealth. (2019, March 19). *Don't wait: 15 reasons to head to the emergency room.* AdventHealth. https://www.adventhealth.com/hospital/adventhealth-new-smyrna-beach/blog/dont-wait-15-reasons-head-emergency-room

Allen, S. (2022, June 2). *10 ways to save time every day that most people ignore.* Grammarly. https://www.grammarly.com/blog/save-time/

ASI Hastings. (2021, August 1). *The most effective way to clean a p-trap.* ASI Hastings. https://www.asiheatingandair.com/info/the-most-effective-way-to-clean-a-p-trap/

Ates, K. (2021, April 7). *Normal wear and tear vs. property damage: a landlord's guide.* Rentspree. https://www.rentspree.com/blog/normal-wear-and-tear

Bank of America. (2022). *Saving money tips - 8 simple ways to save money.* Better Money Habits. https://bettermoneyhabits. bankofamerica.com/en/saving-budgeting/ways-to-save-money

Banton, C. (2023, March 28). *Interest rate.* Investopedia. https:// www.investopedia.com/terms/i/interestrate.asp

Better Health. (2014). *Relationships and communication.* Better Health Channel. https://www.betterhealth.vic.gov.au/ health/healthyliving/relationships-and-communication

Boogaard, K. (2021, December 26). *Write achievable goals with the SMART goals framework.* Atlassian. https://www.atlassian. com/blog/productivity/how-to-write-smart-goals

Boundaries: What are they and how to create them. (2022, February 25). University of Illinois Chicago Wellness Center. https://wellnesscenter.uic.edu/news-stories/ boundaries-what-are-they-and-how-to-create-them/

Brown, T., & Finch, S. (2022, September 27). *How to rent your first apartment: apartment guide and checklist.* Apartment List. https://www.apartmentlist.com/renter-life/first-time-renter-apartment-guide-checklist

Businessman with an affliction quotes by Anas Hamshari. (n.d.). Www.goodreads.com. https://www.goodreads.com/ work/quotes/85599385-businessman-with-an-affliction

CDC. (2017). *CDC - How much sleep do I need? - sleep and sleep disorders.* CDC. https://www.cdc.gov/sleep/about_sleep/ how_much_sleep.html

CDC. (2021a, March 1). *Healthy eating tips*. CDC. https://www. cdc.gov/nccdphp/dnpao/features/healthy-eating-tips/ index.html

CDC. (2021b, May 16). *Benefits of healthy eating*. CDC; U.S. Department of Health & Human Services. https://www. cdc.gov/nutrition/resources-publications/benefits-of- healthy-eating.html

CDC. (2022a, June 2). *How much physical activity do adults need?* CDC. https://www.cdc.gov/physicalactivity/basics/ adults/index.htm

CDC. (2022b, September 13). *Sleep hygiene tips - sleep and sleep disorders*. CDC. https://www.cdc.gov/sleep/about_sleep/ sleep_hygiene.html

Chen, J. (2020, April 9). *Lease definition and complete guide to renting*. Investopedia. https://www.investopedia.com/ terms/l/lease.asp

Clear, J. (2014, January 23). *The marshmallow experiment and the power of delayed gratification*. James Clear. https:// jamesclear.com/delayed-gratification

Collins, C. (2020, April 21). *The importance of self confidence for your success*. Mom's Got Money. https://www. momsgotmoney.com/the-importance-of-self-confidence/

Compound interest calculator. (n.d.). Www.investor.gov. https:// www.investor.gov/financial-tools-calculators/calculators/ compound-interest-calculator

Cuncic, A. (2022, November 9). *How to practice active listening.* Verywell Mind. https://www.verywellmind.com/what-is-active-listening-3024343

Davenport, B. (2020, May 31). *21 examples of healthy boundaries in relationships.* Live Bold and Bloom. https://liveboldandbloom.com/05/relationships/healthy-boundaries-in-relationships

Davis, T. (2018, December 28). *Self-care: 12 ways to take better care of yourself.* Psychology Today. https://www.psychologytoday.com/us/blog/click-here-happiness/201812/self-care-12-ways-take-better-care-yourself

DeNicola, L. (2023, January 11). *Miss a credit card payment? Here's what you can do.* Intuit Credit Karma. https://www.creditkarma.com/credit-cards/i/what-happens-if-you-miss-a-credit-card-payment

Dieker, N. (2022, January 18). *What credit score do you start with?* Bankrate. https://www.bankrate.com/personal-finance/credit/what-credit-score-do-you-start-with/

Do other countries have credit scores? (n.d.). Chase. https://www.chase.com/personal/credit-cards/education/credit-score/do-other-countries-have-credit-scores

Dweck, C. (2016, January 13). *What having a "growth mindset" actually means.* Harvard Business Review. https://hbr.org/2016/01/what-having-a-growth-mindset-actually-means

Feuerman, M. (2017, November 9). *Managing vs. resolving conflict in relationships: The blueprints for success.* The Gottman Institute. https://www.gottman.com/blog/managing-vs-resolving-conflict-relationships-blueprints-success/

Field, B. (2022, November 16). *7 surprising ways to make your relationship even better.* Verywell Mind. https://www.verywellmind.com/7-surprising-ways-to-make-your-relationship-better-5094212

Folger, J. (2022, December 10). *Tips for successful retirement investing.* Investopedia. https://www.investopedia.com/articles/personal-finance/111313/six-critical-rules-successful-retirement-investing.asp

Fontinelle, A. (2018). *8 financial tips for young adults.* Investopedia. https://www.investopedia.com/articles/younginvestors/08/eight-tips.asp

Fontinelle, A. (2021, May 17). *10 reasons to use your credit card.* Investopedia. https://www.investopedia.com/articles/pf/10/credit-card-debit-card.asp

Food for teenagers: meal plan on the cheap! (2021, January 18). Shelf Cooking. https://shelfcooking.com/food-for-teenagers/

Freer, J. (2022, July 1). *Apartment maintenance - what is it and who is responsible for it?* ApartmentAdvisor. https://www.apartmentadvisor.com/blog/post/apartment-maintenance-what-is-it-and-who-is-responsible-for-it

Georgiev, D. (2023, February 28). *How much time do people spend on social media in 2023?* Tech Jury. https://techjury. net/blog/time-spent-on-social-media/#gref

Glowiak, M. (2020, April 14). *What is self-care and why is it important for you?* SNHU. https://www.snhu.edu/about-us/newsroom/health/what-is-self-care

Gomstyn, A. (2019). *Food for your mood: how what you eat affects your mental health.* Aetna. https://www.aetna.com/ health-guide/food-affects-mental-health.html

Gould, W. R. (2021, November 9). *10 red flags in relationships.* Verywell Mind. https://www.verywellmind.com/10-red-flags-in-relationships-5194592

Gupta, S. (2021, December 27). *How to build trust in a relationship.* Verywell Mind. https://www.verywellmind.com/how-to-build-trust-in-a-relationship-5207611

Harvard School of Public Health. (2019, June 3). *Potassium.* The Nutrition Source. https://www.hsph.harvard.edu/ nutritionsource/potassium/

Health care for young adults findings and recommendations from the report investing in the health and well-being of young adults. (n.d.). https://nap.nationalacademies.org/ resource/18869/YAs_Health_Care_brief.pdf

Healthwise Staff. (2022, February 9). *Time management for teens: care instructions.* Myhealth.alberta.ca. https://myhealth. alberta.ca/Health/aftercareinformation/pages/conditions. aspx?hwid=ug6046

Healthy boundaries for teens. (n.d.). Crime Victim Center of Erie County. Retrieved May 13, 2023, from https://cvcerie.org/healthy-boundaries-for-teens/

Hill, L. (2021, April 22). *Breakfast: is it the most important meal?* WebMD. https://www.webmd.com/food-recipes/breakfast-lose-weight

Holly. (2020, July 23). *Creating a house cleaning schedule that works*. Simplify Create Inspire. https://www.simplifycreateinspire.com/daily-weekly-monthly-cleaning-schedule/

How are FICO scores calculated?. (2018, October 19). MyFICO. https://www.myfico.com/credit-education/whats-in-your-credit-score#:~:text=FICO%20Scores%20are%20calculated%20using

How health insurance works. (2020, April 13). Blue Cross NC. https://www.bluecrossnc.com/understanding-health-insurance/how-health-insurance-works

How to change a home air filter. (n.d.). The Home Depot. https://www.homedepot.com/c/ah/how-to-change-a-home-air-filter/9ba683603be9fa5395fab906a15a05f

How to clean the inside of your washer and dryer. (n.d.). Www.appliancewhse.com. https://www.appliancewhse.com/Content.aspx?ID=25

How to improve communication skills in your relationship. (n.d.). The Jed Foundation. https://jedfoundation.org/resource/how-to-improve-communication-skills-in-your-relationship/

How to make a meal plan. (n.d.). Safefood. https://www.safefood. net/how-to/meal-plan

How to understand your costs and key health insurance terms. (2018, March 8). HealthCare.gov. https://www.healthcare. gov/blog/understand-health-insurance-definitions/

How to use a plumbing snake and when it's necessary. (2021, September 28). WM Buffington Company. https:// wmbuffingtoncompany.com/blog/plumbing/when- and-how-to-use-drain-snake/

In and Out Express Care. (2019, March 3). *Top 9 reasons to go to urgent care - common urgent care complaints.* In and out Express Care. https://inandoutexpresscare.com/ top-9-reasons-for-an-urgent-care-visit/

Keech, D. (2022, October 31). *15 home maintenance tasks and repairs everyone should know how to do.* Military by Owner. https://blog.militarybyowner.com/15-home-maintenance- tasks-and-repairs-everyone-should-know-how-to-do

Kellogg, K. (2021, February 10). *How to clean a dishwasher (quickly!).* Architectural Digest. https://www.architecturaldigest.com/ story/how-to-clean-a-dishwasher-with-vinegar

Kilkus, J. (2022, March 27). *Is the mind-body connection real?* Psychology Today. https://www.psychologytoday.com/ us/blog/navigating-cancer/202203/is-the-mind-body- connection-real

Lake, R. (2023, April 28). *How do credit cards work?* Investopedia. https://www.investopedia.com/how-do-credit-cards- work-5025119

Lawler, M. (2022, August 26). *How to start a self-care routine you'll follow.* EverydayHealth. https://www.everydayhealth. com/self-care/start-a-self-care-routine/

Lawler, M. (2023, March 17). *What is self-care, and why is it so important for your health?* Everyday Health. https://www. everydayhealth.com/self-care/

Lyons, M. (2021, December 9). *How to ground yourself: 14 techniques you need to try.* Www.betterup.com. https:// www.betterup.com/blog/how-to-ground-yourself

Making an appointment. (2014, August 21). HealthCare. gov. https://www.healthcare.gov/blog/making-an-appointment/

Manolas, K. (2022, October 25). *Rental scams: how to spot them & what to do.* Avail. https://www.avail.co/education/ guides/a-tenants-guide-to-finding-an-apartment/how-to-spot-a-rental-scam

McQuitty Hindmarsh, L. (2023, March 1). *20+ freezer essentials for a well stocked freezer.* Mums Make Lists. https://www. mumsmakelists.com/freezer-essentials/

Medcalf, A. (2022, August 2). *How to be honest and build trust in a relationship.* Abby Medcalf. https://abbymedcalf.com/ how-to-be-honest-and-build-trust-in-a-relationship-2/

National Institute of Mental Health. (2021). *Caring for your mental health.* National Institute of Mental Health. https://www. nimh.nih.gov/health/topics/caring-for-your-mental-health

O'Shea, B. (2022, August 30). *What is a good credit score?* NerdWallet. https://www.nerdwallet.com/article/finance/what-is-a-good-credit-score

Pant, P. (n.d.). *How much should I save? 50 30 20 Rule.* TIAA. https://www.tiaa.org/public/learn/personal-finance-101/how-much-of-my-income-should-i-save-every-month

Parker-Pope, T. (2019). *How to have a better relationship.* The New York Times. https://www.nytimes.com/guides/well/how-to-have-a-better-relationship

Parrish, M. (2022, May 13). *How to help students develop a growth mindset.* Good Grief. https://good-grief.org/ways-to-develop-a-growth-mindset/

Peddicord, K. (2020, October 2). *12 rules for renting a home oversees.* U.S. News & World Report. https://money.usnews.com/money/retirement/baby-boomers/articles/rules-for-renting-a-home-overseas

Petersen, L. (2019, January 24). *Strengths of compromise as a conflict resolution.* Chron. https://smallbusiness.chron.com/strengths-compromise-conflict-resolution-10502.html

A quote by Eleanor Brown. (n.d.). Www.goodreads.com. Retrieved May 13, 2023, from https://www.goodreads.com/quotes/9752464-self-care-is-not-selfish-you-cannot-serve-from-an-empty

A quote from Nineteen Minutes. (n.d.). Www.goodreads.com. Retrieved May 13, 2023, from https://www.goodreads.com/quotes/75688-everyone-thinks-you-make-mistakes-when-you-re-young-but-i

Ramsey Solutions. (2023, March 15). *How to save money: 22 simple tips*. Ramsey Solutions. https://www.ramseysolutions. com/budgeting/the-secret-to-saving-money

Robinson, L., Segal, J., & Smith, M. (2019). *Effective communication*. Help Guide. https://www.helpguide.org/articles/ relationships-communication/effective-communication. htm

Rose, G. (2023, April 6). *Buying life insurance as an investment*. NerdWallet. https://www.nerdwallet.com/article/ insurance/life-insurance-as-an-investment

Rosen, T. (2021, January 22). *Tips for going to the doctor by yourself as a college student*. Bwog - Columbia Student News. https://bwog.com/2021/01/tips-for-going-to-the-doctor-by-yourself-as-a-college-student/

Rudd, L. (2017, April 12). *How to change a light bulb. Living - Your Home, DIY and Life*. HomeServe. https://www.homeserve. com/uk/living/how-to/how-to-change-a-light-bulb/

Ryan, A. (2020, May 28). *Tips for your young adult and their 1st apartment*. Simply Family Magazine. https:// simplyfamilymagazine.com/tips-for-your-young-adult-and-their-1st-apartment

Saraev, N. (2022, May 19). *The top 10 most common time wasters & how to avoid them*. Day.io. https://day.io/blog/the-top-10-most-common-time-wasters-how-to-avoid-them/

Saving and investing for your future. (2022). University of Minnesota Extension. https://extension.umn.edu/personal-finances/saving-and-investing-your-future

Security deposit laws by state. (n.d.). Rocket Lawyer. Retrieved May 13, 2023, from https://www.rocketlawyer.com/real-estate/landlords/property-management/legal-guide/security-deposit-laws-by-state

Segal, J., Robinson, L., & Smith, M. (2019, March 21). *Conflict resolution skills*. HelpGuide. https://www.helpguide.org/articles/relationships-communication/conflict-resolution-skills.htm

17 relationship communication quotes every couple will love. (2021, February 16). The Healthy. https://www.thehealthy.com/family/relationships/relationship-communication-quotes/

Sharp Emerson, M. (2021, August 30). *Eight things you can do to improve your communication skills*. Professional Development | Harvard DCE. https://professional.dce.harvard.edu/blog/eight-things-you-can-do-to-improve-your-communication-skills/

Sheldon, R., & Wigmore, I. (2022, September). *What is pomodoro technique?*. WhatIs.com. https://www.techtarget.com/whatis/definition/pomodoro-technique

Sheppard, S. (2021, October 25). *How to build a respectful relationship*. Verywell Mind. https://www.verywellmind.com/respect-is-vital-to-building-a-healthy-relationship-5206110

Simeon, D. (2014, March 6). *Want your teen to be more organized? 10 ideas that actually work*. Your Teen Magazine. https://yourteenmag.com/teenager-school/teenager-middle-school/help-your-teenager-get-organized

Soukup, R. (2020, July 7). *How to stock your first kitchen.* Living Well Spending Less®. https://www.livingwellspendingless. com/how-to-stock-your-first-kitchen/

Srinivasan, H., & 2021. (2022, October 21). *When to use a debit card—and when to use a credit card instead.* Real Simple. https://www.realsimple.com/work-life/money/debit-vs-credit-card

Stickley, A. (2022, September 28). *The most effective ways to clean a garbage disposal.* The Spruce. https://www. thespruce.com/cleaning-a-garbage-disposal-2718863

Stretch your protein budget — nourish and exercise your body. (n.d.). Www.ag.ndsu.edu. Retrieved May 13, 2023, from https://www.ag.ndsu.edu/nourishyourbody/stretch-your-protein-budget

The importance of investing early and often. (n.d.). Associated Bank. https://www.associatedbank.com/resource-center/saving/investing-early-and-often

20 biggest time wasters for college students – college girl smarts. (2020, December 9). College Girl Smarts. https:// www.collegegirlsmarts.com/biggest-time-wasters-for-college-students/

Types of abuse. (n.d.). The Hotline. https://www.thehotline.org/resources/types-of-abuse/

Vega, M. (2022, March 23). *Do you need an apartment co-signer? Apartment Living Tips.* ApartmentGuide.com. https://www. apartmentguide.com/blog/do-you-need-an-apartment-co-signer/

Wallender, L. (2022, June 17). *How to unclog any drain.* The Spruce. https://www.thespruce.com/how-to-unclog-a-drain-2718779

Washington state's mandatory auto/motorcycle insurance law. (n.d.). Office of the Insurance Commissioner Washington State. https://www.insurance.wa.gov/washington-states-mandatory-automotorcycle-insurance-law

Wells Fargo. (2022). *Why invest?* Wells Fargo. https://www.wellsfargo.com/goals-investing/why-invest/

What is a credit score? (2020, September 1). Consumer Financial Protection Bureau. https://www.consumerfinance.gov/ask-cfpb/what-is-a-credit-score-en-315/

What is renters insurance and what does it cover?. (2021, October). Allstate. https://www.allstate.com/resources/renters-insurance/what-does-renters-insurance-cover

Williams, R. (2019, March 28). *10 spiritual self-care tips to be happy.* Chopra. https://chopra.com/articles/10-spiritual-self-care-tips-to-be-happy

Wooll, M. (2022, January 11). *Why face-to-face communication matters (even with remote work).* BetterUp. https://www.betterup.com/blog/face-to-face-communication

Money Skills for Teens

Allinson, M. (2023, January 18). *Why is money important in our lives? Robotics & Automation* News. https://roboticsandautomationnews.com/2023/01/18/why-is-money-important-in-our-lives/59144/

Bank of America. (2019). *Creating a budget with a personal budget spreadsheet. Better Money Habits.* https://bettermoneyhabits.bankofamerica.com/en/saving-budgeting/creating-a-budget

Bell, A. (2022, April 7). *What are the 5 purposes of budgeting?* Investopedia. https://www.investopedia.com/financial-edge/1109/6-reasons-why-you-need-a-budget.aspx#:~:text=Having%20a%20budget%20keeps%20your

Blinka, D. (2023, February 2). *How to calculate and compare unit prices at the store.* WikiHow. https://www.wikihow.com/Calculate-and-Compare-Unit-Prices-at-the-Store

Bowling, L. (2019, February 22). *How much should i spend on clothing?* Financial Best Life. https://financialbestlife.com/how-much-should-i-spend-on-clothing/

Braverman, B. (2022, May 10). *Big purchases need major planning. here's where to start | CNN business.* CNN. https://edition.cnn.com/2022/05/10/success/save-for-a-big-purchase/index.html

Drury, P. (2022, January 25). *25+ jobs for teens (with job search advice).* Resume.io. https://resume.io/blog/jobs-for-teens

FarmWell. (n.d.). Financial wellbeing: *Developing a healthy money mindset.* FarmWell. https://farmwell.org.uk/wp-content/uploads/sites/2/2022/03/Financial-Wellbeing-Developing-a-Healthy-Money-Mindset.pdf

Fernando, J. (2023, March 9). *Bond: Financial meaning with examples and how they are priced.* Investopedia. https://www.investopedia.com/terms/b/bond.asp

Frankenfield, J. (2019). *Online banking.* Investopedia. https://www.investopedia.com/terms/o/onlinebanking.asp

Ganatra, M. (2022, September 27). *How to analyze your options before buying an insurance policy.* Forbes Advisor INDIA. https://www.forbes.com/advisor/in/life-insurance/how-to-analyze-your-options-before-buying-an-insurance-policy/

Gongala, S. (2014, July 25). *21 essential life skills for teens to learn.* MomJunction; MomJunction. https://www.momjunction.com/articles/everyday-life-skills-your-teen-should-learn_0081859/

HappyBank. (n.d.). *Financial tips: Six steps to creating a positive money mindset.* Happy State Bank. https://www.happybank.com/resources/six-steps-to-creating-a-positive-money-mindset

Hasty, A. (2023, April 5). *Bank accounts for teens. Compare the Market.* https://www.comparethemarket.com/current-accounts/content/kids-teens-current-accounts/

Hayes, A. (2020, October 3). *Mutual fund.* Investopedia. https://www.investopedia.com/terms/m/mutualfund.asp

Hayes, A. (2022, July 6). Stock. Investopedia. https://www.investopedia.com/terms/s/stock.asp

Jordan, T. (2019, January 14). *The 7 best budgeting methods.* Atypical Finance. https://www.atypicalfinance.com/7-best-budgeting-methods/

Kagan, J. (2023, April 4). *What is an ATM and how does it work?* Investopedia. https://www.investopedia.com/terms/a/atm.asp#:~:text=To%20use%20an%20ATM%2C%20you

Lahunou, I. (2022, June 14). *How to shop smart: 30 ways to make smarter decisions.* Monetha. https://www.monetha.io/blog/rewards/how-to-shop-smart/

Lake, R. (2020, February 4). *How to protect your online banking information.* Forbes Advisor. https://www.forbes.com/advisor/banking/how-to-protect-your-online-banking-information/

Lake, R. (2021, April 9). *What are the different types of bank accounts?* Forbes Advisor. https://www.forbes.com/advisor/banking/what-are-the-different-types-of-bank-accounts/

Langager, C. (2022, August 23). *A beginner's guide to stock investing.* Investopedia. https://www.investopedia.com/articles/basics/06/invest1000.asp

PSECU. (2020, June 5). *How to make good purchasing decisions.* Blog.psecu. https://blog.psecu.com/learn/financial-tips-for-every-stage-in-life/2020/06/05/how-to-make-good-purchasing-decisions

Resnick, N. (2017, July 25). *The 6 best jobs for teenage entrepreneurs.* Entrepreneur. https://www.entrepreneur.com/starting-a-business/the-6-best-jobs-for-teenage-entrepreneurs/296365

Step Change Team. (n.d.). *Credit card debt. what to do if you can't pay.* stepchange. Www.stepchange.org. https://www.stepchange.org/debt-info/credit-card-debt.aspx

Waugh, E. (2022, January 31). *Why is credit important? - experian.* Www.experian.com. https://www.experian.com/blogs/ask-experian/why-is-credit-important/

Which Team. (2023, May 16). *17 ways to save money on your household bills and living costs in 2023 -* which? News. Which? https://www.which.co.uk/news/article/how-to-save-money-on-your-household-bills-aiTGN6b5jZ2N

Wu, A. (2023, May 2). *How to compare prices online (with pictures) -* wikiHow life. Www.wikihow.life. https://www.wikihow.life/Compare-Prices-Online

Social Skills for Teens

A Little Dose Of Happy. (2022, August 15). *9 Tips for cultivating relationships that last - a little dose of happy.* Aldohappy. https://aldohappy.com/cultivating-relationships

Abrahamsen, S. (2019, August 28). *5 Easy ways to track your personal growth.* Little Coffee Fox. https://littlecoffeefox. com/track-your-personal-growth/

Allen, R. (2011, April 1). *How to challenge your beliefs.* https:// www.rogerkallen.com/how-to-challenge-your-beliefs/

Angel, D. (2016, December 28). *The four types of conversations: Debate, dialogue, discourse, and diatribe.* https:// davidwangel.com/the-opportune-conflict/2016/12/28/ the-four-types-of-conversations-debate-dialogue- discourse-and-diatribe

AZ Quotes. (n.d.). *Top 25 first impression quotes (of 109).* Retrieved July 4, 2023, from https://www.azquotes.com/ quotes/topics/first-impression.html#:~:text=You%20 never%20get%20a%20second%20chance%20to%20 make%20a%20first%20impression.&text=You%20only%20 have%20one%20first

Baller, E. (2016, May 27). *10 Ways to cultivate a positive mindset and change your life.* Tiny Buddha. https://tinybuddha. com/blog/10-ways-cultivate-positive-mindset-change- life/

Barclays Life Skills. (n.d.). *What are your strengths? - 5 ways to find out.* https://barclayslifeskills.com/i-want-to- choose-my-next-step/school/5-ways-to-find-out-what- you-re-good-at/

Barrier, J. (n.d.). *8 Strategies for meaningful conversations - improve your skills.* Preach It, Teach It. Retrieved July 6, 2023, from https://preachitteachit.org/articles/detail/eight-simple-strategies-to-have-meaningful-conversations/

Baulch, J. (2016, September 5). *Thought challenging when negative.* Inner Melbourne Psychology. https://www.innermelbpsychology.com.au/thought-challenging/#:~:text=Break%20your%20thoughts%20down%20into

Carnahan, L. (2022, June 2). *How to hold a conversation and build deeper connections.* Vector Marketing. https://www.thevectorimpact.com/how-to-hold-a-conversation/

Cherry, K. (2017). *Understanding body language and facial expressions.* Verywell Mind. https://www.verywellmind.com/understand-body-language-and-facial-expressions-4147228

Cherry, K. (2022, November 8). *How our brain neurons can change over time from life's experience.* Verywell Mind. https://www.verywellmind.com/what-is-brain-plasticity-2794886

Cherry, K. (2023a, February 22). *What are the 9 types of nonverbal communication?* Verywell Mind. https://www.verywellmind.com/types-of-nonverbal-communication-2795397#:~:text=Nonverbal%20communication%20means%20conveying%20information

Cherry, K. (2023b, March 10). *What is self-awareness?* Verywell Mind. https://www.verywellmind.com/what-is-self-awareness-2795023

Cuncic, A. (2019). *Things to start doing if you have social anxiety disorder.* Verywell Mind. https://www.verywellmind.com/social-anxiety-disorder-tips-3024209

Cuncic, A. (2023, February 15). *10 Best and worst small talk topics.* Verywell Mind. https://www.verywellmind.com/small-talk-topics-3024421

Davenport, B. (2022, July 1). *75 Confidence-boosting positive affirmations for teens.* Live Bold and Bloom. https://liveboldandbloom.com/07/mindfulness/positive-affirmations-teens

Davis, T. (2019, April 11). *15 Ways to build a growth mindset.* Psychology Today. https://www.psychologytoday.com/za/blog/click-here-happiness/201904/15-ways-build-growth-mindset

Drillinger, M. (2020, February 25). *6 Ways to make friends when you have social anxiety.* Healthline. https://www.healthline.com/health/anxiety/how-to-make-friends-when-you-have-social-anxiety#2.-Fight

Eatough, E. (2022, January 12). *25 Toxic personality traits to spot in yourself and others.* Betterup. https://www.betterup.com/blog/toxic-traits

Eisler, M. (2019, April 19). *15 Ways to declutter your mind.* The Chopra Center. https://chopra.com/articles/15-ways-to-declutter-your-mind

Elcomblus. (2020, December 18). *Elements of verbal communication.* https://www.elcomblus.com/elements-of-verbal-communication/

Gordon, J. P. (2019, November 7). *Low self-esteem and social anxiety.* Counselling Directory. https://www.counselling-directory.org.uk/memberarticles/low-self-esteem-and-social-anxiety#:~:text=This%20very%20low%20self%2Desteem

Gupta, S. (2022, September 14). *What is self-acceptance?* Verywell Mind. https://www.verywellmind.com/self-acceptance-characteristics-importance-and-tips-for-improvement-6544468

Hailey, L. (2022, November 9). *15 Effective ways to connect with absolutely anyone, anytime.* Science of People. https://www.scienceofpeople.com/how-to-connect-with-others/#:~:text=A%20struggle%20to%20connect%20could

Holland, K. (2018). *Positive self-talk: Benefits and techniques.* Healthline. https://www.healthline.com/health/positive-self-talk

Hull, R. H. (2016). *The art of nonverbal communication in practice.* The Hearing Journal, 69(5), 22. https://doi.org/10.1097/01.hj.0000483270.59643.cc

Incledon, N. (2018, April 11). *How low self-esteem affects relationships.* Peacefulmind.com.au. https://peacefulmind.com.au/2018/04/11/how-low-self-esteem-affects-relationships/#:~:text=Low%20self%2Desteem%20can%20give

Kentucky Counselling Center. (2021, May 14). *How to build mental resilience.* https://kentuckycounselingcenter.com/how-to-build-mental-resilience/

Kottke, J. (2018, May 17). *The respect of personhood vs the respect of authority.* https://kottke.org/18/05/the-respect-of-personhood-vs-the-respect-of-authority

Kropf, J. (2023, May 15). *50 Easy ways to get out of your comfort zone.* Healthy Happy Impactful. https://healthyhappyimpactful.com/ways-get-out-comfort-zone-quotes/

Lawler, M. (2022, August 26). *How to start a self-care routine you'll follow.* Everyday Health. https://www.everydayhealth.com/self-care/start-a-self-care-routine/

Liles, M. (2021, February 21). *101 Uplifting confidence quotes for days you're struggling with low self-esteem.* Parade. https://parade.com/989608/marynliles/confidence-quotes/

Lindberg, S. (2020, November 26). *Self-Improvement goal setting tips.* Verywell Mind. https://www.verywellmind.com/tips-for-goal-setting-self-improvement-4688587

Lumen Learning. (n.d.). *Effective communication.* Lumen Learning.com. Retrieved July 7, 2023, from https://courses.lumenlearning.com/suny-monroecc-hed110/chapter/communication/

Manson, M. (2019, April 11). *5 Skills to help you develop emotional intelligence.* https://markmanson.net/emotional-intelligence

Matthews, D. (2020, January 9). *How to identify your limiting beliefs and get over them.* Lifehack. https://www.lifehack.org/858652/limiting-beliefs

Mayo Clinic. (2020, April 22). *A beginner's guide to meditation.* https://www.mayoclinic.org/tests-procedures/meditation/in-depth/meditation/art-20045858#:~:text=%22Meditation%2C%20which%20is%20the%20practice

Melinda. (2019, June 3). Social anxiety disorder. Help Guide. https://www.helpguide.org/articles/anxiety/social-anxiety-disorder.htm

Merabet, L. B., & Pascual-Leone, A. (2009). *Neural reorganization following sensory loss: The opportunity of change.* Nature Reviews Neuroscience, 11(1), 44–52. https://doi.org/10.1038/nrn2758

Merriam-Webster. (n.d.). *Definition of respect.* https://www.merriam-webster.com/dictionary/respect#:~:text=%3A%20high%20or%20special%20regard%20%3A%20esteem

Merriam-Webster. (2020). *Definition of self-confidence.* https://www.merriam-webster.com/dictionary/self-confidence

Mindtools. (n.d.). *Empathy at work.* https://www.mindtools.com/agz0gft/empathy-at-work

Morin, A. (2022, July 28). *5 Ways to start boosting your self-confidence today.* Verywell Mind. https://www.verywellmind.com/how-to-boost-your-self-confidence-4163098

Nemours Kids Health. (n.d.). *5 Ways to (respectfully) disagree (for teens).* Kids Health. https://kidshealth.org/en/teens/tips-disagree.html

Nguyen, S. O. (2023, January 31). *88 Daily journal prompts on life, love, and gratitude.* Parade: Entertainment, Recipes, Health, Life, Holidays. https://parade.com/1308069/steph-nguyen/journaling-prompts/

NHS. (2021, February 1). *Raising low self-esteem*. https://www.nhs.uk/mental-health/self-help/tips-and-support/raise-low-self-esteem/

Nigam, D. (2023, April 13). *Elements of verbal and non verbal communication*. https://www.linkedin.com/pulse/elements-verbal-non-communication-divakar-nigam

Perry, E. (2022, June 7). *20 Personal values examples to help you find your own*. Better Up. https://www.betterup.com/blog/personal-values-examples

Perry, E. (2023, March 14). *How to build confidence: A guide to doing it right*. Better Up. https://www.betterup.com/blog/how-to-build-confidence

Peterson, T. J. (2022, March 25). *What is self-confidence?* Healthy Place. https://www.healthyplace.com/self-help/self-confidence/what-is-self-confidence

Pollack, J. (2021, April 19). *Tip #7: Challenge your beliefs*. Pollack Peace Building. https://pollackpeacebuilding.com/blog/tip-7-challenge-your-beliefs/

Portland Community College. (2020, March 11). *What are the five conflict resolution strategies?* Climb. https://climb.pcc.edu/blog/what-are-the-five-conflict-resolution-strategies#:~:text=Identify%20specific%20points%20of%20disagreement

Price, C. (2018, January 8). *Strengthening your teen's social and conversation abilities*. Hey Sigmund. https://www.heysigmund.com/strengthening-teens-social-conversation-abilities/

Pyramid Psychology. (2021, June 14). *4 Conversation tips for teens: Getting past the shy.* https://pyramidpsychology. com/how-to-get-past-the-shy-4-conversation-tips-for-teens/

Quizzclub. (2017, April 7). *"You never get a second chance to make a first impression" was an ad slogan for which company?* https://quizzclub.com/trivia/you-never-get-a-second-chance-to-make-a-first-impression-was-an-ad-slogan-for-which-company/answer/152271/

Rao, S. T. S., Asha, M. R., Rao, J. K. S., & Vasudevaraju, P. (2009). The biochemistry of belief. *Indian Journal of Psychiatry, 51*(4), 239. https://doi.org/10.4103/0019-5545.58285

Ratey, J. J. (2019, October 24). *Can exercise help treat anxiety?* Harvard Health Blog. https://www.health. harvard.edu/blog/can-exercise-help-treat-anxiety-2019102418096#:~:text=How%20does%20exercise%20 help%20ease

Raypole, C. (2019, February 25). *How systematic desensitization can help you overcome fear.* Healthline Media. https:// www.healthline.com/health/systematic-desensitization

Raypole, C. (2020, February 27). *Self-Actualization: What it is and how to achieve it.* Healthline. https://www.healthline. com/health/self-actualization

Reach Out. (2019). *Self-esteem and teenagers.* https://parents. au.reachout.com/common-concerns/everyday-issues/self-esteem-and-teenagers

Reynolds, N. (2020, October 12). *10 Important social skills you need to teach your teen now.* Raising Teens Today. https://

raisingteenstoday.com/10-important-social-skills-you-need-to-teach-your-teen-now/

Sander, V. (2021, August 18). *How to improve your social skills - the complete guide.* SocialSelf. https://socialself.com/blog/improve-social-skills/

Sander, V. (2023, January 4). *16 Ways to respond when someone is disrespectful to you.* SocialSelf. https://socialself.com/blog/someone-disrespectful/

Schultz, K. (n.d.). *Self-Image: Definition, issues, & tips.* The Berkeley Well-Being Institute. https://www.berkeleywellbeing.com/self-image.html

Segal, J., Robinson, L., & Smith, M. (2019, March 21). *Conflict resolution skills.* Help Guide. https://www.helpguide.org/articles/relationships-communication/conflict-resolution-skills.htm

Segal, J., Smith, M., Robinson, L., & Shubin, J. (2020, October). *Improving emotional intelligence.* Help Guide. https://www.helpguide.org/articles/mental-health/emotional-intelligence-eq.htm#:~:text=Emotional%20intelligence%20(otherwise%20known%20as

Shah, M. (2022, January 8). *Challenges are what make life interesting and overcoming them is what makes life meaningful.* Set Quotes. https://www.setquotes.com/challenges-are-what-make-life-interesting/

Skills You Need. (2011). *What are social skills?* https://www.skillsyouneed.com/ips/social-skills.html

Smith, J. (2020, September 25). *Growth vs fixed mindset: How what you think affects what you achieve.* Mindset Health.

https://www.mindsethealth.com/matter/growth-vs-fixed-mindset

Smith, S. (2018, April 10). *5-4-3-2-1 Coping technique for anxiety.* University of Rochester Medical Center. https://www.urmc.rochester.edu/behavioral-health-partners/bhp-blog/april-2018/5-4-3-2-1-coping-technique-for-anxiety.aspx

Social Skill Center. (2021, February 19). *The difference between verbal and nonverbal communication.* https://socialskillscenter.com/the-difference-between-verbal-and-nonverbal-communication/#:~:text=There%20are%20two%20primary%20forms

Sonder Wellness. (2022, August 22). *Healthy friendships: 6 Key ingredients.* https://www.sonderwellness.com/blog/2022/08/22/healthy-friendships/

Stenvinkel, M. (2016, October 3). *13 Things to do instead of comparing yourself to others.* Tiny Buddha. https://tinybuddha.com/blog/13-things-instead-comparing-others/

Suni, E., & Dimitriu, A. (2020, September 18). *Anxiety and sleep.* Sleep Foundation. https://www.sleepfoundation.org/mental-health/anxiety-and-sleep#:~:text=Sleep%20deprivation%20can%20worsen%20anxiety

This Way Up. (n.d.). *How to deal with social anxiety.* https://thiswayup.org.au/learning-hub/social-anxiety-explained/

University of Texas. (2020, November 3). *How much of communication is nonverbal?* https://online.utpb.edu/about-us/articles/communication/how-much-of-

communication-is-nonverbal/#:~:text=It%20was%20
Albert%20Mehrabian%2C%20a

Voss, P., Thomas, M. E., Cisneros-Franco, J. M., & de Villers-Sidani, É. (2017). Dynamic brains and the changing rules of neuroplasticity: Implications for learning and recovery. *Frontiers in Psychology, 8*(1657). https://doi.org/10.3389/fpsyg.2017.01657

Wallis, L. J., Virányi, Z., Müller, C. A., Serisier, S., Huber, L., & Range, F. (2016). Aging effects on discrimination learning, logical reasoning and memory in pet dogs. *AGE, 38*(1). https://doi.org/10.1007/s11357-015-9866-x

Warley, S. (n.d.). *How to practice self-awareness.* Life Skills That Matter. https://lifeskillsthatmatter.com/podcast/how-to-practice-self-awareness/

Waters, S. (2021, November 15). *How to carry a conversation — the art of making connections.* Www.betterup.com. https://www.betterup.com/blog/how-to-carry-a-conversation

Westside DBT. (n.d.). *The neuroscience of change—or how to reset your brain.* Retrieved June 28, 2023, from https://westsidedbt.com/the-neuroscience-of-change-or-how-to-reset-your-brain/

Yeager, D. S., Hanselman, P., Walton, G. M., Murray, J. S., Crosnoe, R., Muller, C., Tipton, E., Schneider, B., Hulleman, C. S., Hinojosa, C. P., Paunesku, D., Romero, C., Flint, K., Roberts, A., Trott, J., Iachan, R., Buontempo, J., Yang, S. M., Carvalho, C. M., & Hahn, P. R. (2019). A national experiment reveals where a growth mindset improves achievement. *Nature, 573*(573). https://doi.org/10.1038/s41586-019-1466-

Career Planning for Teens

Boys & Girls Clubs of America. (2022, January 19). The Importance of Goal Setting for Teens. Great Futures. https://www.greatfutures.club/the-importance-of-goal-setting-for-teens/

Carlsson, A. (2023, June 16). Embracing Continuous Professional Development: Unlocking Career Growth and Success. LinkedIn. https://www.linkedin.com/pulse/embracing-continuous-professional-development-career-growth-carlsson/

Columbia University. Connecting Your Self-Knowledge to Career Options. Columbia University Center For Career Education. https://www.careereducation.columbia.edu/resources/connecting-your-self-knowledge-career-options

Columbia University. What to Know Before You Go: Researching Organizations. Columbia University Center For Career Education. https://www.careereducation.columbia.edu/resources/what-know-you-go-researching-organizations

Corhn, D. (2022, June 28). 5 Tips For Helping Teens Plan Ahead For A Sizzling Future Learning Coach Success. Connections Academy by Pearson. https://www.connectionsacademy.com/support/resources/article/5-tips-for-helping-teens-plan-ahead-for-a-sizzling-future/

Crown copyright Province of Nova Scotia (2012, branding update 2015). Guide to Career   Planning With Your Teenager, Explore Careers Nova Scotia. https://explorecareers.novascotia.ca/sites/default/files/2018-06/16-44875%20Post-Secondary%20Guide%20Teenager%20English%20SPREADS%20FINAL-s_1.pdf

D'Monte, A. (2023, February 16). How Industry Mentors & Role Models Impact High School Students. LinkedIn. https://www.linkedin.com/pulse/how-industry-mentors-role-models-impact-high-school-students-d-monte/

Dr. Akos, P. (2020). STARTING EARLY: Career Development in the Early Grades Association for Career and Technical Education. School of Education, University of North Carolina at Chapel Hill. https://files.eric.ed.gov/fulltext/ED610366.pdf

Feder, M. (2022, August 26). 5 Steps to Making a Financial Plan for Your Education. University of Phoenix. https://www.phoenix.edu/blog/5-steps-to-making-a-financial-plan-for-your-education.html

Government of Alberta. (2023). Career Paths and Your Lifestyle. Alberta Alis, maintained by Alberta Seniors, Community and Social Services. https://alis.alberta.ca/look-for-work/career-paths-and-your-lifestyle/

INSIGHT REPORT MAY (2023, April 30). Future of Jobs Report 2023. World Economic Forum. https://www.weforum.org/reports/the-future-of-jobs-report-2023/

Kovacs, S. (2020, January 2). TEENAGE EQ AND ADAPTABILITY. Ambassador Leaders. https://ambassadorleaders.com/toolkit/eq-adaptability

Medically reviewed by: KidsHealth Behavioral Health Experts. Motivation and the Power of Not Giving Up. TeensHealth. https://kidshealth.org/en/teens/motivation.html

MIT. Network & Conduct Informational Interviews. Career Advising & Professional Development. https://capd.mit.edu/channels/network-conduct-informational-interview/

Page, M. team. (2021, November 16). Setting Personal Development Goals in 2022. Jobs and Recruitment Agency in Australia. Michael Page. https://www.michaelpage.com.au/advice/career-advice/career-progression/setting-personal-development-goals-2022

Pearson. (2020, December 10). Leading Students Through a Changing Career Landscape. Pearson. https://www.pearson.com/ped-blogs/blogs/2020/12/leading-students-through-changing-career-landscape.html

PWC, UNICEF, GENERATION UNLIMITED (2021, December). Reaching YES Addressing the Youth Employment and Skilling Challenge. Generation Unlimited. https://

www.generationunlimited.org/reports/reaching-yes-addressing-youth-employment-and-skilling-challenge

Thompson, H. Make Your Action Plan. A Part of the Youth Advocates for Community Health Program. Community Youth Development Division of Extension. University of Wisconsin-Madison. https://youth.extension.wisc.edu/articles/make-your-action-plan/

U.S. DEPARTMENT OF LABOR. Soft Skills to Pay The Bills. United States Department of Labor. https://www.dol.gov/agencies/odep/program-areas/individuals/youth/transition/soft-skills

UNICEF (2022). The 12 Transferable Skills - UNICEF's Conceptual and Programmatic Framework. © United Nations Children's Fund. https://www.unicef.org/lac/media/32441/file/The%2012%20Transferable%20Skills.pdf